Thin, 5c, Stone Farm Rocks. Climber: Tim Skinner. Photo: Ian Smith

Brenva, 5c, High Rocks. Climber: Paul Hayes. Photo: Ian Smith

Climbers' Club Guides
Edited by Bob Moulton

Southern Sandstone

by Mike Vetterlein

Drawings by Ben Bevan-Pritchard

Maps and plans by Don Sargeant

 Published by the Climbers' Club

First Edition (South-East England) 1956, Reprinted 1960
by E.C.Pyatt.

Second Edition (South-East England) 1963
by E.C.Pyatt with Appendix by D.G.Fagan, J.V.Smoker and E.C.Pyatt

Third Edition (South-East England) 1969, Reprinted 1974
by E.C.Pyatt and L.R.Holliwell

Fourth Edition (Southern Sandstone) 1981
by T.J.H.Daniells

Fifth Edition (Southern Sandstone) 1989
by D.B.Turner

Southern Sandstone 1992 (Supplement)
by M.T.Vetterlein

Sixth Edition (Southern Sandstone) 1995
by M.T.Vetterlein

Vetterlein, Mike
Southern Sandstone
Climbers' Club Guides
British Library Cataloguing in Publication Data
A catalogue record for this book is available from the British Library

796.522

ISBN 0 901 601 58 6

Front cover: *Burlap*, 5b, Bowles Rocks. Climber: Robin Mazinke.
            Photo: David Atchison-Jones

Back cover: *Infidel*, 6a, High Rocks. Climber: Mike Eden.
           Photo: Ian Smith

Printed by The Ernest Press, 595 Clarkston Road, Glasgow G44 5QD
Distributed by Cordee, 3a De Montfort Street, Leicester LE1 7HD

Contents

The Climbers' Club   6

Acknowledgements   8

Introduction   9

Historical   21

Bowles Rocks   32

Bulls Hollow Rocks   51

Eridge Green Rocks   60

Harrison's Rocks   81

High Rocks   123

High Rocks Continuation Wall   151

High Rocks Annexe   159

Stone Farm Rocks   165

Minor Outcrops   177

   Bassett's Farm Rocks   177

   Chiddinglye Wood Rocks   180

   Happy Valley Rocks   185

   Penns Rocks   189

   Ramslye Farm Rocks   196

   Under Rockes   199

Other Outcrops (listed alphabetically)   206

Lost Outcrops   217

Other Rock   219

Sea Cliff Climbing   220

Margate	226
Dover	227
Hastings	246
Beachy Head to Brighton	250
Special Considerations for Group Use	262
Climbing Walls	265
Bibliography	268
Graded List of Selected Climbs	271
Index	277
Rescue	288

Maps and Plans

The Sandstone Area – map	front end leaf
The Central Sandstone Area – map	11
Bowles Rocks – West	34/35
Bowles Rocks – East	40/41
Bulls Hollow Rocks	53
Eridge Green Rocks – South	62/63
Eridge Green Rocks – Central	70/71
Eridge Green Rocks – North	74/75
Harrison's Rocks – general map	83
Harrison's Rocks – North	86/87
Harrison's Rocks – North Central	92/93
Harrison's Rocks – South Central	98/99
Harrison's Rocks – South	110/111
High Rocks – general map	125

High Rocks – East	126/127
High Rocks – Central	135
High Rocks – West	139
High Rocks Continuation Wall	152/153
High Rocks Annexe	162/163
Stone Farm/East Grinstead Area – map	165
Stone Farm Rocks – West	168/169
Stone Farm Rocks – East	172/173
Bassett's Farm Area – map	177
Bassett's Farm Rocks	178/179
Chiddinglye Wood Rocks	181
Happy Valley Rocks	186/187
Jockey's Wood Rocks	190
Penns House Rocks	193
Ramslye Farm Rocks	198/199
Under Rockes Area – map	200
Under Rockes	202/203
Dover – North	229
Dover – Main Area	234/235
Beachy Head	252/253
South-East England – map	rear end leaf

The Climbers' Club

The publisher of this guidebook is the Climbers' Club, which was founded in 1898 from origins in Snowdonia and is now one of the foremost mountaineering clubs in Great Britain. Its objects are to encourage mountaineering and rock-climbing, and to promote the general interest of mountaineers and the mountain environment.

It is a truly national club with widespread membership, and currently owns huts in Cornwall, Pembrokeshire, Derbyshire, and Snowdonia. Besides managing six huts, the Climbers' Club produces an annual Journal and runs a full programme of climbing meets, dinners, and social events. Club members may also use the huts of other clubs through reciprocal arrangements. The Club publishes climbing guidebooks (currently 15 in number) to cover most of Wales and Southern England. The Club is a founder-member of, and is affiliated to, the British Mountaineering Council; it makes annual contributions to the BMC's Access Fund, as well as to volunteer cliff and mountain rescue organisations.

Membership fluctuates around 900, and at present there are no limits on growth. Members of two years' standing may propose a competent candidate for membership and, provided that adequate support is obtained from other members, the Committee may elect him or her to full membership; there is no probationary period.

CLIMBING STYLE
The following policy statement on climbing style was agreed in principle at the Climbers' Club Annual General Meeting on 25th February 1990:

The Climbers' Club supports the tradition of using natural protection and is opposed to actions which are against the best interest of climbers and users of the crags. This applies particularly to irreversible acts which could affect the crags and their environs.

Such acts could include: the placing of bolts on mountain and natural crags; retrospective placing of bolts; chiselling, hammering, or altering the rock appearance or structure; excessive removal of vegetation and interference with trees, flowers, and fauna.

The Climbers' Club policy is that guidebooks are written to reflect the best style matched to the ethos and traditions of British Climbing.

GUIDEBOOK DISCLAIMER

This guide attempts to provide a definitive record of all existing climbs and is compiled from information from a variety of sources. The inclusion of any route does not imply that it remains in the condition described. Climbs can change unpredictably: rock can deteriorate and the existence and condition of *in-situ* protection can alter. All climbers must rely on their own ability and experience to gauge the difficulty and seriousness of any climb. Climbing is an inherently dangerous activity.

Neither the Climbers' Club nor the author and editor of this guidebook accept any liability whatsoever for any injury or damage caused to climbers, third parties, or property arising from any use of it. Whilst the content of the guide is believed to be accurate, no responsibility is accepted for any error, ommission, or mis-statement. Users must rely on their own judgement and are recommended to insure against injury to person and property and third party risks.

The inclusion in this guidebook of an outcrop or routes upon it does not mean that any member of the public has a right of access to the outcrop or the right to climb upon it.

Before climbing on any outcrop in this guidebook please read any appropriate access and conservation notes.

Acknowledgements

My thanks are due: to Dave Turner for his 1989 guidebook, which provided the basis for this book, and for his help reading through the manuscript; to the writers of all the earlier guidebooks; to Don Sargeant for his crag maps and plans, and for his advice on the photographs; to Ben Bevan-Pritchard for his drawings; but above all to Robin Mazinke and Tim Skinner, who have given me invaluable assistance in all aspects of the book's production.

The photographs were kindly supplied by: David Atchison-Jones, Chris Eades, Mick Fowler, Robin Mazinke, Luc Percival, Ian Smith, Terry Tullis/Dennis Kemp estate and Gary Wickham. I would also like to thank those who offered photographs which were ultimately not used.

The historical section is based on that written by Bob Moulton in the 1981 guide, and the Sandstone Environment section was written by Mike Eden. Kath Pyke wrote the section on Special Considerations for Group Use.

My thanks must also go to: Steve Durkin (Buzzard), Teresa Hill, John Horscroft, Pat Horscroft, Brian Kavanagh, Bob Moulton, Doug Reid, Ian Smith, Ray Tipton (Tip), Chris Tullis, Terry Tullis, and Gary Wickham; all of whom have contributed to making this a better guidebook.

The Sea Cliff section is based on Chris Mellor's 1994 Interim Guide, which itself was based on Mick Fowler's text for the 1989 guide. Bob Moulton would like to thank: Chris Mellor for making his text available, and Neil Atkinson, Dave Turnbull, Mike Vetterlein, Mick Fowler, Kath Pyke, Frank Ramsay, Phil Thornhill, Dave Wills and Andrew Weilochowski for commenting on the manuscript, and in particular Matt Kingsley and Gary Wickham, who in addition to providing their comments made special trips to Dover for this purpose (in Gary's case this involved the production of a 4-foot long topo!).

Finally both Bob and I would like to thank Ian Smith for his help and advice, and for masterminding the DTP for this book.

MTV 1995

Introduction

This book is a revision of Dave Turner's 1989 Southern Sandstone guide. It remains largely devoted to the Wealden sandstone but again includes a section on chalk and sandstone sea cliff climbing, reflecting the continuing activity of assorted nutters there.

The area remains as popular as ever, with the 'big three' outcrops, Bowles, Harrison's and Stone Farm, continuing to bear a disproportionate amount of traffic. Unfortunately, this popularity has led to a rapid deterioration of the fabric of the cliffs and a general degradation of the crag environment. Seventy years have now passed since the first climbs were recorded in the South-East. If the outcrops are to reach their centenary, let alone another seventy years, it is necessary that climbers adopt a much more responsible approach towards them, and to regard and treat them for what they are – *a precious, non-renewable resource*.

GENERAL
The sandstone outcrops of the Central Weald provide a relaxed and popular playground for climbers in the South-East, as well as for visitors travelling to or from the continent. The pleasant woodland settings and comparatively laid-back attitude in the area contrasts strongly with the generally more serious climbing to be found elsewhere. This is not least exemplified by the local top-roping ethic, itself wholly justified by the friable nature of the rock. There are 'no mind-blowing runouts on impending headwalls' to be had here, unless of course you head for the sea cliffs.

The visitor may be surprised by the number of rules and guidelines but after a short acquaintance with the area the need for these will be apparent. Sandstone is a very soft rock and requires much care to keep it intact as a climbing venue. Please read carefully the section on the Sandstone Environment and the Code of Conduct.

GETTING THERE
Two main roads traverse the area: the A22, London to Eastbourne, which passes through East Grinstead and serves the western area; and the A21, London to Hastings, which serves Tunbridge Wells and the eastern area. Both East Grinstead and Tunbridge Wells can get choked with traffic and it usually pays to by-pass the centre of these towns. The area is well served (at present) by railway lines. From Charing Cross and London Bridge a line runs to Hastings via Tunbridge Wells. From Victoria

another line runs via East Croydon to Oxted, where it divides; one branch going via Cowden, Eridge and Crowborough to Uckfield, the other to East Grinstead. All the major outcrops are within walking distance of stations on these three lines – for train times phone 0171 928 5100.

There is also a preserved railway – the famous Bluebell line. This runs between Sheffield Park and Kingscote, but will eventually run through to East Grinstead. Kingscote station is close to Stone Farm Rocks but at present is unusable as under the conditions imposed by the local residents it is not possible to embark or disembark there. This is likely to change in the future – for more details phone 01825 723777.

Another company known as TWERPS (Tunbridge Wells and Eridge Railway Preservation Society) plans to re-open the line between Tunbridge Wells West and Eridge. If it is successful then there will once again be a halt at High Rocks – for more details phone 01892 862140.

THE AREA
The area is well endowed with good pubs, many of them free houses. There is The Crown and The Junction in Groombridge; The Huntsman, beside Eridge Station; The Boars Head, close to Bowles; and High Rocks Inn opposite High Rocks. All these are indicated on the maps but there are many others of equal worth.

There are plenty of restaurants and cafés in Tunbridge Wells and East Grinstead, and at weekends there is a café in the Harrison's Rocks car-park.

There is a camp-site just north of Crowborough (OS Ref TQ 521 317); and another – The Julie Tullis Memorial Campsite – at Harrison's Rocks. The latter is available by reservation only. To book a pitch contact: Terry Tullis, The Warden/Site Manager, The Bothy, Leyswood, Groombridge, East Sussex, TN3 9PH – telephone 01892 864238 (mobile 0374 243888).

THE OUTCROPS
Harrison's Rocks is the most popular outcrop (as befits its ownership by the BMC) and the most extensive. It can become intolerably crowded at weekends and is suffering badly from erosion. Nevertheless it provides a large number of good climbs at all but the very easiest grades in a pleasant woodland setting, and it has a great sense of history. The next most popular outcrop is Bowles Rocks, which provides a smaller number of climbs than Harrison's but generally of a superior quality and in attractive open surroundings; it is, however, an organised climbing centre but at the time of writing the restrictions on climbers are minimal.

High Rocks is also situated in enclosed grounds but of a very different nature; in this case as part of the grounds of High Rocks Hotel. High

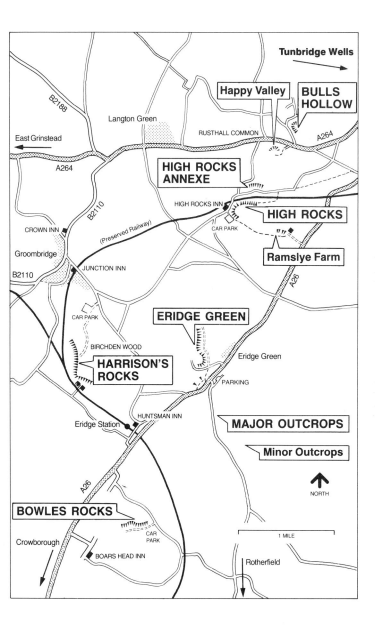

Rocks is almost as extensive as Harrison's but the climbs are less densely packed and, as the name implies, higher – cracks and chimneys predominate and some of the hardest and most impressive climbs on sandstone are to be found here. More reasonable climbing can also be found at High Rocks, and crowding is rarely a problem, but due to the prolific trees and rhododendrons (an advantage in a heatwave) the rock does take longer to dry out than at Harrison's and Bowles.

Close to High Rocks are two smaller outcrops, the Continuation Wall and the Annexe. Both of these provide a selection of short routes mainly in the lower grades. Unfortunately, like the main crag, they are shrouded with trees and tend to be slow to dry.

Bulls Hollow and Stone Farm Rocks provide a stark contrast – Bulls Hollow being almost claustrophobic, set as it is in a hole in the ground; whilst Stone Farm is well-positioned in a picturesque, open setting on an escarpment overlooking a reservoir. Bulls Hollow, when in condition, has a handful of excellent climbs of good length, whilst Stone Farm has lots of short climbs, well-suited to soloing.

The last major outcrop is Eridge Green Rocks, on which climbing is not permitted. It has a large number of climbs set in beautiful woodland scenery, whose unspoilt nature undeniably owes something to the climbing restriction.

THE CLIMBS
For the accomplished climber the rock offers a wide variety of experiences. Some of the best routes are also amongst the hardest, and these provide climbing of the highest standards of difficulty. The climbs are particularly suited to the development of unorthodox techniques and, when top-roping, to the determination of the physical limits of the human body in an attack on a rock problem, completely removed from the difficulties of approach and retreat. The harder climbs can be treated as a succession of boulder problems, this being the method by which most of them were first climbed.

Where the surface is case-hardened and the rock dry, the frictional properties can be very good. The main features are deep cracks and chimneys separated by rounded bulging buttresses. Slabs are infrequent, though there are many easy-angled climbs at Bowles Rocks. The holds tend to be rounded and sloping with few natural incuts, and therefore need, or eventually develop, arm strength, not least because one often cannot trust one's feet.

Southern Sandstone is a reasonable environment for novices, provided they are aware of the need to master new techniques when transferring to rock in mountain or other areas. Stone Farm Rocks is a good place to begin.

First time visitors should not necessarily feel disappointed if they are not satisfied with their performance, as experience seems to greatly improve one's chances of success.

THE SANDSTONE ENVIRONMENT

The sandstone outcrops of South-East England are composed of a particularly soft material and are perhaps the most fragile rocks in the country to be climbed on, using conventional techniques. As they are also amongst the most popular, it is not suprising that there has been some damage as a result of climbing in the area. Whilst some of this damage is almost inevitable there is no doubt that a high proportion of it could be avoided.

Southern Sandstone is, geologically speaking, part of the Lower Tunbridge Wells Sand Formation, and was laid down about 130 million years ago as part of a sequence of ancient river sediments. The rock is exceptionally weak and owes almost all its strength to the development of a thin weathered crust, typically only two to three millimetres thick. Here the sand grains are cemented by a relatively strong quartz cement deposited from pore waters containing minute amounts of dissolved silica. This process took many thousands of years.

The sandstone has weathered to form a number of remarkable features. A peculiar characteristic of the Tunbridge Wells Sandstone is its tendency to form honeycomb-like structures on weathering. These are common features on weathered limestone but the reasons for their formation on sandstone are unknown. There are also polygonal markings, the most notable being at High Rocks. These easily-damaged features formed during the last ice age, several thousand years ago.

Climbing, even without ropes, results in erosion of the rock. The main effects of this erosion are the general wearing away of the rock, particularly on popular climbs, and the breaking of holds. The general wear is probably unavoidable, although its progress can be slowed or halted as described later. The breaking of fragile holds, although normally accidental, is often avoidable by adopting a more thoughtful approach. Some holds have been destroyed by blow-torching, which heats the rock so strongly that the weathered surface develops cracks and eventually breaks off. Other holds have been damaged by abseiling, or as a result of using heavy footwear, or, worst of all, a combination of both. It must also be mentioned that substantial damage to the rock has been caused by non-climbers in the form of graffiti.

Probably the most visible evidence of damage caused by climbing is rope grooves. These result (not surprisingly) from the sawing action of ropes as they drag across the rock surface. This form of damage is easily avoided by arranging the belay so that no moving ropes are in contact with the rock.

Over the last decade or so considerable efforts have been made to repair rope grooves and to slow the rate at which the rocks are being eroded.

Rope grooves have been repaired using mixtures of the ubiquitous sand, to be found at the foot of most climbs, and cement. These repairs have consumed many weeks and months of voluntary work. In some cases the damage has been so bad and affected such a large area that early photographs have had to be studied in order to determine the original shape of the buttress. In conjunction with this work numerous bolts have been placed at the top of Harrison's and Stone Farm Rocks. This should make it easier to set up belays and hence eliminate, or at least lessen, any future erosion.

The most recent repair technique has been the use of surface-consolidating chemicals on areas of severely damaged rock. The principal is that the material penetrates the rock, hardens, and binds the rock together. This material has only been used on areas where the critical weathered surface has been worn away. Repaired rock is almost indistinguisable from undamaged rock. This technique has been used successfully at Harrison Rocks and on a much smaller scale at some of the other outcrops.

The outcrops are also of interest to botanists. The moist and sheltered environment found here is much akin to that of the west coast of Britain, and many of the rock plants are similar to those of that coast. It is believed that such plants have survived in these specialised habitats, well outside their normal distribution range, for about 5,600 years, when the whole country experienced a warmer and wetter climate than now. As a result there are a number of very rare species of mosses and liverworts associated with the rock, for the protection of which (and other features) certain outcrops are designated as Sites of Special Scientific Interest (SSSI). These are pointed out in the text. In the interests of science (and to keep such areas open to climbers) it is important that great care be taken to avoid unnecessary damage to the flora.

With increasing numbers of climbers visiting the South-East it has become more important than ever to conserve the fragile sandstone environment and to take steps to avoid unnecessary damage. For this reason it is vital that the guidelines laid out in the next section are followed at all times.

CODE OF CONDUCT

(1) Think carefully when setting up belays. Your first priority should always be the protection of the rock. If you have insufficient or inadequate equipment for a given climb, then please don't attempt it.

(2) Ensure that the karabiner is hanging over the edge of the crag and that moving ropes don't come into contact with the rock. Resist the temptation to place the krab 'just that little bit higher' to protect the hard finishing moves that are a feature of sandstone climbing.

(3) Slings used for belays should be of a non-stretch type so as to minimise damage when the rope system is weighted.

(4) Try to protect the top of the crag wherever possible. A large piece of old carpet is useful in this respect.

(5) Use the bolts at the top of the crag for belaying wherever possible. Do not allow moving ropes to come into contact with the bolts; always use a sling.

(6) Do not allow moving ropes to come into contact with trees — it will eventually kill them. Always use a sling.

(7) Don't use trees as anchors where alternatives exist. When using trees position the sling as close to the ground as possible so as to minimise leverage. The only exceptions to this are where trees have been equipped with cables, e.g. Two-Toed Sloth at Harrison's.

(8) Do not cut down or prune overhanging trees. Accept that the rock may always be a little damp. Climbing on damp and greasy rock is a necessary sandstone skill.

(9) Do not use herbicides for clearing vegetation from the rock. It will only give a temporary respite, and when regrowth occurs it is the commonest species which re-colonise first, the rare species being eliminated.

(10) Top-roping and soloing are the only acceptable methods of climbing. Do not use pitons, chocks or camming devices. They offer no protection to the climber and cause irreparable damage to the rock when they pull out.

(11) Always wear soft-soled footwear, never heavy boots.

(12) Do not abseil. (See also section on abseiling below.)

(13) Do not lower-off after completing a climb. (See also section on lowering-off below.)

(14) Soloing is the only acceptable way for the first member of a party to reach the summit of an isolated buttress. (See also section on lowering-off below.)

(15) Do not aid-climb. (See also section on aid-climbing below.)

(16) Never blow-torch the rock.

(17) Do not chip or enlarge holds. (See also section on chipping below.)

(18) Use only soft brushes or cloths for cleaning the rock. Never use wire brushes.

(19) Please bear in mind that wet rock is both substantially weaker than dry rock, and more prone to erosion. Sloping footholds are particularly susceptible in this latter respect.

(20) Take care to limit ground erosion on descent paths and at the foot of the crags.

(21) Do not ride mountain bikes at sandstone outcrops.

(22) Don't camp, light fires or stoves, play transistor radios or make unnecessary noise. Please take your litter (and any other) away with you. This includes finger-tape, boot laces, and cigarette ends.

(23) Switch mobile phones off.

(24) Keep dogs under control and remove any waste near the crag.

(25) Don't ice climb.

Please also see the section on Special Considerations for Group Use on page 262.

ACCESS
All the outcrops in this guidebook form part of the inhabited countryside and as such are on private or Forestry Commission land. Climbing is allowed only through the co-operation of the landowners (or perhaps blissful ignorance in the case of some minor crags). At two of the major outcrops there is a payment for climbing.

As in previous editions information is given of outcrops where climbing is not permitted; full details of known access restrictions being noted. This is not intended to encourage climbing on such outcrops but in order to maintain a record of what has been done so as to provide information should a given access situation ever change.

The inclusion in this guidebook of an outcrop or routes upon it does not mean that any member of the public has a right of access to the outcrop or the right to climb upon it.

Moonlight Arête, 4c, Harrison's Rocks, circa 1950. Climber: Johnnie Lees.
Photo: Dennis Kemp

The Thing, 6b(NS), Bowles Rocks. Climber: Chris Murray. Photo: Robin Mazinke.

Before climbing on any outcrop in this guide please read any appropriate access and conservation notes.

ETHICS AND THINGS

Southern Sandstone is unusual in that top-roping is the normal and accepted style of ascent. This ethic has evolved and is maintained because the soft and friable nature of the rock does not lend itself to leading. Conventional protection devices badly damage the rock, and the sandstone will often fail anyway in the event of a fall. It has been suggested that bolts be placed on Sandstone to enable leading, but this would be anathema to most local climbers as well as causing enormous damage; and anyway seems pointless given the ease with which top-ropes can be placed. The choice lies between soloing or top-roping, with the exception of *Temptation* at Bowles which can be led clipping the *in-situ* bolts. A few other routes have been led with normal protection but this practice is not to be encouraged. Soloing is recognized as ultimately the best style of ascent. Soloists should obviously treat all but the best holds with extreme caution. Clearly, top-roping enables one to push oneself to the limit in complete safety (depending on who is belaying!) and rapid improvement is thus possible for beginners. Nearly all the hard climbs were sieged on their first ascents, an approach which pre-dates the current trend on bolt-protected limestone routes – hard climbing under safe conditions.

The use of chalk as an aid to climbing has in the past been the cause of bitter argument in the area, despite its widespread acceptance (or at least widespread use) elsewhere. However, at the crags where the use of chalk was once banned it is now grudgingly tolerated. In general it is suggested that its use be kept to a minimum; that is, use it but don't throw it everywhere.

The softness of the rock raises an ethical problem in that cleaning out a hold is often indistinguishable from enlarging it – brushing the sandstone even just a little too hard can create or remove holds, so please take care.

ABSEILING

Abseiling is best avoided at all times because of the ease with which holds can be broken off and the damage done to the top of the crag by weighted ropes.

There is **a total ban on abseiling at Harrison's, High and Stone Farm Rocks.** Please do not abseil at the other outcrops. If you still feel you must, then please choose your site carefully: pick an area where no climbs exist (or are likely to). Be prepared for a hostile reaction from the locals.

Abseiling is a useful mountaineering skill and as such can form an important part of an introductory course, but the sandstone outcrops of the South-East are totally unsuited to it. A far better alternative is to find a suitable building, which would almost certainly give a longer and thus more exciting descent. Climbing walls are also good venues – see the list on page 265.

LOWERING-OFF
Because of the greater weights involved this practice is even more damaging to the rock than abseiling. What has been said about abseiling, therefore, also applies to lowering-off, i.e. please refrain from the practice.

This should present no problems except when climbing on three isolated buttresses: Isolated Boulder and Hut Boulder at High Rocks and Inaccessible Boulder at Stone Farm Rocks. On these the procedure should be as follows: the first climber solos to the top, sets up the belay and then down-climbs on a slack rope; the rest of the party then follow, ascending and descending on slack ropes. Finally the last climber dismantles the belay and solos down.

CHIPPING
Under no circumstances should holds be cut or chipped. This practice is still going on, particularly at Stone Farm and those involved are pathetic. If you catch anyone doing this please stop them. There is no one here to repair damage and if unchecked the situation will eventually be irretrievable. Many of the routes chipped in the past have now been climbed without using the cut holds and the same will eventually happen to today's adulterations, care of a future generation. Sandstone crags are not slate quarries. Please leave problems you can't do to someone better (or with stickier boot rubber) rather than vandalising the rock.

AID-CLIMBING
The few artificial routes described are rarely ascended and have very little in the way of *in-situ* aid points. Their inclusion is purely for the record and should not be taken as encouragement to aid climb. Many old aid routes have since been climbed free (e.g. *Patella, Kinnard, Temptation, Sossblitz, The King, The Second Generation*). At both Harrison's and High Rocks there is **a total ban on aid-climbing**, largely to prevent the damage that inevitably results.

EQUIPMENT
It is recommended that new ropes are not used for top-roping since the abrasive nature of the rock can quickly ruin them. The ideal rope is the hawser-laid nylon type, not least because of cost. New kernmantel leading ropes are pretty much a waste on sandstone, though tougher

non-stretch caving ropes can be recommended. The belay sling must be of a non-stretch material. To avoid causing or enlarging rope grooves the top-rope should be arranged with a belay sling long enough to allow the (screw gate) karabiner to hang over the edge of the face. Ropes should never be run directly around trees or through *in-situ* bolts because the former will be killed and the latter simply worn through, thus requiring costly replacement. The rock is suffering a great deal from such abuse so please follow this advice and help preserve it for as long as possible.

Only lightweight boots should be worn, such as specialist rock-climbing boots and slippers, training shoes, plimsolls and so on. Heavy duty climbing or walking boots should **not** be worn. Some local climbers favour barefoot climbing which, though uncomfortable initially, can be very useful for cramming toes into small pockets if you like that sort of thing.

The use of a mat or cloth to clean boots is recommended and the practice of blowing sand off holds before using them is well worth adopting.

THE GRADINGS
A numerical grade is given for each climb ranging from the easiest, 1a, rising through 1b, 2a, 2b, 3a, 3b, 4a, 4b, 4c, 5a, 5b, 5c, 6a, 6b, 6c, to the current top grade of 7a. The grade is a measure of the *hardest move* on the climb and takes no account of any other factor. An alternative system, which grades for 'total' difficulty has been used (for the first time) in the Graded List – see page 271. Wherever possible the grade given is the collated opinion of many climbers. The letters NS in brackets after the grade mean that at the time of writing the climb has not been soloed; it has of course been climbed totally free (one hopes) whilst top-roping. Nearly all of the hardest routes have only been soloed after repeated top-roped ascents.

The grades given are for good conditions; those climbs that seem to be in a permanently poor state are often indicated in the text.

It should be borne in mind that repeated top-roping of familiar climbs does tend to reduce their difficulty to the purely physical. Visitors shouldn't be put off by locals who know where all the holds are and have done the routes three million times before. Some can climb 6a or more on sandstone but drop down to about VS when leading elsewhere, so take heart sandstone bumblies.

STARS AND DAGGERS
No, not a section on bitching and back-stabbing by budding super-heroes though that might be more fun.

Stars have been allocated to some routes to pick them out as better climbs than their neighbours and to help indicate those crags or parts of crags worth a look. Clearly, the stars only apply when the routes are in condition, which in some cases is not very often. Three stars have been reserved for the best, two for the very good and one for recommended routes at each grade. The absence of stars does not necessarily mean that a route is not worthwhile, merely that others are better. A certain bias in favour of higher grade routes may be noticed. This is not to put down lower grade climbs but reflects the simple fact that many of the best lines are in the higher grades. The dagger signs (†) have been used to indicate unrepeated routes, for which the grade is more uncertain than most.

NEW CLIMBS

The new routes book is at present kept at Soft Rock, Station Road, Groombridge, which is open at weekends throughout the year and weekday evenings in the summer. It should not only be used to record new routes but also to record changes to existing routes, repeat ascents, solo ascents, comments, wit(?) etc.

A large part of the new routes record is missing – hence the absence of a First Ascents List in this guidebook. However, an embryo list is in existence and gradually, by a slow, painstaking process, the gaps are being filled. If you have any information about first ascents, particularly from the early days of climbing in the South-East, please record it in the back of the current new routes book.

Historical

The earliest known reference by a mountaineer to the sandstone outcrops in the Tunbridge Wells area is in the book *A Tramp to Brighton* by E J Kennedy, president of The Alpine Club from 1860 to 1862. He refers to searching for a specimen of the Tunbridge Filmy Fern (*Hymenophyllum Tunbridgense*) in 1857, '...through woods across meadows towards some crevices in the rocks that I had known some years earlier'. However, he only mentions 'the Tunbridge Wells Rocks', giving no further detail.

The next recorded mention of a sandstone outcrop in South-East England by a mountaineer seems to have taken place around 1908, when Charles Nettleton noticed Harrison's Rocks while passing along the valley below with the Eridge Hunt. He afterwards returned with Claude Wilson but it is not known whether they actually did any climbing.

The first recorded climbing began in 1926, when the possibilities of Harrison's were realised by Nea Morin (*née* Barnard), who had climbed on similar outcrops at Fontainebleau near Paris; a family connection which subsequently led to the introduction of the PA (Pierre Alain) rock-boot to British rock, and later the EB (Eric Bourdonneau). The early explorers also included Jean Morin, Eric Shipton, Gilbert Peaker, Osbert Barnard, E H Marriot and Miss Marples. Among the routes climbed in this period were such classics as *Long Layback*, *Long Crack*, *The Sewer*, *Isolated Buttress Climb* and the excellent *Unclimbed Wall*, which retains the 5b grade to this day. Most of these routes originally had different names. In the late 1920s the same group was active at High Rocks, climbing *Steps Crack* (another 'modern' 5b) and some of the main chimneys. High Rocks has a long history as a pleasure ground, being first popularised in 1670 by James II, when Duke of York.

In 1934 H Courtney-Bryson and M O Sheffield, members of the Mountaineering Section of the Camping Club, produced the first guidebook to Harrison's, listing about thirty climbs. Knowing little of the previous explorations they renamed most of the routes although many of their climbs were in fact new, including the ever-popular *Hell Wall* and *Zig-Zag Wall*. In 1936 Courtney-Bryson went on to produce a new guide, which covered additions at Harrison's such as *Set Square Arête* and *Slab Crack* but which also drew attention to several other known outcrops in the area. This was to be an inspiration to the next generation of sandstone climbers, many of whom had known little or nothing of outcrops other than Harrison's – this still applies in some quarters even today.

Oxford University climbers climbed at High Rocks in 1936-37 and routes described in their journal included the classic *Simian Progress, North Wall* (the first recorded routes on the Isolated Boulder) and *Crack Route* on Hut Boulder.

In the early stages of a long and notable career on sandstone, Ted Pyatt visited High Rocks just before the Second World War with members of the Polaris Mountaineering Club, of whom B N Simmons was particularly active. They knew nothing of the previous work and the outcrop was in effect developed from scratch; *Anaconda Chimney, Boa Constrictor Chimney and Cobra Chimney* (originally A, B and C Chimneys) were among their climbs. Exploration at High Rocks was continued after 1942 by members of the Junior Mountaineering Club of Scotland; Frank Elliot, who had already established a reputation on gritstone was a prominent figure. New climbs during this period included *Shelter Slabs, Swing Face, Python Crack* and *The Helix*.

Little new development took place at Harrison's after the early 1930s until 1941, when Edward Zenthon (of the JMCS) put together a girdle traverse of the outcrop. This was over 300 metres long and, though somewhat broken in continuity and quality in places, was an outstanding achievement. Many of the gaps continued to be filled at Harrison's through the war years, mainly through the efforts of Elliot.

At Eridge Green little climbing had been done until 1941, when visits were made by parties from the JMCS, of which Pyatt had now become a member. The rope grooves at the top of the rocks, particularly on Eridge Tower, bear witness to its early popularity. Elliot again was the outstanding contributor with fine routes such as *Battlements Crack, Barbican Buttress* and *Amphitheatre Crack*. The ascent of the latter was achieved by combined tactics using a chockstone specially imported for the occasion from Dow Crag.

In 1945, a new wave of exploration began at Harrison's under the inspiration of Clifford Fenner, a forester by profession, so giving rise to *Forester's Wall*. Standards were raised considerably by the addition of the fine and elegant *Slim Finger Crack*, which is the first record of a route still retaining the 5c grade. Classics such as *The Niblick, Monkey's Necklace* and routes of similar calibre were also done at this time.

By 1947, JMCS members had added the majority of the climbs at High Rocks Annexe and Continuation Wall. In addition, by this time most of the Stone Farm routes had been done, by either JMCS or PMC members.

After Pyatt's 1947 guide, Harrison's continued to be the most popular outcrop and standards continued to rise as is indicated by the fact that two climbs from this period, *Monkey's Bow* (by Mike Ball) and *Baboon*, are now graded 6a, perhaps the first climbs in Britain to merit this grade. Other notable additions included *Piecemeal Wall* by the Lakeland pioneer, Arthur Dolphin, and *North-West Corner*. Nea Morin was very much involved in this activity and, among many contributors, Johnnie Lees and Pete Warland were outstanding. The former led many of the NSs of the 1947 guide, including *Crowborough* and *Birchden Corners*, and contributed many routes of his own. Notable ascents by visiting climbers included Menlove Edwards's eponymous *Effort*. This was done as an unroped solo, an extremely impressive feat, and perhaps a reflection of the ability required to ascend his Welsh routes of the time without modern equipment. Also in this period Tony Moulam did the first solo of *Slim Finger Crack*, another major achievement.

In the early 1950s, a forceful new group emerged in the form of the Sandstone Climbing Club. The Club was formed in 1951 by Ned Cordery, Salt Sullivan, Mic O'Connor, Doug Stone and Des Entwhistle. They soon moved their attention from Harrison's, where they "often felt outclassed by the earlier inhabitants", to High Rocks (where they had use of the hut that used to exist behind Hut Boulder) so as to work up their standards. The success of this exercise was soon evident and the first generation of SCC climbers was responsible for most of the harder routes at High Rocks in the 1956 guide including *Advertisement Wall*, *Henry the Ninth* and *Simian Mistake*.

Between 1956 and 1963 the SCC monopolised development at High Rocks, adding over seventy new routes; many of these were of the highest standards including four with the new 6a grade in the 1963 guide. John and Paul Smoker, Phil Gordon, Billy Maxwell and Martin Boysen were industrious performers during this period. Among the SCC's routes were *Mulligan's Wall*, *The Lobster*, *Engagement Wall*, *Sphinx*, *Tilley Lamp Crack* and *Effie*. Boysen was one of the first exclusively sandstone-bred climbers to make a real breakthrough onto high standard mountain rock, and subsequently the Alps and further afield. It has been written that he climbed so much on occasions, that afterwards he couldn't use a knife and fork to cut up his dinner. Although there were other notable exceptions, many other sandstone experts failed to adapt their high standards to other types of rock. Indeed John Smoker, one of the most effective SCC members, was once described by Joe Brown, on seeing him climb, as "the cycling window-cleaner".

During this period the SCC were also steadily adding routes at Harrison's and here they were later joined by members of the North London MC, whose routes included *Bonanza* and *Baskerville*. One of their number,

Max Smart, was responsible for *Elementary* and *Far Left* on the Unclimbed Wall, two fine additions.

Bowles Rocks was the only major outcrop to have been omitted from Courtney-Bryson's 1936 guide. Nea Morin is known to have climbed at Bowles shortly after the war and the SCC to have been there in the early 1950s, but it was left to Pyatt to rediscover the Rocks when working on the 1956 guide. In it he made the tantalising comment, "if conditions should change at some future date the outcrop would be an excellent prospect". In 1959/60 the SCC (initially as prospective purchasers of the Rocks) started an intense period of cleaning and they pioneered the large majority of climbs, including some of the very hardest such as the aptly named *The Thing, Hate,* and *Digitalis*; Boysen and John Smoker featured prominently. *The Thing* is probably the first route to now be given the 6b grade. The Bowles Mountaineering Trust purchased the Rocks in 1963, outbidding the initial asking price of £400. One of the unsuccessful bidders was the father of Mick Jagger. Terry Tullis, currently the Harrison's Rocks Warden, and Julie Tullis were both involved with the extensive gardening and cleaning required to make this the excellent climbing area it is today, as well as contributing some new routes. It was at this time that the unfortunate hold-chipping and rock engineering occured on, among others, *Drosophila* (which had already been climbed by the SCC), *Sapper* (admittedly now a fine climb) and the well named *Devaluation.*

Bowles in fact served a wide range of purposes prior to its present role. There is evidence of prehistoric habitation and later smugglers (trading cannons and other iron products for French brandy and cigars) are thought to have used the outcrop as a hiding place. During the 19th century the rocks provided a backcloth to an avenue of trees and a carriageway leading to the house of John Bowles, a Dutchman. Subsequently the Rocks provided the site for a gypsy camp and a rubbish tip. During the Second World War, Bowles was used as a firing range, hence the numerous pock-marks on the Range Wall. In the late 1950s and early 1960s notoriously ferocious pigs had their sties at the base of the Rocks. This seems to be the reason for the large square-cut holes under the base overhangs in the region of Carbide Finger.

One of the most active climbers during the latter half of the 1960s at Harrison's was Trevor Panther, who remains an active sandstone climber to this day. Among his climbs were the fine *Sossblitz* (with Peter 'Soss' Sorrell), albeit with an aid point, *The Knam, Glendale Crack* free, *Crucifix* and *Grant's Wall.* One of Panther's young protégés, Ben Wintringham, climbed the classic *The Flakes* and *Celestial's Reach*, and was also responsible for *The Limpet* and *West Wall Eliminate* (now *Woolly Bear*), though these two climbs are almost certainly much harder now due to the loss of holds. Boysen, on leave from High Rocks, did *Coronation Crack* in 1967, whilst Greg Morgan climbed *Orangutang* in the same period.

Another active group during this period were Les and Lawrie Holliwell, and Robin Harper. They laid strong emphasis on soloing and on using sandstone as training for bigger things. Lawrie Holliwell was to follow Boysen by becoming one of the top Welsh climbers; among his best achievements on sandstone were his solos of *South-West Corner* and *Vulture Crack* – the former being the hardest route to have been soloed at that time. It is now even harder since a crucial large hold broke off at the top!

Little history is known about Bulls Hollow; the 1947 guidebook described twenty routes and little else was added up to 1963. Between then and 1968 the number of routes was doubled by Les Holliwell when working on the 1969 guide, though many of the routes may have been climbed before. Some of the hardest and most worthwhile routes were among the additions including *The Wall*, an atypical route for sandstone and one of the best at Bulls Hollow.

During relaxations in the access restrictions a considerable number of routes were quietly added at Eridge Green by the Holliwell group, though once again much of this was probably a question of formalising previous, unrecorded, SCC activity.

A lull in development followed the 1969 guide until a wave of new route activity commenced in late 1971. Between 1971 and 1975 by far the most active pioneers were Nigel Head and Gordon DeLacy. They can probably be credited with around half of the 150 odd new routes contained in the 1981 guide; particularly notable among their routes were *Nightmare* and *Fandango Right Hand* at Bowles; and *Adder* (free) and *Dysentery* at High Rocks. In the late 1970s Mick Fowler, another climber who established his reputation in North Wales and elsewhere (including the chalk climbing described later in this book), was responsible for advancing the standards of sandstone climbing by adding many high grade, good quality climbs. With routes such as *The First Crack* (free), *Honeycomb* and *Infidel* at High Rocks, and *Sandstorm* and *The Crunch* at Eridge Green these included some of the earlier 6bs on Southern Sandstone. During the 1970s Boysen, on periodic visits, climbed *Sandman* (on which his reach was a great asset) at Bowles and *Boysen's Crack* at High Rocks.

Adder and *The First Crack* were two of a number of old aid climbs to have been climbed free, giving some of the most impressive lines on Southern Sandstone and some of the hardest climbing of the time. Important solo ascents in the 1970s and early 1980s included the

Harrison's *Coronation Crack* by Stevie Haston and *Hate* by Fowler. *The Thing* was led by Andy Meyers, with a Friend and a nut for protection, and after a number of falls, when he apparently came dangerously close to the slab beneath at times. *Digitalis* and *Serenade Arête* were soloed by Ron Fawcett, on a rare visit to Southern Sandstone when he soloed "all but two or three of the routes at Bowles on sight" – despite this quote there were 16 NSs in the subsequent guide to Bowles!

Following Tim Daniells's 1981 guide a number of very good but necessarily hard routes were done at the major outcrops. Most of the smaller, less frequented crags were also further developed. One of the major and most able contributors, particularly in the early 1980s, was Guy McLelland. Of his numerous ascents a number are outstanding. At High Rocks he climbed two major additions with the hugely overhanging and impressive *Judy* and subsequently the less imposing but equally fine *Salad Days*. David Jones was also active during this period and, often climbing with McLelland, put up a number of important new routes as well as numerous fillers-in. His most difficult contribution was *Time Waits for No One* at Bulls Hollow which, though very short, provides some sustained technical climbing. Of his other routes, *Harlequin* (Chiddinglye Wood), *Meridian* (Under Rockes) and *Kathmandu* (Stone Farm) stand out. Together with McLelland he accounted for most of the new additions recorded at Penns Rocks and Ramslye Farm. Furthermore, he soloed extensively, removing the NS suffix from numerous 5b and 5c routes. Other climbers active in this period and subsequently include Barry 'Rambo' Knight, Chris Arnold, Dan Wajzner, Martin Crocker, Martyn Lewis, and Frank Shannon – all of whom contributed to the development of the area in various ways.

One of the few major lines remaining at Harrison's was picked off by McLelland with very little effort. This was a free version of Crisis – *What Crisis?* – which retained an aura of difficulty (of the 7a type) for a number of years, though it is now climbed frequently, and has even been soloed. In the same period Dan Lewis climbed *The Republic*, another fine addition to the Harrison's repertoire, while his talented brother Martyn created *Karen's Kondom*, named after a (strange?) sculpture he had done.

In addition to McLelland a number of other climbers were active at High Rocks in the mid-1980s. In particular, Boysen caught out the regulars with his ascent of the superb *Krait Arête* (pronounced Krite), which had repelled the efforts of many strong climbers; he himself had been trying it on and off for 25 years. Subsequently, Boysen managed another major line with *Moving Staircase*, the name reflecting the sloping nature of the crux footholds. A year or two later Gary Wickham found some motivation and picked some plum routes here, including the highly problematic *Kinda Lingers* and the excellent *Nemesis*; the latter perhaps stimulated by Matt Saunders's ascent of the adjacent *A Touch Too Much* – a good route with a name appropriate to its first ascentionist.

Perhaps surprisingly, Bowles Rocks continued to give some excellent new routes. The impressive wall of *Temptation* was climbed by Dave Turner who subsequently led the route, sticking his neck out and clipping all the many bolts on the way. On the same wall the old aid climb *Kinnard* was turned into a very sustained free climb by Paul Hayes, thus creating one of the longest roped climbs on sandstone.

The discreet activity continued at Eridge Green; the best routes being once again the work of McLelland. *The Beguiled* is a tendon-ripping problem on a steep wall, while in contrast *Diagonal* is a delicate, technical proposition. At Stone Farm a few surprisingly good new routes were climbed in the mid-1980s. Ed Stone put up the very tricky *Birdie Num-Nums*; McLelland powered up the extremely strenuous *Guy's Route* – which is dangerous even on a top-rope – and Barry Franklin created the technical *Illusion*. Sadly, a large number of chipped holds have appeared here, a reprehensible practice which can only be condemned.

Bassett's Farm, a small but fine outcrop omitted from Daniells's guide because he couldn't find it, was 'rediscovered' by Ian Mailer and friends. Between them all the worthwhile lines were climbed before its location was revealed, including the fine *Karate Liz* and *Dislocator* by Mailer, and *Dan's Wall* courtesy of Dan Lewis.

In 1987, while working on his guidebook, Turner set to work on some of the more obvious remaining lines. At Bowles the Patella- Digitalis wall provided yet another fine climb – *Nutella* – while the much-eyed line on the Engagement Wall at High Rocks gave the highly gymnastic *Dyno-Sore*. An altogether different proposition was a wall in the Grand Canyon which required a protracted effort before it finally yielded *Cool Bananas* – the hardest route on sandstone at that time. At Harrison's Turner later climbed *Lager Frenzy* – 'the last great problem' of the crag. Panther's 1986 Harrison's guide provided the incentive, claiming it would require a "superman... rocknast" to free-climb it.

The early and mid-1980s saw a number of notable solo performances. Dan Lewis managed some of Harrison's harder routes, including *Celestial's Reach, Forester's Wall Direct*, and *The Mank*. At Bowles he made a frightening unroped ascent of *Sandman*, with a somewhat worried person below to divert his 13-stone frame from the boulder should he have come unstuck. Again at Bowles Hayes soloed *Patella*, a highly insecure proposition. Returning to Harrison's, *Right Unclimbed* received a solo ascent from Wickham – impressive because the crux is very easy to fluff – while *Grant's Wall* and the precarious *Grant's Groove* received similar treatment from Mailer. Furthermore, Fowler returned once again to sandstone and made a very impressive ropeless ascent of his own route, *Infidel*.

In 1987 Saunders risked a lot with his solos of first *Temptation* and then, to top that, *Carbide Finger* – still the hardest route in the South-East to have been soloed. Indeed, his first attempt on the former ended with a broken ankle. Carbide Finger, undergraded and certainly the most difficult climb in Daniells's guide, has now had a number of ascents.

The publication of Turner's guide led to a re-assessment of the remaining possibilities. Hayes was the first to make the book out of date. In the summer of 1989 he climbed two major lines: the bizarrely named *More Cake for Me* at Eridge Green – superb climbing up an unlikely-looking wall – and *Unforgettable*, an imposing arête at High Rocks. He also eliminated the aid points from Ping Pong to produce the short but desperate *Whiff Whaff*.

The summer of 1990 proved to be exceptionally hot and dry. All the outcrops dried out completely and an unprecedented new route boom ensued.

At High Rocks Jasper Sharpe succeeded in free-climbing one of the few remaining aid routes to produce *The Second Generation*, the finest addition for almost a decade. This was originally 'ascended' in the 1970s using a plethora of wooden-wedges and expansion-bolts, the area of rock being chosen on the assumption that it could never be climbed conventionally. Turner, who was narrowly beaten to the first ascent, then climbed the hideously thin groove opposite to create *Chimaera*, the first, and so far only, route to warrant the grade of 7a. The climb remains unrepeated to this day despite concerted efforts by the locals and occasional visits by 'stars' from other areas.

The weekend that Chimaera fell proved to be one of frenetic activity. Wickham climbed the technical *The Purvee*, a climb unlikely to see a lot of traffic; and *Fungal Smear*, which, unusually for sandstone, features hard slab-climbing. Paul Widdowson added *Too Hard for Dave*, and Hayes climbed the pumpy *So What?* The pick of the routes, however, was another Turner creation – *Renascence*, a steep unrelenting climb with a nasty sting in its tail.

The rest of the development that year proceeded at a (slightly) more sedate pace. Widdowson was the most prolific activist, accounting for a suprising number of hard routes, amongst which *Kraken*, *Slowhand*, and *Telegram Sam* stand out. Wickham gave *Missing Link* an independent start and eliminated the aid-point; and in doing so created a fine route – one of the longest at the outcrop. Turner's final route of the year was the esoteric *Tubby Hayes is a Fats Waller*. Sadly this turned out to be his last route in the South-East, as first injury and then migration to Sheffield removed him from the sandstone scene. Undoubtedly the finest sandstone climber of his generation he was responsible, together with Wickham, for setting a standard of difficulty which, five years since his departure, has yet to be equalled, let alone surpassed.

Eridge Green also saw much activity. The decaying vegetation, a legacy of the 1987 storms, was obligingly cleared by the owners, and great swathes of rock emerged from the gloom. In the frantic scramble for new routes that ensued, nearly every buttress received attention. The father-and-son team, Oliver and Guy Hill, developed the Steelmill buttress with four good routes of a suprisingly reasonable standard; *Genesis* and *Poofy Finger's Revenge* being perhaps the pick. Widdowson put up four quality routes; on an early visit he accounted for *Lou*, a fingery, highly technical proposition on one of the newly unearthed buttresses; and *Lazy Chive*, a climb with a frustratingly hard finish. Later he added *Zugzwang*, a fine crack-line, and *Nonpareil*, the hardest route at the outcrop, which involves wall-climbing at its most thin. Other notable routes were: Mike Vetterlein's *Prowess*, a route that is probably harder to set up than to climb; Sharpe's *Flail Trail*, the only route to fall in the Amphitheatre; Andy Hughes's *Mellow Toot*; and Alan Grigg's *Meaty Thighs*.

With the return of more typical weather the pace slowed at High Rocks. Sharpe added two short desperates, *I'll Be Back* and *Ponytail Pearson*, before he too moved out of the area. The evergreen Boysen hobbled up *Senile Walk* in the Stygian gloom of Bell Rock Transverse Passage. Vetterlein climbed the intricate *Educating Airlie*, and Wickham, after over two years of effort, the grossly overhanging *Bone Machine*.

A few climbs were un-earthed at Harrison's (literally, in some cases). Widdowson powered his way up *Powder Monkey* and Theseus Gerard added the thuggish *Oliver James* to the same buttress. Steve Quinton climbed two fine routes: *Dr. Pepper*, an extremely thin wall climb, and the fiercely impending *Lager Shandy*.

At Bowles Robin Mazinke climbed what is undoubtedly the hardest route at the outcrop, *Them Monkey Things*. A route of this name was climbed by Jonny Woodward (of *Beau Geste* fame) and first appeared in the 1981 guidebook at the grade of 6a! However, confusion then set in as to its exact location, with the locals eventually settling for the wrong line – a line well to the right of Woodward's route. Fifteen years of unsuccesful repeat attempts then followed, during which Woodward's actual route was climbed and renamed as *Boiling Point*. Chris Murray added two routes to the last sizeable area of unclimbed rock: *Knucklebones*, a painful route up a line of old bolt holes, and *Coast to*

Coast, a short but sustained high-level girdle. The latter climb opened up the possibility of a girdle traverse of the whole outcrop. This was duly done by Mazinke, who, a few months earlier, had proved himself something of a traversing expert with his girdle of Bulls Hollow Rocks. Of the outcrops where complete traverses are possible, only Harrison's now remains to be done, although it is doubtful if there are sufficient hours of daylight, or enough people willing to act as belayers/dogsbodies, for this mammoth undertaking.

Mazinke was also the main activist at Penns Rocks, where, during an all-too-brief relaxation of the access restrictions, nearly forty routes were put up (although some of these had probably been done before but left unrecorded).

The early 1990s saw a continuation of high grade soloing, of which the most impressive was undoubtedly Murray's ascent of *What Crisis?* at Harrison's. At the same outcrop he also soloed *The Limpet*, whilst Quinton accounted for *Karen's Kondom* and *The Republic*. Other notable solos were *Sputnik, Meridian, Reach for the Sky, Crucifix* and *Fly by Knight* – all the work of Tim Skinner – *Forgotten Crack* by Wickham; and *Double Top* and *Higher Purchase* by Doug Reid.

The most prolific soloist, however, was John Patterson, who accounted for some 30 routes of 6a or above. These include *Nightmare, White Verdict* and *A Lady in Mink* at Bowles; and *Stubble* and *Wailing Eliminate* at Harrison's. His finest routes, however, were at Eridge Green, where the brittle rock, dampness, and isolation all work against the solo climber. Here, in a series of brief but intense campaigns, he soloed, amongst others, *Diagonal, Sandstorm, Slug, The Beguiled, Waffer Thin, Lou, Steelmill*, and *Steamroller*.

The future for new-routeing on sandstone does look a bit bleak. There are now virtually no gaps for new climbs at Bowles, Bulls Hollow and Stone Farm, whilst at Harrison's gaps that do exist tend to be where the rock is heavily vegetated. Only at High Rocks and Eridge Green is there any real scope, and even here it will need a summer on a par with 1990 before any real progress is made. It seems that for the foreseeable future soloing will be the pre-eminent activity. A glance at the graded list is sufficient to see that a considerable number of routes of 6b and above have yet to be soloed. Some of these are clearly out of the question while at the same time routes such as Krait Arête, Salad Days, Judy and Boonoonoonoos are all reasonable propositions; and then there's always Moving Staircase!

Finally, and most importantly, a great deal of extra care is needed to minimise erosion, otherwise Southern Sandstone will cease to be.

Bowles Rocks

Bowles Rocks

OS Ref TQ 542 330

The rocks are situated about a mile south of Eridge station and are marked 'Outdoor Pursuits Centre' on the Landranger OS map. The usual approach is from the A26 between Tunbridge Wells and Crowborough – see the map on page 11. The turn off to Bowles is about half a mile south of Eridge station and is signposted 'Bowles Outdoor Centre'. The entrance to the rocks is on the right, half a mile along this road.

Bowles is owned by the the Bowles Outdoor Centre and is run as a non-profit making charity. The Centre is mainly concerned with courses of instruction, of which climbing is a major part. They also operate a dry ski slope which can be used by the public. If you are interested in these aspects then contact: The Director, Bowles Outdoor Centre, Eridge Green, Tunbridge Wells, East Sussex, TN3 9LW – telephone 01892 665665.

A scheme known as 'Open Climbing' operates, meaning you can climb anywhere that is not required by the Centre's instructional courses. It is occasionally necessary to close the rocks completely, but this is extremely rare; it is a good idea to check with the office in advance.

The Centre charges for climbing; the present rates being £1.30 a day (£0.80 after 2 pm) or £19.20 for a yearly season ticket. There is a bar in one of the chalets by the ski slope, and a vending machine for hot and cold drinks in another.

The main part of the crag is the cleanest and most continuous wall in the region. The rock is generally harder and consequently less sandy than at other outcrops, and its open nature and southerly aspect often means that it is the only dry crag in the area. As a result Bowles is very popular and can become unpleasantly crowded.

There are a number of routes with cut holds and it is hoped that no more of these will appear, as has been the case for some time. Most of the vandalised routes can be climbed on natural features only. The Centre discourages the use of chalk on easy routes and asks that it be used sparingly, if at all, on the harder ones.

To minimise damage to the rock caused by moving and stretching ropes, it is essential, when top-roping, to use a non-stretch belay sling and to position the karabiner over the edge of the crag. If you see these instructions being

ignored please make polite or stronger suggestions as to the correct procedure.

The climbs are described starting at the end furthest from the public car-park, beginning with a low boulder just right of the staff car-park and in front of the toilets. This has a slab running from bottom left to top right and has two little problems:

1 Bull's Nose 4c
The arête below the top of the slab. Pull up on good holds and then mantelshelf over the nose to finish.

2 Badger's Head 4b
Climb the protruding ironstone knobs about a metre right of the last route.

Past several low boulders, and immediately behind the left-hand end of the chalet, is:

3 Hibiscus 3b
Two mantelshelves on the blunt, overgrown arête.

4 Helter Skelter 5a
Climb the diagonal gash to a horizontal break; finish on small holds.

The next feature is an easy descent chimney. The slab on the right gives some pleasant little routes:

★**5 Chalet Slab Left** 3b
Go straight up the left side of the slab on the ironstone protrusions. The slab to the left leading into the chimney is 3a.

★**6 Chalet Slab Direct** 5c
Climb the centre of the slab past a large ironstone knob. At the top move left a little and surmount the overhang. Traversing off before the overhang reduces the grade to 4b.

7 Chalet Slab Right 5b
Climb the right-hand side of the slab to an awkward mantelshelf onto the ramp. Finish straight over the steep wall above; very hard for the short. The wide crack on the left is an easier alternative finish, making the climb 4c.

★**8 Mohrenkop** 5c
A strenuous climb up the front of the tall block right of the slab.

9 Two Step 5b
Mantelshelf onto a ledge on the right of the block; move right on this until good holds on top can be reached and then mantelshelf again. A poor route.

Away to the right, past a gully and a few boulders, is Problem Slab, providing a number of short problems. Beyond this is:

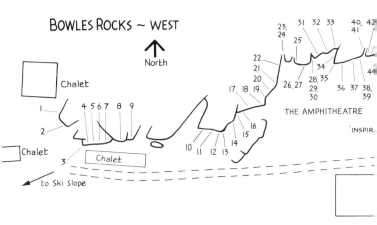

BOWLES ROCKS ~ WEST

North

Chalet

Chalet

Chalet

to Ski Slope

THE AMPHITHEATRE

INSPIR...

10 Roman Nose 4b
A couple of moves up the very short wall just right of a short thick flake.

★ 11 Umbilicus 5c
Start on the left side of a long ironstone edge; stand up on this and then climb the left arête of the impending wall above. Mantelshelf to finish.

12 Geoff's Route 6b
A severe problem. Climb the wall a metre right of *Umbilicus*. From the slab finish painfully up the short wall. There is a 6b boulder problem just right of the start.

13 Blue Moon 6a
Make a strenuous mantelshelf onto the nose. Finish direct to the holly tree. There is a 6a problem on the little wall immediately to the right of the start.

14 Court's Climb 4c
Move left from the corner and mantelshelf onto a large ledge. Move back right to finish. Often greasy.

15 Grotty Groove 2a
Climb the grotty groove.

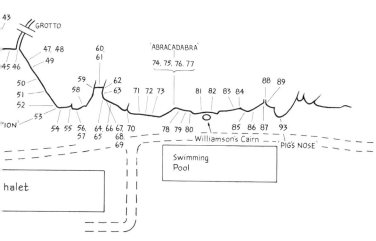

16 Running Jump 2b
Immediately right of the corner. A leap and two mantelshelves – beat 2.3 seconds! This can be climbed less energetically but is less fun that way.

★ 17 Scirocco Slab 4b
The steep slab 2 metres right of the previous route. A number of variations are possible between this and the next route at 5a or thereabouts.

★★ 18 Netwall 4a
Start right of the last route, and just before the slab changes direction. Follow the cut holds trending rightwards to the top. A number of variations are possible, including a more direct finish and a harder direct start.

19 Corner Layback 4c
Layback (take it easy), move right and jam to finish. Alternatively, climb the wall directly to the jamming crack – 4b.

The original route of the next piece of rock, **Aphrodite** *6a, takes the vague nose just right of Corner Layback to the break, followed by a swing right to join:*

20   Zoom   6b
A powerful dynamic move on undercuts about 3 metres right of
Corner Layback leads to the break; continue straight up.

21   Santa's Claws   4c
Follow the artificial line of granite holds grouted in the rock. Tricky
start, especially for the short.

22   Knucklebones   6b†
A tendon-ripping climb up the line of boltholes. Move left at the break
and finish by the rhododendron.

23   Coast to Coast   6b
Climb *Chelsea Chimney* until it is possible to reach out left for the
horizontal break. Traverse strenuously leftwards, past the
rhododendron, and finish as for *Santa's Claws*.

24   Chelsea Chimney   2a
This is straightforward when climbed inside but is much harder as a
layback.

The easy way up and down this area of the rocks is **Reclamation
Gully** *1a, which bounds the left side of Reclamation Slab. The slab
features five routes:*

★ **25   Reclamation Slab Left**   3b
Climb straight up the left edge, using this as required. The further right
you go, the harder it gets.

*There is an eliminate up the centre of the slab which avoids all cut (that
is big) holds on the upper half –* **Reclamation Slap** *5c(NS).*

★★ **26   Reclamation Slab Right**   2b
A very popular route with beginners. Follow the line of cut holds up
the right side of the slab.

27   Mental Balance   5b
Follow the line of the previous route but avoid all the cut holds. Very
delicate and probably impossible for the short.

There is an eliminate climb up the extreme right-hand side of the slab –
Compact and Bijou *6a.*

28   Cenotaph Corner II   5b
The crack bounding the right-hand side of the slab gives a short
technical jamming problem; has nothing in common with its Welsh
namesake.

The next steep wall features three good routes:

★ **29   High Traverse**   4c
Start easily up the rib left of the banana-shaped depression and
traverse right along the high-level break to finish up the corner of
Babylon.

30 Slyme Cryme 6a
Start as for the previous route but take the square-cut overhang on its right-hand side. A boulder problem direct start is possible using small ironstone holds.

★★ **31 Banana** 6a
Surprisingly, this climbs the banana-shaped depression to the break – don't slip. Continue up the crack above and finish with some difficulty.

An eliminate between Banana and Drosophila, **Proboscis** 6a(NS), *is worthwhile but independent only for the finishing moves over the bulge.*

★★ **32 Drosophila** 5b
Go straight up the fine wall on good but, unfortunately, chipped holds. At the top trend right to finish, but not as far as the tree stump of *Babylon*. Be careful when positioning your rope so as to avoid taking a flyer into the right wall. There is a good direct finish – 5c(NS).

★ **33 Babylon** 4b
An enjoyable climb up the corner crack. Usually damp.

34 T.N.T. 5c
Climb delicately up the centre of the smooth and often greasy wall. A bit of a damp squib.

★ **35 Coathanger** 5c
The overhanging arête. Start on the left and then swing onto the arête. Finish carefully up the edge on its left-hand side. There is a reachy direct start – also 5c.

Just to the right is the overhanging Fandango Wall, a favourite place to get pumped, and with some frustratingly hard boulder problems – see route descriptions. There are a number of short but worthwhile low-level traverses – see also Icarus below. On the very lowest break is **Tobacco Road** 6b, *which starts in Skiffle and finishes either up Fandango Right Hand, or continues, at the same level, across to T.N.T. as* **Nicotine Alley** 6b. *At mid-height there is* **Sugarplum** 6a, *which also starts in Skiffle and goes all the way across to Coathanger. Otherwise, use your imagination. It is possible to climb on every square inch of this wall and routes have been claimed thus. Only the original and best are described here:*

★★★ **36 Fandango** 5c
Start with difficulty up the centre of the wall. At the first break move left and go up to the top overhang. Swing right to an awkward mantelshelf finish. A spectacular route. A direct start is 6a. One can also go straight up from the start, taking the overhang at its widest point – 6a.

★★★ **37 Fandango Right Hand** 6a
Climb *Fandango* to the break but then move right and go up to the

overhang. Move right then back left round the overhang and finish straight up – all very strenuous. A direct start up to the curved flake just to the right is 6c.

38 Pastry 5c
Climb the easy crack for two metres; move left a metre or so and then pull over the bulge. From here trend right to finish just right of the nose, but without moving into the chimney. A direct start is possible just left of the chimney at 6c.

An alternative line is **Poff Pastry** 6b. *Follow* Pastry *over the bulge but then trend left almost to* Fandango Right Hand. *Finish on the left side of the nose.*

39 Icarus 6a
Start as for *Pastry* but after pulling over the bulge make a rising traverse leftwards onto *Fandango Right Hand*. Move left to gain a standing positon on the ledge of *Fandango,* and then go on round across *Coathanger* and *T.N.T.* Descend *Babylon* (33) for 2 metres and then traverse along a line of handholds across *Banana* to easy ground.

⋆⋆ 40 Skiffle 3a
The twisting crack. Easier than it looks.

⋆ 41 Orr Traverse 5c
A very good low-level traverse of increasing difficulty. Start at *Skiffle.* Cross *Mick's Wall* and move easily right on good holds to the pedestal of *Digitalis* (51). Step down and then across to *Inspiration* (53). Either move right and pull over the bulge (crux), Orr (5b) go up the overhanging crack of *Inspiration* and then step right. Step down and continue on to, and across, Meager's Slab. The traverse can be continued; see *Pegasus* (69) etc.

42 Mick's Wall Arête 6a
Climb the blunt arête immediately right of *Skiffle.* Finish left of the crack of *Mick's Wall.*

43 Mick's Wall 5b
Somewhat eliminate moves just left of centre of the wall lead to the overhang. Move left to the nose and up the awkward crack to finish. A direct finish seems possible over the roof but has not yet been done.

⋆⋆ 44 Kemp's Delight 4b
An enjoyable route up the centre of the wall about a metre right of the last route. Follow good but chipped holds up to the overhang and then traverse right into the chimney to finish.

45 Mick's Wall Variation 6a(NS)
Awkward moves up the wall immediately left of the chimney lead to a bulge; finish direct.

46 Grotto Chimney 2b
Climb the chimney to the grotto and then finish easily up the earthy
ledges. The finish can be avoided by a pleasant ramp leading out
right.

*The next sweep of rock features some of the best and most impressive
climbs at Bowles.*

★ **47 Patella** 6a
Just right of *Grotto Chimney*. Climb directly past the small old bolts;
surmount the overhang and layback up the crack above. If you feel
the kneed to use the bolts as holds – the original method – the climb
is slightly easier.

★★ **48 Kinnard** 6b(NS)
A totally free version of a mysterious aid route. Climb *Patella* to the
bulge and then hand-traverse the high-level break all the way to
Inspiration. Finish up this. Sustained, strenuous and Kinnard, but not
technically demanding.

★ **49 Nutella** 6b(NS)
A wicked move on tiny finger pockets a metre or so right of *Patella*
leads to the high-level break. Hand-traverse strenuously right until
below a vague groove; finish up this with another desperate move.

*The next feature is an obvious line of large ring-bolts on the wall above
a pedestal. This gives an A1 aid route or arm-over-arm thuggery using
the bolts as holds – 5b. Please take care not to damage natural holds
because:*

★★★ **50 Temptation** 6b
Free climbs the line of bolts directly to the top starting from the
pedestal – the temptation is to grab the bolts. An impressive and
technical climb, which can be led.

★★★ **51 Digitalis** 6a
An airy and heart-quickening route. From the pedestal go up and
right on good holds until a fingertip layback is reached (crux). Move
right and mantelshelf over the nose as for *Inspiration*. An undercut
direct start is possible to the right.

A direct finish to Digitalis *on the left side of the nose is rumoured but not
confirmed.*

★★ **52 Serenade Arête** 6a
The impressive arête gives a fine sustained climb marred only by its
proximity to *Inspiration*. Start on the left and move onto the arête on
the good breaks. Move slightly right and pull onto the sloping ledge.
Finish as for *Inspiration*.

★★ **53 Inspiration** 5c
A varied climb with a spectacular (frightening?) finish. Climb the

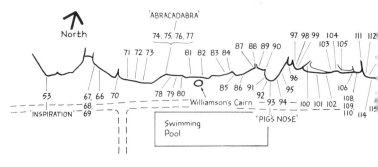

awkward wide crack just right of the arête and the easy staircase to
the roof. Move left to the airy sloping ledge on the arête and finish
with a difficult mantelshelf.

★ 54 The Thing   6b(NS)
A sticky tape job but no fetishists please. Follow *Inspiration* to the top
overhang, then use a horizontal flake to gain a jam at the lip.
Vaguely strenuous thugging follows. Swinging off is more fun than the
climbing.

★★ 55 Juanita   6a
The crack in the roof right of *The Thing*. Start with a hard pull onto the
slab directly beneath the crack. Climb straight up the wall to the roof
and then with a surge of adrenalin go out over it.

★★ 56 Sapper   4c
A popular and unusual trip. Start by stepping onto the right arête from
Yoyo. Traverse left to the staircase of *Inspiration* and follow this to the
roof. Move right beneath the crack of *Juanita* and squeeze up the
body-sized hole at the back. Alternative starts include a hard pull over
the overhang 2 metres left of the arête (5c) or the initial crack of
Inspiration – 5b.

57 One Nighter   6c(NS)
Get it? The roof 2 metres right of *Juanita*. Climb up to the roof any
way you like and then, using pockets as undercuts, gain the
horizontal break – interesting if you face outwards. Finish with a
skin-ripping grovel onto the top.

★★ 58 Burlap   5b
Climb the front face of the square-cut arête straight up to the
overhang and finish delicately up the wall to the right of this. It is

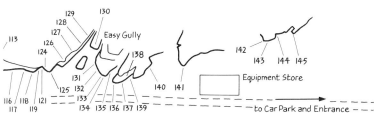

BOWLES ROCKS ~ EAST

possible to climb the thin sliver of wall between the arête and *Yoyo* at 6a(NS).

The next feature is a steep recessed wall, known as Meager's Slab.

★★ 59 Yoyo 4a
The crack bounding the left side of the slab. Take care not to jam your feet in too well.

60 White Verdict/The Ly'in 6b
Two overlapping eliminates up the centre of the slab, slightly to the left and slightly to the right respectively. Both inflict pain on the finger joints. Use of the arêtes is forbidden.

61 Meager's Right Hand 5c
Climb the right-hand side of the slab using the right edge until it is possible to move left to the centre. Finish straight up.

62 Sing Sing 3a
The crack crack bounding the right side of the slab slab. This is a thrutch when climbed by chimneying, but is much harder, though more pleasant, when bridged on the outside – take your pick.

63 Manita 5c
Climb the impending wall immediately right of *Sing Sing* on small pockets. Pull onto the ledge and finish as for *Jackie*.

★ 64 Jackie 5b
An enjoyable technical climb up the rounded arête right of the recessed slab. From the wide ledge climb the steep little slab round to the left. Alternatively, grovel over the left end of the steep wall at 5c.

★ 65 Murph's Mount 5a
Start in *Sing Sing* and traverse right, past *Jackie*, onto the slab. Climb

straight up the middle of the slab, and at the big ledge traverse left to re-join *Sing Sing*. Starting as for *Jackie* is also 5a.

66 Nero 5c

Pull onto the slab as for *Jackie* or, better, start 2 metres right with a jump for the break. Climb the middle of the slab to the ledge and the centre of the steep wall above.

★67 Salamander Slab 5c

Start as for *Nero* but then move diagonally right to the top right-hand corner of the slab. Climb the impending headwall moving slightly left to finish at the birch tree.

There is a direct start to Salamander Slab – **Cheese Sandwich** 6a. *Start a metre left of* Perspiration; *gain the first break with the hands, move left a bit and pull with difficulty onto the slab.*

The next wall is undercut by large overhangs and is interlaced with routes upon which numerous variations are possible. A number of ring-bolts are present, enabling some routes to be led – use only the in-situ bolts and chockstones because conventional protective devices will badly damage the rock (and you when they pull out).

★★68 Peter's Perseverance 5a

A fine outing. Start as for *Murph's Mount* (65) but carry on traversing to the corner-crack. Continue the traverse and then go straight up the face past a large pocket to a bolt runner. Finish up the wide crack by the tree stump.

★★★69 Pegasus 5a

A very worthwhile extension to *Peter's Perseverance*. Follow that route to the large pocket but then continue traversing, past a delicate step down, to the niche and bolt runner on *Abracadabra* (77). Make a rising traverse past a limestone chock to a block and bolt belay on the broad ledge. The traverse can be continued at two levels to *Charlie's Chimney* (88). It may then be extended, 5b, across *Hate* (90) as a hand-traverse, round *Pig's Nose* (93) and into *Birch Crack* (96). This last section is completely unprotected.

A number of variations can be made on the extension to Pegasus. *The first, 5a, is an easier finish across* Hate. *Descend* Charlie's Chimney *and cross* Hate *at the level of the first horizontal break to eventually join* Chelsea Traverse *(107). The second is at a lower level and is 5c. Traverse right from* Abracadabra *just above the overhangs, following* Target *into the cave; cross* Devaluation *(86) by the obvious difficult hand-traverse to eventually join the low-level traverse across* Hate.

★70 Perspiration 5c

Is the word. Start beneath the overhanging crack; up-thrutch it and then continue more easily to the overhangs. Either traverse right a little and finish up the crack, or make the route more sustained by continuing directly up the headwall right of *Salamander Slab*.

There is an eliminate, **Boiling Point** 6b(NS), *taking the roof immediately right of* Perspiration.
71 Them Monkey Things 6c(NS)†
A powerful route, the hardest at the outcrop. Climb the sandy roof 2 metres right of *Perspiration* to the short vertical crack; gain and somehow use a good but small layaway hold at the top of this to reach the good breaks above and easy ground.
★★ 72 Carbide Finger 6c
The thin crack in the widest part of the roof gives a powerful and sequency series of moves on side pulls and undercuts.

The next roof-crack to the right has been aided but is rarely ascended. However, just right there is:
★ 73 Cardboard Box 6b
Gain the thin horizontal flake under the roof. Leap for a right handhold and then make some hard, unpleasant moves to stand up. Finish up *Swastika* or *(Recurring) Nightmare*.

The next three routes are described as starting up Abracadabra *but some prefer to start from* Williamson's Cairn *and traverse in above the bulge.*
★ 74 Swastika 5b
A fine exposed route. Start as for *Abracadabra* but at the first break traverse left for 5 metres and go up a shallow groove in the centre of the front face. Exit via the wide crack by the tree stump.
★ 75 Nightmare 6a
Follow *Abracadabra* to the ledge then traverse left for 3 metres; climb the steep wall on the left side of the blunt nose to a difficult mantelshelf. Finish as for *Swastika*.
76 Recurring Nightmare 6b(NS)
The logical finish to *Cardboard Box*. Climb the bulging wall 2 metres right of the blunt nose on *Nightmare*, with a long reach for a flat ironstone hold. Finish direct.
★ 77 Abracadabra 5a
Straight up the despicably-awkward wide crack. Some find this harder than *Cardboard Box*! Continue much more easily to the top.

To the right is Range Wall, which is undercut and rotten at the base. Most of its routes start by stepping off the cemented pillar – Williamson's Cairn.
78 Conjuror 6a
Levitate up the sandy bulges just right of *Abracadabra* and follow a

direct line to the top avoiding both *Abracadabra* and *Ricochet*.
Perhaps a wandering line would be more appropriate?

*The next four routes start from Williamson's Cairn but were originally
climbed direct or by traversing in from* Abracadabra:

★★ **79 Ricochet** 4b
Start on the cairn and go up to the first foot-ledges. Traverse left for
about 3 metres and climb the pock-marked wall directly to the top.

★ **80 Four-by-Two** 5a
Start as for *Ricochet* but traverse for only 2 metres before climbing
straight up.

★ **81 Pull Through** 5b
From the cairn go straight up the wall on cut holds to finish up a
groove on the right. An unpleasant direct start just right of, and
without touching, the cairn is 6a – mind your back.

★★ **82 Lee Enfield** 5c
A Stirling route. Start on the cairn, then climb the wall diagonally
rightwards finishing via the niche at the top. Pulling on the bolt
reduces the grade to 5a.

★★ **83 Target** 5c(NS)
Climb up the left wall of the cave, then swing round onto the front
face. Climb directly up the wall above, keeping just right of *Lee
Enfield*. Finish awkwardly to the right of the niche. A sandy direct
start is 6b.

★ **84 Cave Crack** 5a
Start in the back of the cave. Move out right beneath the roof and
continue straight to the top. There is an an alternative start up the
right wall of the cave – also 5a.

★ **85 E.S. Cadet Nose** 5b
Climb the rounded arête right of the cave, avoiding the previous route
by keeping on the front face after the start. Go straight up to finish. A
direct start on the front face is 5c.

There is a very hard eliminate up the wall right of E.S. Cadet Nose –
Skallagrigg 6c(NS).

★★ **86 Devaluation** 5b
The centre of the wall. A pleasant climb despite the many cut holds.

The final hard move of Devaluation *can be done by a figure-of-four move
– that is, put both hands on the jug then put the left leg up between them
and over the right hand. Udge your weight upwards until eventually a
sitting position on the right hand is reached. Reach the next break with
the left hand thus entirely avoiding intermediate holds. The left-handed
will find it easier to put the right leg over the left hand. Either way this
requires some practice but can be very elegant when perfected.*

★ **87 Sandman** 6b

The blunt right arête of the wall is easier for the tall and utterly desperate for the short. From the wide ledge either traverse off left or climb the overhangs above near their left end; more 6b.

It is entertaining to jump from the wide ledge on Sandman *to the juggy break on* Love/Hate *and finish up the latter.*

★ **88 Charlie's Chimney** 3a

Climb the crack to the roof; traverse left and finish up the short corner.

★ **89 Love** 6a(NS)

A good route despite its eliminate nature. Climb the arête right of the chimney to a cave. Surge up the overhanging crack to finish (you).

★★★ **90 Hate** 6a

An awkward move onto the first break is followed by thin moves up the centre of the wall. Pull over the overhang and finish up the crack above. The wall just to the right has similar but slightly harder moves.

★★★ **91 Pig's Ear** 5c

Climb the shallow curving crack to the overhang; move slightly right and then pull over the roof. Finish more easily in the same line.

92 T.T. 5b

Climb the wall immediately right of the previous route to the ledge below the overhang. Either step right and finish up *Pig's Nose* or go left to join *Pig's Ear*.

★★★ **93 Pig's Nose** 5a

Another popular classic. The fine arête is followed easily to the ledges below the top overhangs. Summon up courage, breathe deeply, and launch over the bulges above.

94 Koffler 6a

The wall just right of the arête gives one very hard move, after which the difficulties soon ease. Much easier for the tall. Finish up the gully wall of the top block. The grade is 5b if the breaks running right from *Pig's Nose* are used.

95 Gully Wall 5a

The layback flake on the left wall of *Birch Crack*. At half-height abandon the flake and climb the earthy ledges above.

The next climb provides the usual descent route for this area of the rocks.

96 Birch Crack 1b

A straightforward chimney climb with a triangular slab at its base.

97 Chris 5c

The wall midway between the chimney and the next crack, trending slightly left then back right to a mantelshelf and easy ground.

★ 98 Kennard's Climb 4a
Not Kenneasy. The first crack right of the chimney. Move right at its top and finish with a strenuous mantelshelf.

99 Rib 5c
The sandy bulges just right of *Kennard's Climb*.

★ 100 Dib 4a
Climb the overhanging crack and then move left, just below the ledge, to an ironstone hold. Mantelshelf onto the ledge and then follow easy ground to the top.

★ 101 Corbett Slab 4a
Climb the centre of the pock-marked wall right of *Dib* to the ledge. Continue up the right-hand side of the slab and then go up easy rocks above.

102 The Scouter 3a
Climb the blind crack right of the pock-marked wall to a broad ledge; walk left to an obvious groove and follow this, past some ancient ironmongery, to reach easy ground. The overhang above is 5b.

103 Nelson's Column 5a
Start just right of *The Scouter* and climb the wall without using holds on the next route.

★ 104 Dival's Diversion 5b
After a hard start go delicately up the wall about a metre left of *Funnel*. Using the same start as *Funnel* reduces the grade to 4b.

★★ 105 Funnel 4a
A fine route, with thought-provoking moves. An obvious scoop in the upper part of the face marks the line; start a little left of this at a short (pink?) crack, or more directly.

106 U.N. 5c
Start a metre right of *Funnel* and climb delicately up the wall. Mantelshelf onto the wide ledge and then finish straight up the front of the top block.

107 Chelsea Traverse 4a
A technically interesting low-level traverse. Start as for *U.N.*, then traverse left along the lower ledges to the slab at the foot of *Birch Crack*.

★★ 108 Wells's Reach 3a
Bridge up *Harden Gully* for 3 metres and then climb the crack on the left to the wide ledge below the roof; from here move back right into the gully and so to the top.

★ 109 The Wrecker 6c(NS)
Well named – a subtle blend of technicality and mindless brutality. The roof is climbed at its widest point using the obvious fist-sized

crack. A fist jam here can numb your right thumb for two months. Fun, fun, fun.

★ 110 One of Our Buzzards is Missing 6b(NS)
Another hard roof climb. Start on the prow just right of the shackles and then move left to the blunt arête. Finish up this.

★ 111 Harden Gully 2a
Climb the chimney to the broad earthy gully.

★ 112 Sylvie's Slab 4b
A pleasant slab to the right of *Harden Gully*. Finish up the wide crack at the back of the big ledge, if you so desire.

★ 113 Six Foot 4c
Start 3 metres right of *Harden Gully*. Climb the wall on slot holds, trending slightly left to finish at the top of *Sylvie's Slab*.

★ 114 Larchant 5a
Climb the wall just left of centre, past some cut holds, to finish on the broad ledge.

★ 115 Hennessy Heights 5b
Go straight up the wall a metre right of *Larchant* – a good climb despite the cut holds.

An **August Variation** 5c *takes the wall just left of* October, *though it is hardly majestic.*

★ 116 October 4c
Climb a thin crack on good sharp holds, and go straight up to the finish of *Fragile Wall*.

★★ 117 Fragile Wall 4a
A popular route. Start direct or by traversing in from the right or left. Go up the obvious break at the right-hand end of the wall on enormous holds.

★ 118 Fragile Arête 5a
Climb the direct start to *Fragile Wall* and then go delicately up the arête.

There is an extremely strenuous ultra-low-level traverse between Fragile Arête *and* Harden Gully. *Keep the hands below the level of the first break* – 6a.

119 Escalator 5a
Two metres left of *Renison Gully*. Go straight up on small holds with a mantelshelf to finish. A route has been squeezed in just before the corner – **Elevator** 5a.

120 Pop's Chimney 4b
The short chimney above the ledge provides a finish for any of the last four routes.

121 Renison Gully 3a
Follow the corner crack to the wide ledge. Traverse easily left to finish.

★ 122 Lawson Traverse 4a
A worthwhile outing. Start up *Harden Gully* and traverse strenuously right to *Renison Gully* with the feet at about 2 metres.

123 The Lawson Extension 5b
From *Renison Gully* to *A Lady in Mink*, with interesting sections crossing *Seltzer*, *Encore* (rounded hand-traverse), and *Rad's Cliff*.

★ 124 Finale 6a(NS)
Climb easily up the wall right of *Renison Gully*. Pull leftwards with great difficulty onto the wall above the roof and so to the top.

★ 125 Alka 4c
Go up the nose on good rounded holds and continue up the obvious wide crack above.

★ 126 Seltzer 5b
The wide kinked crack to the right of the last route. Finish up the thin crack right of *Alka*.

127 Encore 5c
Climb the wall 2 metres right of *Seltzer* to the ledge. Continue straight up the impending wall to a mantelshelf finish.

128 Zugabe 6b
Climb the short wall right of *Encore* and continue to the second ledge via a large ironstone knob. Climb the blunt arête above on its right-hand side to finish at the beech tree.

129 November 1b
An easy gully to the left of the block.

130 Baby Boulder 4b
The front of the block between the two gullies. It is possible to step left from the top of the block and climb the steep wall at 5c.

The next gully used to provide an easy descent route but because of erosion problems this should **now be avoided.** *Please use the steps at the right-hand end of the crag.*

131 Ballerina 4a
Prance delicately up the steep slab right of the gully.

132 Red Peg 2a
Follow a worn crack and mantelshelf onto a broad ledge; continue straight up to finish over or around a little nose.

133 Claire 3a
Ascend the bulging front of the buttress on rounded holds. Finish up the left edge of the little slab.

Carbide Finger, 6c, Bowles Rocks. Climber: Robin Mazinke. Photo: Chris Eades

Pig's Nose, 5a, Bowles Rocks. Climber: Teresa Hill. Photo: Robin Mazinke

134 Barham Boulder 4b
Start just to the right of the last route and go up diagonally right to the ledge. Finish as for either of the last two routes.

135 Rad's Cliff 4a
Start 2 metres left of the gully. Move right on the first break and go up to the terrace. Finish up a short wall below the holly tree.

Just to the right of an earthy gully there is a tall block. The next route goes up the front nose:

136 Bovril 4b
Climb the nose largely on its right-hand side. At the ledge move left into the gully and pull back right onto the upper block to finish. Ma mightn't approve of this.

137 Wally 4b
A direct line up the wall right of *Bovril*. It is also possible to start just to the right and climb the wall trending slightly rightwards – 5a.

138 Oliver's Twist 5c
This takes the pocketed wall right of *Wally* using the obvious undercuts. At the ledge climb the impending wall left of the square-cut chimney.

★★ **139 Nealon's** 4c
Bridge up beneath the big diagonal overlap to the ledge. Exit up the square-cut chimney.

140 A Lady in Mink 6a
Climb the easy wall right of *Nealon's* to the ledge; pull onto the wall above with some difficulty and make a hard lock to reach the top. The blunt undercut arête to the left of the finish is 6b(NS).

The rocks now become considerably less continuous and more overgrown:

141 Mercator's Projection 3a
Climb easily up the centre of the next buttress and then cross a broad ledge to finish awkwardly from left to right on the overhanging boulder.

The next feature is a small isolated rock mass just before the chapel is reached. This is the somewhat overgrown Bowles Buttress, on which there are four short routes:

142 Pat's Progress 4a
A few awkward mantelshelves, starting from the front of the buttress.

143 Dubonnet 4b
Start to the right of the previous route, s'il vous plâit, with a mantelshelf, then continue straight up.

144 William's Layback 2a
The flake-crack below the stunted tree.

144A Free Willy   3a
Climb the wall right of *William's Layback*, and below the holly tree.

145 Index   4b
On the arête of the small block. Start from the left; curl the index finger around the stalactite/mite and then mantelshelf. A direct start is 5b.

★★ **146 Girdle Traverse**   6b(NS)†
There are very good opportunities for traversing at Bowles. The complete girdle from *Roman Nose* (10) to *A Lady in Mink* (140) is a very tough proposition, the crux being the reversal of *Coast to Coast* (23). However, a more reasonable and enjoyable (★★★5c) expedition is to follow *Orr Traverse* (41), and then *Pegasus* (69) as far as *Charlie's Chimney* (88). From here cross *Hate* (90) at a low level, step across *Birch Crack* (96), then follow *Chelsea Traverse* (107), *Lawson Traverse* (122), and *The Lawson Extension* (123).

Bulls Hollow Rocks

OS Ref TQ 569 394

The rocks are situated adjacent to Denny Bottom on Rusthall Common, one mile west of Tunbridge Wells.

From Tunbridge Wells take the East Grinstead road (A264) along the north side of Tunbridge Wells Common. Take the first right some 300 metres past the Spa Hotel. The outcrop lies in the wood right of this road, 150 metres from the junction. Parking is available on the road adjacent to Toad Rock; for this, turn right again at the signpost to Toad Rock.

The outcrop is L-shaped, averages about eight metres in height and, as the name implies, lies in a hollow. The ground at the foot of the rocks is in places rather quaggy. The quality of the rock is variable because most of the faces have been quarried in the not-too-distant past. In some areas holds crumble very easily.

Unfortunately, the outcrop is rarely in condition largely due to its secluded aspect and the plentiful shading trees (to quote the last guidebook: "Waders and a small sailing craft are recommended when climbing at Bulls Hollow and, remember, don't feed the crocodiles"). Despite this, the central area in the region of *The Wall* provides a concentration of excellent routes.

To minimise damage to the rock caused by moving and stretching ropes, it is essential, when top-roping, to use a non-stretch belay sling and to position the karabiner over the edge of the crag. As the trees above the rocks tend to be well back from the edge, a second rope used as a long sling is necessary here. If you see these instructions being ignored please make polite or stronger suggestions as to the correct procedure.

At the far left end of the main crag is a bulging overhanging nose. The first route starts up the slope to the left of this:

★ **1 Waistline** 5a
A high-level traverse along the break above the large overhang. Step off the tree roots and climb to the break. Traverse right to the arête and an awkward finish. The small tree at the top is not allowed. The break can be hand-traversed at 5c.

2 Broken Crack 3a
The cracks to the right of the large overhang leading to a tree. A bit awkward.

3 The Chasm 3b
Go up to a cave in the centre of the face, either direct or by
traversing in from the right. The finish is straightforward.

4 Uncertainty 5c
A disgusting route, not to be recommended. Start 2 metres left of the
large tree and climb the shattered wall into the groove; finish up this.

5 Tree Climb 2a
Two wide cracks lead to a tree with exposed roots.

6 Sandcastle 5c
Climb directly up the overhanging sandy nose just right of the tree of
Tree Climb.

7 Yew Wall 5b
Climb the short crack to the right of *Sandcastle* until it is possible to
move onto the ledge on the left. Pull over the bulge (hard for the short)
then trend leftwards to the small yew tree.

★ **8 Poltergeist** 5c
Climb onto the ledge right of *Yew Wall* and then up the flake- crack
and wall above. A good route when clean and dry.

9 Yellowstone Wall 3b
Climb straight up a sandy crack just to the right of a pair of
tree-stumps on the ground.

10 Yellowstone Crack 4b
Another sandy crack 3 metres right of *Yellowstone Wall.*

11 Taurus 5b
The arête just right of *Yellowstone Crack.*

12 Minotaur 6a(NS)
Climb the obvious diagonal overlap left of the passageway on poor
holds. Finish with a long reach. Previously a peg route.

Next is a wide passage leading to the top of the crag.

13 Caught between Two Stools 5b
The slimy, slabby buttress in the depths of the passage.

In the right wall near the entrance is:

14 Bridge Crack 4b
Climb awkwardly into the niche on the right and continue up the
crack above. An alternative from the niche is to bridge up at 4a.

★ **15 The Scoop** 6a(NS)
A very technical climb up the concave wall just right of the passage
entrance.

★★ **16 Possibility Wall** 4b
The steep sandy slab with well-worn holds and a thin finish. Very
good when dry.

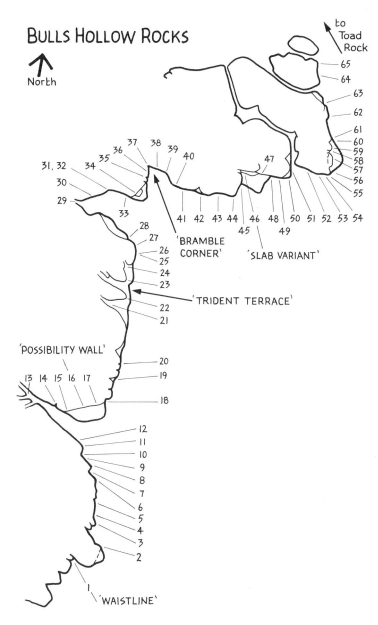

★ **17 Impossibility** 5b
Step carefully up the steep slab right of *Possibility Wall*. Lives up to its name when greasy.

18 Sentry Box Arête 5b
Start round the arête on a ledge 2 metres up; swing left and climb the arête on its right-hand side without touching the large tree.

19 Sentry Box 4b
Climb straight up the wall to a triangular niche; exit past the tree.

20 Yew Break 1a
An obvious staircase with a tree in it. Follow this rightwards.

To the right is a very rotten green wall. This has been climbed on but is extremely unpleasant and not worth describing. At its right end is Trident Terrace, which can easily be gained on the right. The following unsatisfactory routes start on the terrace:

21 Trident Left 1b
An easy break at the left-hand end of the terrace. Start up the tree roots.

22 Neptune Arête 4a
A short arête to the right with an awkward finish.

23 Trident Arête 3a
A somewhat artificial line to the left of *Trident Chimney*.

24 Trident Chimney 2b
At the right-hand end of the terrace.

Back on the main wall, to the right of the terrace is:

25 Apis Variation 5c
Climb the unsound wall right of *Trident Chimney*. Finish up the bulging nose to the left of the short crack.

26 Apis 4b
Start as for the last route but then move into the short crack. This leads to a small tree and the top.

On the left wall of the next bay is:

27 Moss 5b
The wall between *Apis* and the beech tree. Climb the centre of the wall on rounded mossy holds.

28 Cellar Wall 2a
Follow the wide ledges rightwards to the slabby upper section.

29 Coal Cellar 2a
A freak climb (aren't they all?) through a hole between the two converging walls at the back of the bay. It is apparently considered unsporting to use the tree roots to assist the undignified entry. Finish up the wall ahead.

The right wall of the bay starts with:

30 Blasphemy 4a
A short, rather dirty crack in a V-groove.

31 Solo 4b
The sandy centre crack with a small overhang at the top. Climb the crack to the overhang; move left onto the wall and finish via some loose rock. An alternative start, 4c, can be made from the crack on the right; this is followed to mid-height, where a move left joins the other line.

32 The Buzzard and the Purple Fish 6a(NS)†
Start between the two alternative starts of *Solo*. Climb the pillar without touching either crack. Finish direct, and avoiding the big pinch at the top of the ramp of *Conway's Variation*.

At the right end of the wall is a pedestal; the next route starts just left of this:

★ **33 Conway's Variation** 3b
Climb onto the pedestal on the left side and follow the diagonal ramp leftwards to the top.

★ **34 Conway's Buttress** 3b
Surmount the pedestal from the right and continue up the short corner to the top. Alternatively climb the crack on the right to finish at a small tree.

★★ **35 Conway's Crack** 4b
Climb up the twin cracks in the centre of the left wall of the bay.

36 Hanging Crack 5c
Start just left of *Bramble Corner*. Climb the short wall to gain the steep finger-crack. Formerly a peg route.

The next series of routes provides a concentration of some of the best climbs on the outcrop:

★★★ **37 Bramble Corner** 4c
An excellent crack climb. Go straight up the cracks at the back of the bay.

★★ **38 Knott** 5c
An enjoyable crack climb. The obvious thin crack to the right of *Bramble Corner*; it gets wider in the upper part. Another old peg route.

★★★ **39 The Shield** 6a(NS)
Climb directly up the centre of the wall between *Knott* and *The Wall* trending slightly right at the top. Very sustained and technical. Finishing direct is 6b(NS).

★★★ **40 The Wall** 5c(NS)
One of the best climbs at the rocks. Make an awkward mantelshelf

onto the broad shelf. Move up right, then back left to a ledge in the middle of the wall. Continue to the top trending right.

41 Caesar 5c
The square-cut arête right of *The Wall*. Approach from the right from the recess of *Centurion's Groove*.

★★ **42 Centurion's Groove** 4c
A pleasant route. Head straight up the wall to a recess and then follow the shallow groove to the top.

★★ **43 Pseudonym** 5c
A tricky climb that is high in its grade – a pseudo-6a? Climb the thin crack left of the nose to a small sloping ledge. Either go straight up the wall or, easier, trend right to finish.

★★ **44 Broken Nose** 5b
Climb directly up the prominent nose. Move slightly right to finish. The grade assumes that the tree is not used.

45 Slab Chimney 3a
Climb the overhanging square-cut corner to the large platform; continue up the chimney and crack left of the narrow slab.

★★★ **46 Slab Variant** 4c
Ascend the broken lower wall to the large platform, then climb the narrow slab ahead. At the top it is possible to step across to easy ground on the left – taken this way the climb is 3b. The route proper continues straight up the whitish upper wall on the right.

★ **47 Time Waits for No One** 6b(NS)
The centre of the upper wall right of *Slab Variant* gives an unusually thin and highly technical sequence of moves. Start on the platform, either direct or, better, by stepping across from the slab.

48 Full Moon 5a
Gain the large platform as for *Slab Variant*. Move right into the yew tree and climb the sandy crack behind it.

49 Eyewash 5b
The steep wall a metre left of the arête. Usually very greasy.

50 Triangle Arête 5b
Climb directly up the arête left of the passage. Normally greasy.

The passage provides an easy way up or down and a route:

51 Triangle Climb 2a
Climb the chimney formed by the passage, either inside or near the entrance.

On the wall right of the passage is:

52 Handle with Care 6a
Start in the centre of the wall and then move left along the ledge to a

niche. Climb straight up the crack to an awkward finish. A direct start to the niche gives a more sustained climb.

53 Crossply 5b
Start as for the previous route but at the ledge move right to a bulge and a short slanting crack. Climb this and finish on the wall above the gangway.

54 The Bitch and the Meal Ticket 5c(NS)
Climb the overhang a metre right of *Crossply*. Continue straight to the top via the thin crack.

Round the corner to the right is a wide shelf at head height.

★★ **55 Gangway Wall** 3a
Climb the short wall at the extreme left end of the shelf; move up and left to the prominent gangway. Follow this to the top.

56 Square Cut 5c
Climb onto the shelf as for *Gangway Wall* but then climb the obvious right-angled arête above.

57 Overhanging Crack 4c
The obvious overhanging crack with a little cave at the bottom. Rotten rock but good jams.

58 Sandy Wall 5b
Start as for *Overhanging Crack* but move right and pull strenuously onto the wall; continue straight up on good holds.

59 Avalanche Arête 6a
The undercut arête right of *Sandy Wall*. Pull strenuously onto the arête and go straight up to a difficult mantelshelf finish.

60 Fortuitous 5c
The short steep wall a metre right of *Avalanche Arête*.

61 Avalanche Route 3a
Climb a short rotten wall to a groove and follow this to the top.

62 Birch Tree Wall 3b
Start a metre left of the fallen tree, and go straight up the groove.

63 Birch Tree Buttress 2a
The groove opposite the fallen tree.

The next buttress has a tree growing out of it at about two-thirds height.

64 Toad Wall 2b
Straightforward but sandy. Climb the centre of the wall left of the tree. An alternative start is in the depression to the left trending right to finish.

65 Toad Arête 4c
The arête to the right of the tree.

★ **66 Girdle Traverse**   6a(NS)†

The girdle traverse of the whole outcrop was once possible, but the recent felling of the tree in the gap between *Minotaur* and *Bridge Crack* has split the climb into two sections. It is, however, still an adventurous and worthwhile outing, requiring lots of ropes and a patient belayer. Start below *Waistline* and traverse rightwards at a low level to *Minotaur*. Continue traversing until the ledges peter out, then step down to the ground. Regain the rock on the other side of the gully. Carry on to *Yew Break* and either cross the friable wall or, better, go up *Yew Break* and behind the two trees on the ledge and then across the arête to Trident Terrace. Keep low across *Apis* and then climb *Coal Cellar* to the sloping shelf. Step right to the small tree and, using this, step across the passage. Move down and right to the foot of *Conway's Buttress* and then keep at a low level until *The Wall* is reached. Climb *The Wall* for a few moves and then move right, across *Caesar* and down to the recess of *Centurion's Groove*. Move diagonally right to the top of *Broken Nose*. Descend this until a tree can be reached around the corner. From the platform climb down and hand-traverse across *Eyewash* and then continue to the shelf of *Gangway Wall*. Continue easily at a low level until *Toad Arête* is reached. Finish with a jump across to the adjacent boulder.

Eridge
Green Rocks

Eridge Green Rocks

OS Ref TQ 555 356

The rocks are situated close to the Tunbridge Wells-Crowborough road (A26), three miles south-west of the centre of Tunbridge Wells and 300 metres west of Eridge Church.

The rocks are private and climbing is strictly forbidden. However, as in the past, occasional discrete visits have been made by various people, resulting in the new routes described. The description of routes is purely to serve as a record in case the access situation should ever change, and does not imply that anyone has the right to climb here. The crag is a designated SSSI.

The main area map (page 11) shows the best approach to the rocks, that is: park where indicated, cross the main road diagonally left to the wooden gate and then follow the path rightwards until it joins another path at an oblique angle. A left turn leads to Elephant's Boulder and Columnar Buttress – two small buttresses that mark the start of the outcrop. A right turn leads to the metalled road that runs between Eridge Church and Warren Farm. From the road the main part of the outcrop can be seen through the trees. **Do not** approach the crag along the road or park at the foot of the rocks. A dirt-track (not a public right-of-way) runs below the entire length of the outcrop.

The nature of the outcrop as a whole is very varied. Its height ranges from five to ten metres and the condition of the rock varies from clean and solid to lichenous and friable. Both the top and the bottom of the rocks are heavily vegetated and, due to the lack of climbers, a few routes have completely disappeared beneath the plant life. However, the quality of the routes is largely good and the outcrop has a unique atmosphere, which seems to gain much from it being little frequented. Reaching the top of the crag is often a problem; the best ways-up are indicated in the text.

To minimise damage to the rock caused by moving and stretching ropes, it is essential, when top-roping, to use a non-stretch belay sling and to position the karabiner over the edge of the crag. If you see these instructions being ignored please make polite or stronger suggestions as to the correct procedure.

The first climbs are on Elephant's Boulder. This can be reached by turning left at the junction of the two paths and walking for about 450 metres. The boulder is on the right just before the path re-joins the main road.

1 Heffalump 2a
A minuscule route up the easy-angled rock on the right side of the equally short passage.

2 Elephant's Tail 3b
Start in the gully on the left and then step round to the front and up.

3 Y Crack 4c
Why not? The obvious Y in the front of the boulder.

4 Elephant's Head 5c
Start up the left end of the sheer wall just round the corner from *Y Crack*. Finish up the slabby arête.

★★ **5 Diagonal** 6b
A fine-looking wall with equally good climbing. The right-to-left overlap, with a tricky exit at the top.

★★ **6 Mammoth Wall** 5b
Climb the flake-crack right of *Diagonal*. Move left to finish via small ledges.

There is an alternative finish to Mammoth Wall, *which moves right at the top of the flake-crack* – **Wall E. Mammoth** 5c(NS)†.

7 Tusk 5b(NS)
The disgusting slanting crack on the right of the buttress. Start by traversing in from the crack of *Mammoth Wall*.

8 Trunk Route 3a
The short crack and arête approximately 15 metres right of *Mammoth Wall*.

About 300 metres further right a rounded white buttress can be seen (vegetation permitting). This is Columnar Buttress.

9 Columnar Buttress 4a
This is the main route, and is centred on the huge stalactite.

10 Primrose 4c
The rounded flake just right of the last route.

The first climb at the left end of the main outcrop is:

11 Close to You 6a(NS)
Climb the wall using the two metal holds at the bottom and the large flake at the top.

★ **12 Siesta Wall** 5b
Go up an overhanging crack and trend right to finish. An eliminate boulder problem takes the nose just to the right at 6b.

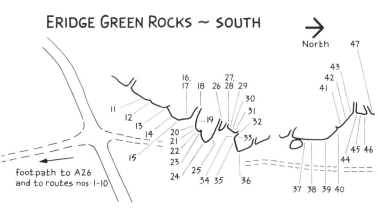

ERIDGE GREEN ROCKS ~ SOUTH

North

footpath to A26
and to routes nos: 1-10

13 Innominate Crack 5b
The obvious crack. Finish right or left or straight up – where else?

14 Last of the Summer Wine 5c
Climb the bulges 2 metres right of *Innominate Crack* moving slightly
right onto the slab. Climb the slab and finish up the short crack of
Equilibrium Wall.

15 Big Fat Tart 5c
Start in the shallow groove immediately right of the last route. Go
straight up the wall and slab keeping left of the large pocket. Finish
over the rounded top via a finger-pocket.

★ 16 Equilibrium Wall 5b
Start just left of *Boulder Chimney*. Climb the lower steep section to a
narrow ledge. Move diagonally leftwards up the slab and finish in the
crack on the left.

★ 17 Hottie 6a(NS)
The impending pock-marked wall immediately left of *Boulder
Chimney*. Start as for *Equilibrium Wall* but then climb up to an
undercut flake and finish with some difficulty.

18 Boulder Chimney 2b
An awkward-width chimney.

19 Nuthin' Fancy 5c
Climb the narrow wall between *Boulder Chimney* and *Libra* without
using the arête.

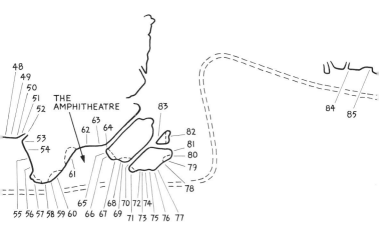

20 Libra 5c
Climb the blunt arête mainly on its right-hand side.

21 Too Short 5c
The arête 2 metres right again. Climb the bulge and gain a standing
position on the arête. Move slightly left and then finish straight up,
keeping your right hand and foot on the arête.

22 Trainer Drainer 5c
Pull over the bulge just left of *Hanging Crack*. Move left and up
towards the arête, then make a hard move back right to finish.

★★ 23 Hanging Crack 5a
The crack to the left of the large jutting prow. The initial overhang is
surmounted by some strenuous moves on good holds. Once in the
crack it is comparatively straightforward.

★★ 24 Prowess 6b(NS)
A quality route which climbs the large jutting prow. Start on the right
and then move left onto the nose at mid-height.

★ 25 Nonpareil 6c(NS)
This desperate route, the hardest at the outcrop, takes the
blank-looking wall 2 metres right of *Prowess*. Move slightly left to
finish.

26 Flake Crack 3a
The crack – featuring a flake?

The right-hand arête of Flake Crack *can be climbed at* 6a.

27 Bivouac Chimney 1b
Before the obvious cave.

28 Geronimo 4b
The right arête of *Bivouac Chimney.*

29 Truncate 3a
The short wall left of the cave.

30 Parisian Affair 6a
The short wall above the left-hand side of the cave entrance. Holds on *Truncate* are not allowed.

31 Too Short to Mention 6a
The roof right of *Parisian Affair.*

32 Cave Chimney 2b
The dingy chimney that miraculously appears on entering the back of the cave.

It is possible to walk through Cave Chimney *and reach the top of the crag and hence gain access to the tops of routes 11 to 36.*

33 6.0 a.m. Route 4b
Start from the right-hand side of the cave and climb the crack. The top is rather overgrown.

34 Condom Corner 6b
The wall immediately right of *6.0 a.m. Route* using the rounded flake to start.

35 Safe Sex 6a(NS)†
The short wall 2 metres right of *Condom Corner.*

★**36 Dr. Kemp's Cure** 6a(NS)
The rounded arête; much harder than it looks.

Twelve metres further on there are some boulders close to the track offering a few short problems. The next route is on the main wall behind and right of these boulders.

37 Tree Climb 4c
Immediately right of the boulders is a short nose with a small tree in it. There is a short 1a climb just to the left – **The Slab.**

★**38 Thin Layback** 5b
To the right is a series of small layback holds. This gives a nice little climb with reasonable finishing holds.

39 Scratch 6b(NS)
The wall 3 metres right of *Thin Layback.* Very hard to finish.

40 Amnesian 5b
The slimy, cracked groove opposite a large oak tree. An instantly forgettable route.

The Pillar, 5c, Eridge Green Rocks. Climber: Tim Skinner. Photo: Ian Smith

Asterix, 5c, Eridge Green Rocks. Climber: Robin Mazinke. Photo: Ian Smith

★ **41 Moments of Pleasure** 6c(NS)

Climb the diagonal overlap right of *Amnesian* and then continue in the same line to a thin finish on the rounded top. The flakes hidden from view around the left arête are on *Amnesian* and not allowed.

42 Woodstock 6b(NS)

Climb the wall right of the previous route and 1½ metres left of the arête. Finish by using the branch resting on the top.

43 Dutch Cap Arête 6b(NS)

The blunt arête. A boulder-problem start leads to a big hold. Continue directly up the scooped, cracked arête.

Next is a slightly cleaner wall with a large roving tree branch in front of it.

44 Mosquito 4c

Climb the arête on the left of the wall on good holds.

45 Tiger Moth 5a

Climb the centre of the wall on good holds.

46 Buzzard's New Saw Gets Christened 5a

Climb the arête right of the last route on its left-hand side.

Next is an easy gully, which gives access to the tops of routes 37 to 61.

47 Sadness is: 35 and Living at Home 5c(NS)

The wall and rounded slab. A large undercut enables one to finish delicately on the right (avoiding the tree).

★★ **48 Rota** 4a

A good jamming crack leads to a twiggy finish.

★★ **49 Demon Wall** 5c

Climb straight up the clean pock-marked wall to an obvious curved flake. Finish with difficulty. A good route.

★ **50 Easy Life** 6b

A highly technical route up the blunt arête right of *Demon Wall*.

51 Tallywackle's Climb 6a

The wall left of the chimney with a dyno for the small tree to finish – OAPs should note that a dyno is a wild lunge in disguise.

52 Descent Chimney 3b

Straightforward but thrutchy.

53 Bulging Corner 5c

The arête right of the chimney is awkward to start. At the top move round left into the chimney but don't use the opposite wall.

★ **54 Enigma** 6b

The centre of the steep wall right of *Bulging Corner*. Technical and fingery climbing leads to a small overlap just below the top. Move strenuously left and finish at the small tree.

★ **55 Long Man's Neighbour** 4b
The groove on the right. Approach either from the left or, with more
difficulty, direct. A good and varied climb.

56 Long Man's Slab 5b
Start 2 metres right of the last route and pull onto the vegetated
ledge. Continue up the mossy slab and finish directly up the headwall.

At this point the rocks extend out to the track.

★ **57 Scirocco** 6b(NS)
The left-hand arête. Climb the bulges and then the arête above,
mostly on its right-hand side. The grade assumes that the large bucket
hold on *Sandstorm* is not used.

★★★ **58 Sandstorm** 6a
A fine route. Pull over the overhang and move left with difficulty to a
large pocket. Go up and right into the shallow scoop and follow this
onto the wide ledge. Finish direct on very poor holds with a belly flop
– not recommended – or traverse left and use the tree branch.

★★★ **59 The Crunch** 6b(NS)
The impressive blunt arête right of *Sandstorm*. Start direct or more
easily by a long traverse in from the right. Go straight up the arête on
well-spaced jugs and small layaway holds to some undercut pockets
just below the top, then traverse left and finish up *Sandstorm*. A direct
finish seems possible but would be unpleasantly rounded and sandy.

*Next comes the Amphitheatre – an impressive arena with steeply
impending walls and swathes of unclimbed rock. Unfortunately the top
is overhung with copious vegetation and the bottom is, at present, a mass
of brambles and saplings.*

★★★ **60 More Cake for Me** 6a(NS)
A magnificent climb that takes the flake system in the wall right of *The
Crunch*. Move right at the top to finish left of the vegetated scoop.
Sustained but not nearly as difficult as its appearance suggests.

★ **61 Amphitheatre Crack** 5b
The obvious wide crack is reminiscent of Curbar's Right Eliminate. The
lower portion is awkward and can be very green, whilst the upper
section is strenuous.

62 Slug 6a
On the back wall. Start by stepping off the right-hand side of the
large boulder. Very strenuous and greasy.

★ **63 Flail Trail** 6b(NS)
Climb the arête right of *Slug* by desperate slapping and optimistic
lunges. Finish up the scoop on the left. A good route when dry.

64 Amphitheatre Chimney 3a
A typical High Rocks-type chimney – in other words a megathrutch.
Climb with foot and knee anywhere, facing either way.

★**65 Branchdown** 5c(NS)
The mossy right arête of *Amphitheatre Chimney*.

★**66 Leech** 5c
The mossy scoop left of *Forgotten Crack*. Approach from the left.

★★**67 Forgotten Crack** 6a
The curving crack. The difficulty is getting over the bulge and into the
main crack.

★**68 Smile of the Beyond** 6b
The undercut arête right of the last route. Approach from the right via
several hard moves. The wall and short crack above the start provides
a slinky alternative finish – **Bernadette** 6b.

69 Caped Avenger 6c(NS)†
The wall right of the start of *Smile of the Beyond*. A desperate
boulder-problem start leads to the crack of *Bernadette*; finish up this.

70 Torpedo Route 3b
The next chimney is hard to start due to the absence of the right wall
for a metre or so. The finish up the front is straightforward. It is also
possible to go straight up inside the chimney without the torpedo
move.

71 Getafix 6a
Climb the blunt arête to the right of *Torpedo Route*. A massive leap is
needed at the start.

On the steep slab to the right is:

★**72 Locust** 5c
Swarm up the flared crack; step slightly left on the top ledge and
make an exhilarating mantelshelf over the bulge using a large
rounded boss.

73 Finance 5c
A pleasant eliminate on the slab immediately right of *Locust* – the big
layaway hold close to the crack at half-height is kosher. Finish up the
short crack.

★**74 Higher Purchase** 6b
The centre of the slab between the two cracks. Move slightly right at
the top and finish over the bulge close to *Dusk Crack*.

★**75 Dusk Crack** 4c
Right of the steep slab.

★**76 Meaty Thighs** 6b(NS)
Climb the rounded arête right of *Dusk Crack* mainly on its left-hand
side.

★★ 77 The Beguiled 6b
A brilliant little route. The left-hand end of the impressive pocketed wall round the corner from *Dusk Crack* is terribly technical, tendinous and tiring.

78 Hour Glass 5b
Six metres right of *The Beguiled* is a niche at ground level. Climb out of the niche and jam up to the jungle.

★★ 79 Snail Trail 6b(NS)
Another fine route. Using undercuts, make a dynamic move out of the right side of the niche of *Hour Glass*. Continue directly up the wall above, making use of the obvious large undercut/sidepull near the top.

★★ 80 Zugzwang 6b(NS)†
Climb the crack round the arête from the previous route. Finish with the mother of all rockovers.

81 Emerald 6a(NS)
Just right of *Zugzwang* is a leftward-leaning ramp. Climb this and the buttress above to finish on the right-hand arête. An enjoyable route when dry.

Right of Emerald *is a short gully, which provides an easy way to the top and access to routes 62 to 83. The next buttress is a detached block, on the front of which is:*

82 Sandstone Hell 6a(NS)
Climb the frighteningly unstable buttress over the small roof and up the flake-crack on the left. Move right and finish with a desperate mantelshelf. Those climbers who don't own a JCB may wish to decline however.

Round the corner to the right is:

83 5.11 Crack 6a
A pleasant route up the crack-system left of the large chimney.

Beyond 5.11 Crack, and past some very green buttresses, is another easy way to the top, convenient for routes 62 to 83.

The next routes are 150 metres further right and beyond the S-bend in the track. A small boulder is passed before the first sizeable buttress is reached.

84 Greasy Slab 3b
A pleasant climb up the left edge of the small slab. The carpet of moss and slime that gave the route its name has long since gone.

85 Embarkation Crack 3b
Climb with the right leg in. There is a short climb up the wall on the left using the obvious slots – 5c.

86 Middleclass Ponce 5c(NS)
Climb the wall just right of the arête using snappy undercuts and pockets.

87 Spot the Dog and the Breath of Death 4b
The centre of the wall left of *Yew Crack*.

88 Yew Crack 3b
This is almost completely blocked by a tree whose roots form an unavoidable 'chockstone' at the finish.

89 Tortoise on a Spin Out 6b
A short technical climb below the yew tree right of *Yew Crack*. Finish by wrestling with the tree.

90 More Funkey than Monkey 6a
The overhang and groove right of the last route. Deceptively difficult.

91 Thrutch 6a
The sandy light-coloured arête. Start just left of the arête and pull over the overhang with difficulty to good holds; easier climbing leads diagonally left to the top.

★ 92 Earthrise 6a(NS)
The extreme left-hand end of the wall right of *Thrutch*. Start where the horizontal break ends at a vertical crack. Head up, and slightly left, passing two large slots just below the top.

93 Empty Vee 6a(NS)
The wide corner-crack. Very strenuous.

To the right is a steep wall. At the right end of this, on good pocketed rock, is:

94 Triceratops 6a(NS)
Start just right of the arête (but left of the wide ledge); pull up and make very strenuous moves round onto the front face. Finish straight up.

95 Impacted Stool 5c
Start on the wide ledge. Gain the large elliptical hold and then dyno for the holly tree. Finish by slithering off right into the slimy groove. A short, painful and thoroughly disgusting route.

★ 96 Brian's Corner 5c
The corner-crack gives an elegant bridging exercise.

On the next nose is:

97 Kinetix 6b(NS)
Climb the left-hand wall, close to, but not touching, the arête. A powerful and dynamic series of moves.

★★ 98 The Pillar 5c
Start on the right-hand side and move up onto the ledge; continue up the front face then move delicately left to the edge and finish straight

THE PILLAR

up. A good route on excellent clean rock. It is possible to climb the front face without recourse to either arête – 6a(NS).

On the steep wall to the right is:

★ **99 Waffer Thin** 6b
A highly entertaining (and explosive?) route. Gain the break and make a very hard rockover move to stand up on it. From the good hold on the left jump for the next one and finish strenuously.

★★ **100 Obelisk** 6a
Another fine climb on good clean rock. Climb directly up the sharp arête.

101 Mein Herr 6a(NS)
The thin sliver of a wall right of, and completely avoiding, *Obelisk*.

102 Slanting Crack 4a
The wide (distinctly not slanting) crack right of *Obelisk*. This is easy until it narrows near the top. An earthy finish.

★ **103 Nigel Mantel** 6a(NS)
The well named slab immediately right of *Slanting Crack*. An easy start leads to a frustrating mantelshelf finish.

★★ **104 Stirling Moss** 6a
A thoroughly enjoyable climb up the wall left of the central groove – thin and technical but with holds in all the right places.

★★ **105 Scooped Slab** 5b
Start at the right end of the wall and climb diagonally left to the groove in the centre. The finish is rounded and very awkward. A direct start is also 5b.

ERIDGE GREEN ROCKS ~ CENTRAL

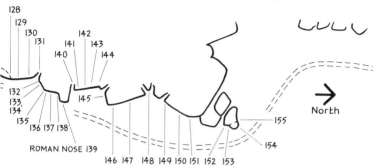

106 Snap, Crackle...POP!...Splat 6a
Start as for *Scooped Slab* but go straight up to the impending, pocketed wall. Undercuts and a dynamic move enable the top to be reached.

★ 107 Afterburner 6a
Climb the right arête on its front face.

108 The Nail 6b(NS)†
Climb the thin crack immediately right of the arête past an old stump to a small niche. Finish direct.

109 Black Crack 3b
The very short corner is hard to start and a tight thrutch all the way.

On the attractive sandy coloured buttress to the right is:

★★ 110 Mellow Toot 6a(NS)
Start up the short discontinuous crack. Move slightly right at the break and then trend back left to finish with a long reach.

★ 111 Yellow Soot 6a(NS)
The wall left of *Dilemma*. Strenuous climbing on slightly sandy rock leads to a shallow scoop and a tricky finish.

112 Dilemma 6a
Start just left of the forward point of the broad arête. Trend slightly right onto a sloping ledge and then finish over the bulge.

113 **Ken Clean Air System** 6b(NS)
Climb directly up to the sloping ledge of *Dilemma*. Finish over the bulge.

★ 114 **Iron Man Tyson** 6a(NS)
Climb the wall just right of the next arête. Finish up the yellow sandy groove.

115 **Communist** 5c(NS)
Follow the steep slab to the overhang. Traverse left and finish as for *Iron Man Tyson*.

116 **Polly Ticks** 5c(NS)
An unpleasant climb up the arête right of the previous route. Badly overgrown at present.

Just to the right, and behind the rhododendron thicket, is an easy gully which gives access to routes 94 to 123. Just right again is:

117 **The Pink Pengster** 5b(NS)
Start at the undercut niche. Climb the wall above on flakes. The line of flakes just to the right of the curving tree is 4b.

118 **Tweedle Dee** 5b
Start 2 metres left of the blunt arête. Climb easily up the wall moving slightly right to finish.

119 **Tweedle Dum** 5c(NS)
The blunt arête.

★ 120 **Stem Son** 6a(NS)
An enjoyable route up the open groove.

★★ 121 **Lou** 6b
The cracked arête is gained from the right and climbed with some difficulty.

122 **Toadstool Crack** 4a
The short crack.

Right of Toadstool Crack *is a small buttress with three short problems:* **Just Cause** 4b(NS) *a metre right of the crack;* **Just C.I.A.** 5b *up the centre; and* **Just Ice** 5b *up the flakes on the right.*

★ 123 **Backyard** 4c
The narrow, straight crack bounding the left side of an impressive wall.

The next buttress provides a concentration of some of the finest routes at the outcrop.

★★ 124 **Genesis** 6a
Climb the left-hand end of the wall on small positive holds. Start from the small right-facing corner.

★★ 125 Steelmill 6a

Takes the fine flaky wall just left of an obvious groove running down from the top. Hard to finish.

★ 126 Touch Down 6a(NS)

The wall right of the groove. Follow the obvious twin cracks just below the top and then move left into the groove. Often greasy.

★ 127 Scorpion 6a(NS)

Start 2 metres right of *Touch Down*. Climb slightly right to the large alcove. Move back left and finish up the thin crack right of the twin cracks of *Touch Down*.

★★ 128 Lazy Chive 6b(NS)

Move directly up to the right-hand end of the large alcove. Climb the improbable-looking wall on the right, moving slightly left at the top to a perplexing finish.

★★ 129 Revelations 6a(NS)

The discontinuous finger-cracks and flakes 2 metres right of the last route.

★★ 130 Poofy Finger's Revenge 6a(NS)

The blunt arête 2 metres right again.

131 Green Bollard Chimney 3a

Three metres right again is another High Rocks-type chimney.

It is possible to walk up the inside of Green Bollard Chimney. *This provides convenient access for routes 124 to 144.*

★ 132 Antoninus 5c

Climb the wall immediately right of *Green Bollard Chimney* via the flaky crack.

133 The Great Bald Turkey Meets a Dwarf with a Problem 5c(NS)

Start as for *Hadrian's Wall* but instead of traversing right head straight up the wall, passing undercuts just below the top.

★★ 134 Hadrian's Wall 5b

A rising traverse from just right of the foot of *Green Bollard Chimney* to the top just left of *Asterix*. The traverse line can be reached from directly below, halfway along.

★★ 135 Asterix 5c

The clean-cut arête. Start round to the left and then climb directly up. A pleasant climb.

★ 136 Fly by Knight 6a

The slabby wall just right of *Asterix*. Delicate balance moves lead to large layaway holds just below the top.

ERIDGE GREEN ROCKS ~ NORTH

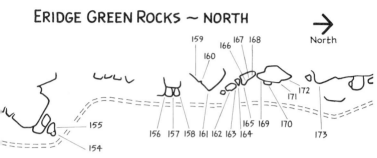

137 Achilles' Last Stand 6b(NS)
An eliminate up the wall between *Fly by Knight* and *Remus* without touching either.

★★ 138 Remus 4c
The narrow crack to the left of the nose. Another pleasant climb.

139 Roman Nose 5a
The nose between the cracks. Start up *Remus*, then step right onto the nose; thin layaways then lead to the top. A direct start over the roof is 6b.

140 Romulus 5b
The deeper crack to the right of the nose. The start is awkward, but the difficulties ease once the crack is reached.

The next four routes are on the wall right of Romulus, *the condition of which is quite variable:*

★ 141 Good Route...Poor Line 6a(NS)
The vague line of grooves a metre or so right of *Romulus*.

★ 142 Good Route...Good Line 5c
The groove-line just right of the last route, initially taking the obvious flake-crack.

143 Layaway 5b
The shallow scoop 5 metres right of *Romulus*. Currently in very poor condition.

★ 144 Hipposuction 5b
The rightward-leaning groove just right of *Layaway*. Pleasant climbing despite the greasy nature of the rock.

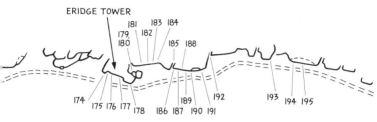

The next buttress has three short routes but, unfortunately, is completely obscured by a dead tree.

145 Capstan Wall 4a
Follow the line of the crack on the left of the buttress on good holds.

★ **146 Concorde** 5b
Climb straight up the arête.

147 Shanty Wall 5a
Go straight up on small lichen-covered holds, then step across to a rake on the right and so to the top.

The next four routes are of poor quality and are hidden behind dense undergrowth:

148 Bugbear Buttress 5a
Straight up the centre. Short but strenuous.

149 London Corner 2b
Two routes close together.

150 Jughandle 2a
On the wall to the right.

151 London Wall 2b
Just right again, and in some contrast to its eponymous northern counterpart.

On the next block, which is close beside the track, there are four routes:

152 Fruits 5c(NS)
The glacis and steep slab close to the left-hand end of the buttress. Holds on *Eric* are not allowed.

153 Eric 5a
Start by a ledge just left of the front nose. Go up and trend left to the top.

154 Life in the Old Dog Yet 6a(NS)
The arête is climbed mainly on its left-hand side.

★ **155 Fandango** 5c
Start right of the nose, and go straight up. The only obvious feature is a welcome horizontal break at mid-height, before a strenuous finish. An interesting route.

Sixty metres further right, there is a little buttress shaped liked a clenched fist.

156 Keystone Face 4c
The face left of the chimney. The final move is on small holds and is currently obscured by a tree.

157 Keystone Crack 1b
Go easily up the obvious chimney.

158 Keystone Wall 3b
The buttress right of the chimney.

Next is a series of five small buttresses. On the first is:

159 Paisley 5b
Climb the short wall left of the crack passing two strange metal wedges.

160 Hartleys 4b
Jam up the obvious crack in the centre of the wall.

161 Flutings 4b
A steep climb on good holds, which starts on the arête and finishes either on the front or side wall.

On the second buttress is:

162 Fontainebleau 5c
Is somewhere else and bears little resemblance to this. A strenuous flake-crack, very undercut at the base, and awkward to start. Quite a grinder.

163 Oliver and His Amazing Underpants 6b†
The short, hard finger-crack right of *Fontainebleau*.

164 Fernkop Crack 5b
Difficult to start, due to the absence of the right wall at the bottom. Rather vegetated.

On the third buttress is:

165 'Hyphenated' Jones 6a(NS)
The wall immediately right of *Fernkop Crack*. Climb strenuously up the steep lower section, and then delicately up the top slab.

166 Short Work 5c
Climb the leftward-leaning flake and finish up the slab above.

167 Sonny Dribble Chops 5b
Start up the twin cracks and finish on the vegetatated arête.

168 Brighton Rock 6a
The wall a metre right of the last route. The cracks are not allowed.

On the fourth buttress is:

169 Wobble 5b
Climb the short slab and then finish via the obvious flake.

170 Pedestal Wall 4b
A small platform jutting out from the wall is easy to attain. The wall above is also easy apart from the final move.

★ **171 Elastic Headbands** 5b
The wall right of *Pedestal Wall* provides good entertainment and an interesting mantelshelf finish.

172 Another Wet Bank Holiday 5c
The crack right of *Elastic Headbands*. Friable and usually greasy.

On the fifth buttress is:

173 Crackpot 4b
The crack in the centre.

Continuing along the track one comes to a prominent semi-isolated buttress – Eridge Tower. A very long sling or a second rope is needed for the belay.

174 Optical Racer 5b
Climb the centre of the wall left of the start of *Barbican Buttress*. Step left and rock over into the scoop left of the final slab. Finish direct.

★★ **175 Barbican Buttress** 4b
Climb the corner-crack to a ledge at the foot of a narrow slab; finish up this.

★ **176 Steamroller** 6a
Straight up the centre of the impending, pock-marked wall.

★★★ **177 Battlements Crack** 5a
Climb the crack to the overhang; move left and continue up another crack to finish with increasing difficulty. An excellent climb.

★★ **178 Portcullis** 5c
Another good climb. Go up the crack to the niche below the square, block-shaped overhang. Pull over this on sandy holds to the top. A variation finish takes the left wall of the Tower after the niche – 6b(NS).

179 Eridge Tower Route 5a

A scramble up the lower part leads to the upper overhanging crack, which is climbed on sandy holds.

180 Tower Girdle 5b

The Tower can be girdled just below the overhanging top portion.

On the low green wall immediately right of, and set back from, Eridge Tower is:

181 Moroccan Roll 5c(NS)

Climb the wall at the left-hand end via a shallow groove, a flake and the pock-marked wall.

182 Shirt Rip 5c

One metre right of the last route is a thin slanting crack leading up to a small scoop.

183 Pillow Biter 6b(NS)†

An eliminate climb on the wall to the right. Don't use the scoop at the top.

184 Three Hands Route 5b

The greasy crack 2 metres right of *Shirt Rip*. Good when dry.

The next route is 10 metres further on and just right of a large yew tree growing on top of a small buttress:

185 Honest Toil 4a

The short thrutchy chimney. The left arête is 5c.

186 Slave Labour 6a(NS)†

The large flake immediately right of *Honest Toil*. The finish is hideously rounded.

187 Liz's Layback 6a(NS)

The short corner-crack to the right of the last route.

187A Poetic Justice 6a(NS)

The wall right of, and not touching, the previous route. Finish slightly right.

188 Dougnacious 6a(NS)

Climb the steep pocketed wall to the right of a greasy, flared crack.

189 Clear Conscience 6a(NS)

The arête left of *Twin Slabs*. Climb the lower slab keeping left of the large holds on *Twin Slabs*. From the broad ledge climb the flake-crack to a problematic finish over the rounded top.

★**190 Twin Slabs** 5b

Follow the large worn holds up the slab to the halfway ledge, and then bridge up the square-cut shallow chimney to a thin finish.

★**191 Tiger Slab** 4b

Climb the lower slab to the broad ledge. Follow the short crack until it peters out and then step left and climb the thin upper slab. An alternative (5b) finish goes up right from the top of the crack.

192 Green Crack 2b
Obscured by rhododendrons and appropriately named.

Close to the track again is:

193 Gully Rib 3b
The obvious easy-angled rib where a small buttress projects near to the track.

194 Cave Corner 5a
The lower wall is climbed at its most forward point a metre left of the low wide cave. Continue up the upper part by a steep slab on the left.

195 Cave Climb 5b
Take the lower wall immediately above the cave. From the terrace move slightly left and climb the steep slab.

Harrison's Rocks

Harrison's Rocks

OS Ref TQ 532 355

The rocks are situated about one mile south of Groombridge, along the west edge of Birchden Wood and close to the preserved railway line between Groombridge and Eridge. They are named after a former owner, William Harrison, who manufactured firearms here until 1750.

They are approached by heading south from Groombridge, passing the old station on the left. At the first fork turn right and after 200 metres turn right again down a narrow lane signposted to Harrison's Rocks. A car-park with toilet facilities is soon reached, beyond which motor vehicles are not permitted. There is a donations box at the car-park exit. This money is put towards the maintenance of the toilets, the car-park and the rocks themselves. (The toilet block, incidentally, serves as a useful little climbing wall; on sight the Gents is 6b, the Ladies a little easier.)

The Julie Tullis Memorial Campsite is located at the northern end of the car-park. Pitches are available by reservation only and can be booked by contacting the Warden (for details see below). At weekends there is a café in the car-park.

The continuation of the approach road as a dirt track leads from the car-park through Birchden Wood and past another signpost to the rocks. One usually arrives at the top of the gully between routes 91 and 92. When you are familiar with the outcrop please try to vary your means of descent so as to minimise erosion in this gully.

Harrison's Rocks remains the best known of the outcrops described in this guide. This is due to the large number of good climbs at most grades of difficulty. There are, perhaps thankfully for most, far fewer chimneys than at High Rocks. The rocks face west and can be a sun-trap in the summer – trees permitting – making them a very pleasant evening venue. The rock is not always as sound as it may appear even on the more popular routes. Care should therefore be taken when soloing and in the positioning of top-ropes – large apparently solid blocks at the top of the crag are often not as stable as they seem.

Harrison's Rocks is actually owned by climbers. It was purchased by the British Mountaineering Council (BMC) and is held in trust by the Sports Council. The intention is solely to preserve the climbing facilities. To this end, the following conditions have been drawn up by the BMC/Sports Council Management Committee for Harrison's Rocks.

1. It is essential that only friction boots, trainers or plimsolls are used by climbers. **Boots** cause irreparable damage.

2. A sling, karabiner and *in-situ* bolt should be used at all times when top-roping. Make every effort to ensure that any **running** rope is not in contact with the rock, otherwise the rope will quickly wear grooves (and your rope will suffer too). The belay bolts have been put in for your benefit. Please use them.

3. Abseiling should not be attempted, nor should climbers be lowered off after they have finished the climb. Both practices cause **damage**.

4. Free-climbing only should be practiced. Pitons, modern protection chocks and camming devices should not be used because the rock is too soft.

5. Please refrain from using chalk out of respect for the ethics of the crag and the wishes of the majority of users.

6. Please do not camp, light fires or stoves, play radios or make unnecessary noise.

7. Harrison's can claim to be the cleanest crag in the country. Please take litter back to the car-park refuse bins.

8. Please approach the rocks from the Groombridge entrance, which is the only authorised access to the site.

9. Access to the car-park is through Forestry Commission land, and Forestry Commission bye-laws, exhibited at the car-park and elsewhere, must be observed.

10. All parking should be at the car-park. Please do not park on, or obstruct, the access road. The track from the car-park to the rocks belongs to the Forestry Commission and visitors do not have permission to drive their vehicles on it. A general speed limit of 15mph applies to all roads and to the car-park.

11. Please leave a donation towards the upkeep of the rocks, car-park, and facilities on your way out. £1 per vehicle is suggested.

12. All the property below the bottom path is **private**. Any trespassing puts a strain on the fragile truce that has been built up between ourselves and our neighbours over the past decade. If you are in charge of a group using the rocks please make sure that your party is aware of this. Large groups wishing to use the rocks should, in the first instance, get in touch with the Warden. Visitors needing advice or assistance, or experiencing difficulties when using the rocks or the car-park facilities, should get in touch with **Terry Tullis, The Warden/Site Manager, on 01892 864238, or his Mobile number, 0374 243888, or write to: The Bothy, Leyswood, Groombridge, East Sussex, TN3 9PH.**

The imposition of rules is clearly anathema to most climbers but is entirely necessary because of the fragility of the environment. Serious deterioration has already occurred, partly because of heavy use, but mainly because of bad practices. The Rocks are suffering badly from

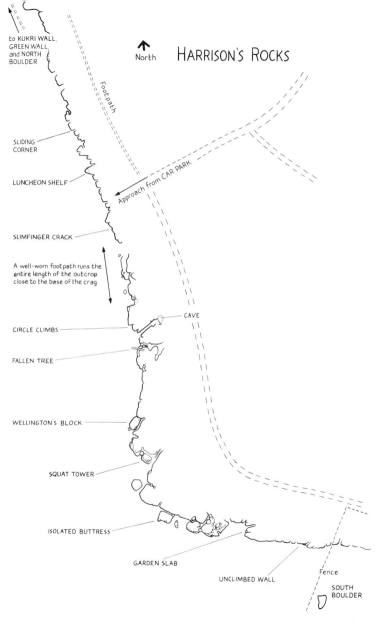

North

HARRISON'S ROCKS

to KUKRI WALL,
GREEN WALL,
and NORTH
BOULDER

Footpath

SLIDING
CORNER

LUNCHEON SHELF

Approach from CAR PARK

SLIMFINGER CRACK

A well-worn footpath runs the
entire length of the outcrop
close to the base of the crag.

CIRCLE CLIMBS

CAVE

FALLEN TREE

WELLINGTON'S BLOCK

SQUAT TOWER

ISOLATED BUTTRESS

GARDEN SLAB

UNCLIMBED WALL

Fence

SOUTH
BOULDER

erosion due to moving ropes at the tops of climbs; and heavy foot traffic at the bottom, which has led to a drop in ground level below some routes. The typical result of this is progressively easier finishes to some routes and harder starts to others. The rope grooves are regularly cemented but with care this should not be necessary. Unfortunately, it is more difficult to check the ground erosion though steps have been taken. These consist of laying down extensive amounts of gravel to improve drainage and shoring up the paths with planks and stakes. So far this seems to have been a successful policy.

To minimise damage to the rock caused by moving and stretching ropes, it is essential, when top-roping, to use a non-stretch belay sling and to position the karabiner over the edge of the crag. If you see these instructions being ignored please make polite or stronger suggestions as to the correct procedure.

The first climbs are to be found on the North Boulder, which is some way left of the main crag and sports a number of boulder problems.

On the side facing the main crag there is a 3a, with 5b problems to either side. The centre of the passage wall gives a 6b lunge for a jug. The arête to the right is 6a. The north face has a 5a problem using a large undercut, a 5b problem up the centre, and another 5b with undercuts just to the right. The right arête is the same grade. The west face has a 6a over the nose on the left, a 5c up the flutings in the centre and three 6b problems gradually working right.

Twenty-five metres right of the North Boulder, and past some low buttresses, is Sandown Crag. It has a tree stump on the right at the top. There are three short routes:

1 The Ramp   2b
At the left end of the buttress is a ramp. Follow this leftwards to a dirty finish.

2 D.J. Face the Music   5b
A thin and technical problem up the steep wall between the ramp and the crack.

There is a nano-eliminate between D.J. Face the Music *and* Central Route *– 6a.*

3 Central Route   3a
A pleasant and worthwhile route up the crack-line in the centre of the buttress.

There now follows an area of low buttresses, easy-angled slabs and intermittent faces. With its plentiful belays and negligible exposure this is a good place for the complete beginner. The one recorded route in

*the area is to be found on a slabby buttress about 50 metres right of
Sandown Crag.*

4 Usurer 3a
Despite the name this is a climb of little interest. Climb the right-hand
end of the slab, past the sapling, to finish right of the holly bush.

*About 20 metres further on is Green Wall, which is now quite open and
thus very often dry. There is a large beech stump just left of centre at the
top, and two grooves on the right-hand side. Recent ground excavation
has added a couple of metres of blank rock to most of the routes. This
has had the effect of making some of the climbs rather unbalanced in
that they have desperate boulder-problem starts but relatively easy
finishes. At the left-hand end of the wall is a yew tree; three metres right
of this is:*

5 Photinia 6a
The leftward-slanting crack. Approach from the left with a hard
mantelshelf.

6 Teddy Bear's Picnic 6b(NS)
This is far from being a picnic. Climb the wall 1½ metres right of
Photinia, starting with a desperately hard mantelshelf and then
continuing straight up the pleasant upper wall.

7 New Hat 6a(NS)†
The wall just to the left of the descending tree root. Jump to start;
move slightly right and then rockover onto the break. Finish left of the
descending root and without using it.

8 Central Groove 5c
Make some awkward moves to gain the groove right of the tree
stump. Move right to finish.

★**9 Dynamo** 5c
Climb straight up the wall between the two grooves.

★**10 Usurper** 5b
Start just right of the right-hand groove. Climb the lower wall and then
move left into the groove. Continue straight up.

Another 10 metres right is Kukri Wall with four routes:

10A Penknife 5a
The extreme left-hand end of the buttress. Mantelshelf onto the ledge
and finish direct to the tree.

11 Breadknife Buttress 4b
Climb the wall a metre or so left of *Kukri Wall*. Tricky at the top.

12 Kukri Wall 3b
Climb the faults in the middle of the wall.

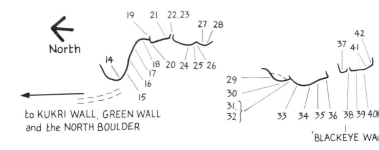

to KUKRI WALL, GREEN WALL
and the NORTH BOULDER

'BLACKEYE WA

13 Kukri Wall Direct 4c
Climb the middle of the right wall on small holds. Somewhat
obstructed by the holly tree.

*More broken rocks follow, after 50 metres of which Eyelet Wall is to be
found.*

14 Ringlet 5b
Start just right of the bulging arête. As soon as possible move across
left onto the arête. Finish up this. A direct start is possible – also 5b.

15 Twiglet 6b(NS)†
Start slightly to the right of *Ringlet* and climb straight up to the bulge.
Climb over the bulge using an undercut on the left.

★ 16 Eyelet 4b
A strenuous problem on good holds up the square-cut bulge. The
Eyelet itself disappeared years ago.

17 Singlet 5b
Climb straight up to the tree stump.

18 Dave 3a
Mantelshelf and then go up the crack to the tree roots.

19 Don 2a
A short wide crack in the corner.

20 Toad 5c
The nose to the right of *Don*.

21 Elastic 5c
Climb awkwardly up the centre of the wall left of *Tight Chimney*.

22 Tight Chimney 3a
Face right and climb with the left leg in, if you want to that is.

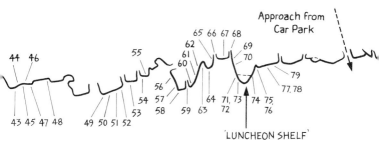

Approach from
Car Park

65 66 67 68
62
61   69
60   70
55
44 46   79
                                                          77, 78
              56
           54 57   64 71, 73 74 75
        53 58   59 63   72   76
43 45 47 48   49 50 51 52

'LUNCHEON SHELF'

.L`

HARRISON'S ROCKS – NORTH

23 Tight Chimney Slab 4b
Climb *Tight Chimney* to the first ledge and then traverse rightwards
until just beyond the nose. Finish up the slab. A direct start is possible
at about 6a.

24 Sullivan's Stake 5c
A tricky climb up the centre of the triangular wall.

25 Gilbert's Gamble 4b
Gain a ledge just left of *Ejector* and go delicately to the top.

★ 26 Ejector 4a
The groove in the centre of the face. Aptly named.

27 Sand Piper 6a
The thin cracks in the steep slab just right of *Ejector*.

28 Shytte 6b
The blunt nose right of *Sand Piper*.

*Further along the path is a short buttress with a chimney on its left-hand
side. Left of this is:*

29 Trip of the Psychedelic Tortoise 6a
The short wall and overlap gives a deep and meaningful experience,
man.

30 Carrera 5c
The steep slab left of the chimney. Start on the left; move right and
then back left to finish.

★ 31 Open Chimney 2b
This can be done facing either way or not at all.

*The buttress right of Open Chimney has five routes on large rounded
holds:*

★ 32 Cottonsocks Traverse 4b
From the foot of *Open Chimney* make a gradually ascending traverse rightwards until the break below the top is reached. Finish up *Root Route 2* or a little further right.

33 Root Route 3 5b
A strenuous climb up the rounded nose right of *Open Chimney*.

34 Root Route 2 6a
Start at a deep positive pocket hold in the middle of the wall; stand up on this with difficulty and then continue up moving a little left to finish.

35 Root Route 1½ 5a
Start 2 metres right ot *Root Route 2* and go straight up.

36 Root Route 1 4a
Start at the right end of the wall and gain the first break. Traverse left to join and finish as for *Root Route 2*. A direct line from the start to the tree roots is 2b.

The next buttress has some short problems of some technical interest for those who have done all the longer ones:

37 Soft Rock 6b
Climb the left-hand side of the buttress without using the arête on the left.

38 Blackeye Wall 5c
Climb the thin crack until it is possible to hand-traverse left on a rounded ledge. Mantelshelf awkwardly into the niche and then finish with ease. A direct finish is possible at 5c(NS).

★ 39 Slanting Crack 5c
The diagonal line in the centre of the wall. Much harder than it looks.

★ 40 Counterfeit 5c
Forge up the wall immediately left of *Right-Hand Crack* on small finger holds.

★ 41 Right-Hand Crack 4a
The wide crack with a holly tree at the top.

42 Serendipity 5c
The wall immediately right of *Right-Hand Crack*, finishing over the block and without using the crack on the right.

There is a short 3a climb on the wall right of Serendipity.

The next buttress is small and vegetated and has two cracks in its upper part. This is another area where there has been excavation at the base of the cliff, and, as with the routes on Green Wall, this has made the starts of some of the climbs very hard indeed.

43 **Smear Campaign** 5c(NS)
Climb the lower wall and then the flake-crack at the left-hand end of
the buttress.

44 **Wisdom** 6a
The thin lower wall and the left-hand crack.

45 **Fang** 6a
Climb the centre of the bulging wall between the two cracks.

46 **Incisor** 6a
The lower wall and the right-hand crack.

47 **Stranger than Friction** 5b
A direct line up the wall right of *Incisor*. Hard to finish.

The short crack right of the last route is **Steph** *4a. The next climb is a
few metres right on a short green slab, somewhat hidden at the top of
a slope:*

48 **Weeping Slab** 5a
A steep slab that is usually wet and impossible. Also known as 'The
Monk's Slippery Slide'.

*A little further on, the line of the rocks is more continuous than previously.
The next feature is Slanting Holly Buttress with four routes. At present
there are no bolts on the top so please take great care when setting up
the rope so as to prevent damage to the rock.*

49 **Corridor of Uncertainty** 6b
The blank-looking wall at the left-hand end of the buttress.

50 **Sticky Wicket** 5c
Bowl up the obvious crack to the right of the last route. The finish can
be a bit greasy and unpleasant.

51 **Rotten Stump Wall** 5c
Climb the next short crack on its right side; make a long reach to the
next break, and then continue to the top. Another route that is often
greasy.

★ 52 **Sliding Corner** 5b
Start in the chimney right of the buttress, move left and then straight
up on awkwardly placed holds. A start directly below the arête is
possible at 6a†. The thin crack on the wall to the right has also been
climbed – 6a.

53 **Fingernail Crack** 1b
The short crack on the left-hand side of the steep slab.

54 **Dinosaurus** 5b
On the buttress right of the steep slab. Go up the gully for 2 metres
and then move right onto a wide sloping ledge. Step up and right
onto a break and finish on the front face. It is possible to climb
straight onto the sloping shelf at 6a(NS)†.

55 Smiliodon 5c
A direct start to *Dinosaurus*. Climb the crack in the centre of the wall to the break. Move right to layaway holds and then back left to finish. It is 6a when climbed direct all the way.

Next is a broad gully with a wall on its right side:
56 Tomcat/Simon's Wall 5c
The left end of the wall. Start behind the holly bush and go up on small holds.

57 Panther's Wall 6a
Climb the wall left of the arête of *Snout* using the obvious undercuts. A highly technical route.

58 Snout 5b
Climb the rounded arête at the end of the wall with some awkward balance moves. Finish easily.

★ **59 Snout Crack** 3b
This is best done facing left, and gives a straightforward and surprisingly good route.

60 Guy's Problem 6a
The arête right of *Snout Crack*.

61 Mantelpiece 5c
A short problem which climbs into and out of the niche left of the tree.

62 Inimitability 6a(NS)
A short problem immediately left of *Beech Corner*.

63 Beech Corner 3a
The tree gets in the way but the climb up its left side is strenuous. The line on the right side of the tree is 5a.

★ **64 Blue Peter** 5c
Climb the prominent arête, starting on the left, then moving right, and finally back left to finish up the shallow groove.

★ **65 Blue Murder** 6b
Climb the impending crack in the left wall of the bay, easily at first but then with increasing difficulty. From the break either finish directly above the crack or move strenuously a little to the right and then go up.

66 Slab 3b
Not a slab at all, more of a contorted chimney really. The wide crack on the left of the slab. The kink is the tricky bit.

★★ **67 Slab Direct** 4c
A nice and (therefore?) unusual climb for sandstone. Make a delicate step onto a large foothold in the centre of the slab and climb directly to the top.

★68 Slab Crack 5b
The corner-crack provides a fine exercise in jamming and bridging.

★69 Lager Frenzy 6c(NS)
Can be had, but most will resign themselves to a hangover of some sort. Climb the peg-scarred cracks in the centre of the overhanging wall. At the break move left and reach for the top. Move back right and finish with a mantelshelf on a jug.

70 Lager Shandy 6b(NS)†
Climb the crack right of the last route to the ledge. Dyno for an obvious jug, then power up the fiercely impending arête.

★71 Celestial's Reach 6a
Start on the right edge of the wall. Go up to the main break with difficulty, then step left and finish more easily up the wide crack. Alternatively, swing left from the bottom of the crack and finish up the steep nose on good but well-spaced holds, 5c.

72 Stardust 6a(NS)
Follow *Celestial's Reach* to the break, then move right and pull over the bulge to finish up the shallow groove.

To the right is the Luncheon Shelf which can be gained in a number of ways. The various finishes can be combined with any of the starts.

73 Hangover II 6a
Start immediately below the left edge of the overhang. Make a hard move up to gain a ledge; hand-traverse right to the centre and then mantelshelf onto the Luncheon Shelf. **The Centre Finish** 6a is the logical continuation, and makes use of a large pothole and small fingerholds above.

A strenuous variation to Hangover II *is* **Hangover I** 6a. *Start as for* Celestial's Reach *but then hand-traverse right to join and finish as for* Hangover II.

★★★74 Hangover III 6a
Do people ignore you? Want to get noticed? Start at the right-hand corner of the overhang. Make a long reach to a slanting jug, swing out left on the break and traverse to the centre. Mantelshelf with difficulty onto the Luncheon Shelf. Finish either up *Luncheon Shelf*, or by the **Nose Finish** 6a(NS) a metre to the left.

A good direct line on Hangover III *goes straight up from the slanting jug using a heel-hook in the break on the left.*

75 Luncheon Shelf 6a
Start as for *Long Layback* but at the top of the parallel cracks traverse left onto the wide shelf – 5a. Finish up the headwall about 2 metres left of *Long Layback*.

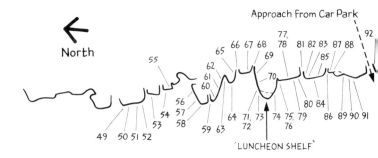

Approach From Car Park

★★★ 76 Long Layback 5a
A classic climb up the big corner with the parallel cracks. The start is now very polished.

★★★ 77 The Flakes 6a
Another classic route. Pull into the niche right of the corner then go up gradually right to the roof using the thin flakes. Hand-traverse right to the leaning crack and finish awkwardly up this. Please try to minimize rope abrasion to the rock on the left of the final crack.

★ 78 Flakes Direct 6a
Start as for *The Flakes* but instead of moving right go straight up the crack above the niche. Finish directly over the top overlap. Holds on *Long Layback* are avoided entirely.

★★ 79 Coronation Crack 6a
Follow the thin crack in the middle of the wall to join and finish as for *The Flakes*. The middle section gives precarious jamming for the technician or a powerful undercut move for those of the ramboid tendency.

★★ 80 The Limpet 6b
A good but eliminate climb that is now almost a trade route. Climb the arête left of *Dark Chimney* almost totally on its left-hand side. At the top overlap either finish direct or swing left for a metre and then go up.

A strenuous traverse has been made along the high-level break of The Flakes wall by starting up Dark Chimney *and finishing up* Long Layback – **Vampire's Ledge** 5c.

★★★ 81 Dark Chimney 2a
The classic easy route of the rocks is also a very popular climb – the

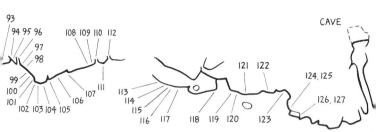

HARRISON'S ROCKS ~ NORTH CENTRAL

adjectives popular and classic don't always go together, particularly with Sandstone chimneys.

82 Dark Chimney Buttress 5a
Climb the left-hand end of the wall right of *Dark Chimney*. Move right onto the ledge and finish straight up.

There is a freak route that overcomes the blank wall right of Dark Chimney Buttress by an outrageous leap – **Icarus** 5a-7a. *The grade depends on your build.*

83 Nut Tree 6b
The very rounded arête at the right end of the wall is touch and go.

84 Spout Buttress 5c
The crack just right of the arête. Very hard to start.

85 Spout Crossing 5b
Climb the recess right of the last route to the first ledge. Either finish direct with further difficulty, or (the original finish) move right into *Windowside Spout*; go up this for a metre and then traverse right to finish as for *Pelmet*.

★ 86 Windowside Spout 2a
The obvious chimney.

There is a multiplicity of routes on the next wall, of which Bow Window *is the original. This is distinguished by a 'milestone' block at the foot and a 'triangular pocket hold' on the smooth wall above.*

87 Casement Wall 5b
An eliminate climb on the wall immediately right of *Windowside*

Spout. Go straight up to the Pelmet ledge and continue up the jamming crack to the top.

★ 88 Pelmet 5b
Take a direct line up the wall 1½ metres left of *Bow Window* and then finish up the jamming crack. The triangular pocket may be used for the right hand but it can be avoided. Alternatively, climb the first 5 metres of *Bow Window* and then hand-traverse across to the crack.

★★ 89 Bow Window 4a
A justifiably popular climb. Start on the milestone and follow the obvious break via the triangular pocket to beneath the overhang; pass this on the right to finish up an easy wide crack.

There are two alternative finishes to Bow Window. The first moves left below the overhang and climbs the flake-cracks (5c); and the second pulls straight over the overhang – also 5c.

90 Finger Stain 5c
Climb the middle of the convex wall right of *Bow Window*.

★ 91 Sashcord Crack 4a
Short but good, which is what counts. Never mind the quality... Climb the centre of the bulging wall left of the descent gully. Finish up the wide crack on the left or traverse off right. The small block directly above the crack is 4b.

There is a 6a problem on the wall right of Sashcord Crack.

At this point a steep, well-worn path leads to the top of the rocks. This is the usual descent route when approaching from the car-park. To the right of this is:

92 Yosemite Big Wall Climb 5b
Climb the buttress immediately right of the descent gully, trending leftwards to finish.

93 Giant's Staircase 2a
This consists of three tiers, the second of which is a tricky balance problem.

94 Arrow Crack 2a
Straightforward. Finish up the short wall above.

95 Gardeners Question Time 6a
The short wall just right of *Arrow Crack*.

96 Longbow Chimney 2a
Another straightforward but often greasy route.

The wall to the right has eight routes:

97 Grist 6a
Climb the arête just right of *Longbow Chimney* using an obvious

pocket at mid-height. Mantelshelf and then climb the short wall above. Starting from the boulder is not allowed.

★ 98 Quiver 5c
Climb the line of flakes just right of *Grist*. Awkward to start.

An eliminate has been squeezed in between Quiver *and* Toxophilite – **That Man's an Animal** 6b(NS).

★ 99 Toxophilite 5c
The next line of flakes below the large tree at the top of the crag.

★ 100 Little Sagittarius 5c
Start below the next flake along. Make an awkward mantelshelf onto the wide ledge. Move delicately up to a thin layback hold and then make a difficult step right into a scoop. Finish straight up to the beech tree. An alternative, better, and more logical finish, is to continue straight up instead of stepping right into the scoop.

★★ 101 Sagittarius 5a
Start directly beneath the overhanging arête. Hand-traverse the first break leftwards until a restful standing position can be gained. Step up the slab delicately to a scoop and exit on the right to an easier finish. A start a metre to the left is 5b, while a metre left again is 5c.

102 Archer's Wall 5c
Start just left of the overhanging arête and go straight up in the same line to the top, where else?

103 Archer's Wall Direct 5c
Start directly below the overhanging arête and go straight up it, including the final move.

★ 104 Stupid Effort 5b
Start as for the previous route but go straight up trending slightly right to a ledge; from here make an awkward mantelshelf onto the next sloping ledge. Step left to the edge and finish up this.

★★ 105 Long Crack 4b
Start in the corner and follow the crack. It is most difficult in the constricted centre section. Either continue easily up the crack or move left and join *Stupid Effort*.

★★ 106 What Crisis? 6c
A technical and powerful route. Gain the chipped peg-hole in the wall right of *Long Crack* and somehow use this to reach the crack above where another very hard move follows. (The climb was formerly **Crisis** 6a(1pt). Please do not aid sandstone routes with pegs etc. because of the inevitable damage the rock suffers as a result.)

★★★ 107 Slim Finger Crack 5c
A classic climb which can be done with great elegance. Climb easily up to the ledge and then, using hand-jams, gain the crack. Layback

up the crack and finish up the pleasant groove above. Alternatively, finish over the bulge on the right.

★ 108   Vulture Crack   5c
Climb the steep crack to the break. Move out left and carrion up the wall on small holds. An interesting diversion is to continue moving left past *Slim Finger Crack* and *What Crisis?* and then finish up *Long Crack* – **Missing Link** 6a(NS).

109   The Sting   6a
Start on the undercut wall just right of *Vulture Crack* and go directly to the top. Bee careful with the holds.

110   Horizontal Birch   3a
The birch disappeared years ago. Climb the crack to the overhang and traverse out left to finish.

111   Jumping Jack Flash   6b(NS)
Climb the blunt arête right of the previous route to the platform. Get established on the impending wall above then leap like a salmon for the top.

112   Downfall   4b
Climb the next crack to a platform and then go up the impending wall on the left. This is somewhat easier than it looks.

Next is a bay with a low wall at the back which gives some worthless problems. The Pig Tail Slabs follow with three routes, which are very popular with instructional groups:

★ 113   Left Edge   2b
Guess where this goes? Climb the left end of the slab.

114   Original Route   2a
Either go directly up the centre of the slab 2 metres right of the edge or, start a little further right and step left into the line.

115   Big Toe Wall   3b
Do the right-hand start to the last route but then continue to a standing position on the second break. Traverse right for a metre to a hidden layaway and then go straight up.

116   Greasy Crack   4a
The wide greasy crack above the large tree stump. Best avoided at all costs.

★ 117   Giant's Ear   5a
Climb the obvious ear-shaped flake at the right end of the face. From the platform there are two possible finishes, often climbed as routes in themselves. The first is 3b taking the centre of the wall, and moving right to finish. The second is a direct finish to the first – 4a.

118   Junend Arête   1b
An artificial line up the right edge that is ideal for novices. Start by a

Tempestivity, 6c(NS), Harrison's Rocks: John Patterson on the first ascent.
Photo: Luc Percival

Birchden Corner, 5c, Harrison's Rocks. Climber: Robin Mazinke. Photo: Ian Smith

large boulder; climb up to the holly tree on the platform and then continue to the top in the same line.

A low greasy wall now follows with three poor routes:

119 Fallen Block Mantelshelf 4a
Mantelshelf into the triangular niche from the left, whence a tallish person can just reach the edge with the fingertips – otherwise tough luck. The fallen block itself is buried in the undergrowth at the foot of the buttress.

120 Fallen Block Eliminate 5b
Climb the short wall just right of the previous route using small pocket holds. Continue over the bulge above to a hard finish.

121 Fallen Block Wall 5a
Start up a crack behind the fallen block; hand-traverse left for 3 metres, then move into the triangular niche and continue more easily to the top.

A little further on is:

122 Snake's Crawl 1a
A weird little route which enters the rock via a hole to the left of *Little Cave*, or by another further left, and then emerges halfway up the face. Finish up the short wall above. The furthest left hole seems to be getting smaller and is now only suitable for anorexics.

123 Little Cave 2a
The wide chimney.

The wall now becomes higher and is in the form of huge blocks.

★ 124 Signalbox Arête 5b
A good route. Traverse in along a broad ledge from the bay on the left to the steep blocky nose. Climb this on good holds finishing with a hard mantelshelf. It is possible to wimp out at the top by traversing rightwards to the tree and then up – 4a.

125 Sinner's Progress 5a
A worthwhile route if in condition. Start as for *Signalbox Arête* but continue along the ledge of *Sinner's Wall*, behind the sapling and into the cleft. Go up a metre to a ledge and traverse right along this before moving down to the niche of *Saint's Wall*. Continue across *Left Circle* and *Right Circle* and then descend to the ground at the foot of *Short Chimney*. Known as **Saint's Decline** if taken in reverse.

126 The Bishop and the Actress 6a(NS)†
Climb the greasy crack to the platform; move right and then climb the wall above via the obvious twin-cracks. Finish up the slab to the tree.

127 Sinner's Wall 3a
Start as for the previous route but carry on traversing to a sapling in

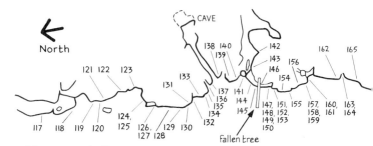

HARRISON'S ROCKS ~ SOUTH CENTRAL

the next crack on the right. Follow the crack easily to the top. There is an ungradeably greasy direct start up the thin crack below the sapling. It is also possible to go straight up the chimney above the start.

128 In Limbo 6a
After the initial moves of *Saint's Wall* climb the bulges to the left of the niche. From the large platform climb the flake-crack and overhang above. It is possible to avoid *Saint's Wall* entirely but this involves an outrageous (and ungradeable) running-jump.

129 Saint's Wall 5c
Start at the left-hand end of a low horizontal break. Using this gain the next ledge with some difficulty. Move right into the niche and exit from this up the cracks above. A start can be made at the right end of the initial break using a shallow rounded pocket, 6a.

130 Glendale Crack 6b
To the right is a thin peg-scarred crack. Climb this to gain the usually greasy and thus deceptively difficult ledges above.

A variation finish to Glendale Crack *has been climbed –* **Gretta** 6b(NS). *After the initial hard section traverse left along the first break to the next thin crack. Climb this to the top.*

131 A Killing Joke 6c
The blunt arête right of the previous route has a vicious boulder problem start. The rest is considerably easier.

The next two routes were originally done as one climb – **Circle**. *This followed* Right Circle *to the top, descended* Left Circle *to the first break,*

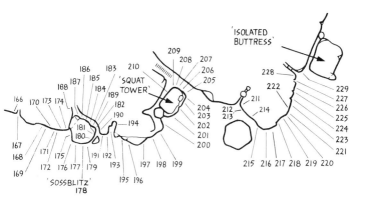

traversed back into Right Circle, *and then repeated the process* ad
infinitum, *or until "one got giddy and fell off".*

132 Left Circle 6a
A groove in the wall left of the corner marks the line, which only just
merits the grade. The initial moves are very thin, after which the
difficulties rapidly ease.

A micro-eliminate has been climbed up the wall between the Circle routes
– **Take That Effing Chalk Bag Off, or I'll Nick Your Rope and
Give It to Terry 'The Chainsaw' Tullis and He'll Keep It For
Ever and Ever** 6a.

★★ **133 Right Circle** 4a
A straightforward climb up the corner apart from the tricky and
strenuous start.

134 Bloody Sunday 5c
The narrow wall immediately right of *Right Circle.*

135 Good Friday 5c
The front nose gives steep climbing on poor holds.

136 Small Chimney 2b
Very few positive holds; face either way.

137 Small Wall 5b
Two tricky layaway moves, the first using a good layaway hold very
close to the chimney. It is possible to start on the right and step left
into the line.

To the right is an easy way down.

138 Long Stretch 5b

The front of the block between the two passages. Much harder for the short.

On the low block right of the passage is:

139 Coffin Corner 4c

A grave problem to be taken seriously. Start at the foot of the passage, gain the first break and move right to finish.

140 The Bolts 6b(NS)

Climb the sandy bulges on the front of the boulder. Mantelshelf or belly-flop to finish.

On the right side of the block is the St. Gotthard Tunnel which gives:

★★ **141 St. Gotthard** 4b

A varied route of some interest. Climb the chimney to the top of the low block. Step across right onto the main wall and traverse right for 2 metres. Move up, then go diagonally left on good holds to an awkward move into a recess and easier ground.

Through the St. Gotthard Tunnel and up on the right is a steep wall below the finish of St. Gotthard:

142 Long Reach 5a

Another inspired piece of route-naming. Ascend the left end of the wall on good holds with (surprise, surprise) a long reach for the top.

★ **143 Simplon Route** 4a

Climb the wall to the recess of *St. Gotthard* either by bridging or as a face climb.

Back on the main wall is:

144 The Nuts 6a

Climb the thin crack to the right of *St. Gotthard* with great difficulty. From the large ledge move a little left and then monkey up the steep wall above.

145 Pascale 6a(NS)

Start at the bottom of *The Nuts*. Move up and right onto the blank-looking wall, and head straight up to the tree on the broad ledge. Finish up the white, overhanging nose.

146 Rowan Tree Wall 6a

The crack left of the next recess and below the leaning tree. A hard, and usually greasy, start leads to the crack. From the upper ledge climb the slab on the right using small holds – you could try using big ones but they aren't there.

The next feature is a wide recess with two cracks on either side. The right-hand crack is The Sewer, *which provides the start for the next three routes, all of which move left after the initial crack:*

147 Sewer-Rowan Connection 5b
Follow *The Sewer* to the top of the initial wet crack. Step left across
the base of the wedge-shaped block and continue leftwards until the
crack of *Rowan Tree Wall* is reached; finish up this.

148 Pipe Cleaner 5b
Start as for *The Sewer* but hand-traverse left along the first line of
stalactites until one metre left of the arête. Move up and climb the
short wide crack to cross *Sewer-Rowan Connection*. Finish straight up
to the ledge then up the right-hand side of the slab.

★**149 The Sandpipe** 4b
Start as for *The Sewer* but at the top of the initial wet crack step
across the base of the wedge-shaped block into the crack on the left;
follow this to the platform and finish up the crack.

★**150 The Sewer** 4c
A fairly popular route, guaranteed to drain your strength. Climb the
wet crack and continue up the pod right of the wedge-shaped block
to a platform. Finish straight up the crack above.

The next three climbs also share a common start with The Sewer *but all
move right along the first break:*

151 Cannibals 6a(NS)
After the wet crack of *The Sewer* step right and climb the arête.
Bushwhack over the top bulge.

152 Sewer Wall 5c(NS)
Start as for *The Sewer* but from the top of the wet crack traverse right
onto the wall and climb the next crack to the upper ledge. Traverse
right and finish up the awkward crack.

★★★**153 Monkey's Necklace** 5b
A long route well worth the rope manoeuvres. Start as for *Sewer Wall*
but continue the traverse round the nose for a further 6 metres to a
second more obvious crack – Monkey's Necklace Crack; climb this
then trend diagonally right to the top. There is a powerful direct start
to the Monkey's Necklace Crack – **Primate Shot** 6b(NS).

★**154 Powder Monkey** 6b(NS)
Start 4 metres right of *The Sewer* by a low horizontal break. A series
of hard moves lead to the base of a thin crack right of *Sewer Wall*.
Climb the crack to the big ledge, then surmount the overhang at its
widest point.

★★**155 Orangutang** 5c
Start at some undercut ledges below and left of the Monkey's
Necklace Crack. Go up to the traverse line of that route and then
continue up the bulging wall trending slightly rightwards. An
alternative finish is to move left along the Monkey's Necklace traverse

and climb the improbable-looking wall just right of the crack of
Powder Monkey.

★★ 156 Oliver James 6b(NS)
A powerful and sustained route which starts 1½ metres left of the
start of *Monkey's Bow* and continues straight up, via an obvious
pocket.

★ 157 Monkey's Bow 6a(NS)
Start just left of the right edge of the front wall and gain a standing
position on the small pedestal on the right. Hand-traverse left towards
the Monkey's Necklace Crack and finish up a short crack just right of
it.

158 Baboon 6a(NS)
This is similar to the previous climb but traverses along the next break
up.

159 Moonlight Variation (Brookslight) 6a(NS)
Start as for the previous two routes, but carry straight on up the
impending wall keeping a metre or so left of *Moonlight Arête*. A
direct start is possible.

★★★ 160 Moonlight Arête 4c
A fine route straight up the scooped wall 2 metres left of the gully.
Start with an easy traverse in from the gully.

★★ 161 Starlight 4c
Start as for *Moonlight Arête*, but then climb the broad arête to the
right.

*The next passage provides an easy way down. A short problem has
been climbed on the left side of the gully –* **Matt's Fingertip** *5a.*

*The series of walls right of the gully has been the site of a recent clearance
operation, which has removed much vegetation both at the top and the
bottom of the cliff, although some of the lower sections are still very
greasy. Only time will tell whether or not the rock retains its current
condition and any of the following routes gain sufficient popularity to
realise their potential quality. If so, some of the Noisome routes will no
longer deserve their names.*

★ 161A Tempestivity 6c(NS)
The left-hand side of the blank-looking wall right of the easy way
down. Climb up to the break and make a long, powerful move to
reach the obvious vertical slot. Finish direct with another desperate
move.

162 Bostic 6a(NS)
A problem of adhesion. The bulging greasy arête at the right end of
the wall and immediately left of *Noisome Cleft No.1*. This route very
rarely sees an ascent for obvious reasons.

163 **Noisome Cleft No.1**   2b
Climb the crack to the top, moving onto the left side when necessary.
In good conditions the slab above *Bostic* may be climbed.

164 **Noisome Wall**   5b
Start as for *Noisome Cleft No.1*, but at the first break climb
diagonally right. Finish up the crack and over the boulder above to a
birch tree.

164A **Noisome Wall Direct**   6a(NS)
Start just right of *Noisome Cleft No.1* and climb up to the break of
Noisome Wall. Use undercuts to stand up on the second break, then
move slightly left and finish up the slab.

165 **One-Two Traverse**   6a
Barely worthwhile – should be One-Two Avoid Traverse. Start at the
top of *Noisome Cleft No.1*. Descend the cleft a metre or so to a thin
break for the feet. Traverse along this; step down at the crack in the
centre and continue traversing to *Noisome Cleft No.2*.

166 **Plagiarism**   6a(NS)†
Climb the wall a metre left of *Noisome Cleft No.2*. Finish with a hard
rockover to reach the birch stump.

167 **Noisome Cleft No.2**   3a
The wide crack in the corner.

168 **The Sod**   6a
A bugger of a route. The dirty greasy crack right of *Noisome Cleft
No.2*. Follow the slimy crack to near the top, then either bushwhack
off left or continue straight up. Originally 5c (2pts.), using two slings
for aid.

169 **Sharp Dressed Man**   6a(NS)
Start at the blunt arête 2 metres right of *The Sod*. Head for the small
tree and finish to the left.

170 **Squank**   5b
The dog-leg crack just right of the previous route.

171 **Tubesnake Boogie**   5b
The wall just right of the previous route.

172 **El Loco**   5c(NS)
Start 2 metres left of *Passage Chimney*. Climb the greasy wall
trending leftwards to a niche. Continue straight up and finish either
direct or to the left. The niche can be reached from the left at 5b.

173 **Ten Foot Pole**   5c
Start as for the last route but continue straight up to finish over the
bulge 1½ metres left of *Passage Chimney*.

174 **Passage Chimney**   2a
The chimney left of the Block. The climb goes up the outside on well
worn holds. The inside can be taken as an easy, though usually

muddy, way down. The passage can be chimneyed or grovelled at any point along its length.

Next is the Wellington Block, which sports some excellent hard routes and a couple of good lower grade routes to boot. The first route takes the steep wall right of Passage Chimney:

175 Forester's Wall Direct 6a
Climb the wall just left of centre to the break and then continue to the top in the same line, keeping left of the crack of *Forester's Wall*. The first break can also be gained from the right.

A line has been climbed directly up the arête to the right, crossing Forester's Wall *at the break and then continuing straight up as for the direct finish to* Forester's Wall – **Indian Summer** 6a(NS).

★★ 176 Forester's Wall 5b
A good climb. Start on the right side of the arête; move up to a small ledge on the arête, then swing left and make strenuous moves up to a wide ledge. Traverse left to the middle of the face and climb the crack. Finish with a hard mantelshelf. A direct finish is possible before the traverse – 5c.

★ 177 Bonanza 5c
Follow the previous route to the ledge on the arête. Go up a little, then traverse right for about 2 metres. Finish over the bulges with difficulty.

There is a direct start to Bonanza, which climbs straight over the fierce-looking roof – 6b(NS)†.

★★★ 178 Sossblitz 6a
A pumpy little number. Start in a niche to the left of the arête. Climb up to the roof and then move out right onto a ledge. Continue straight up over the bulges.

★★ 179 The Republic 6b
The front nose of the Block gives a fine route with hard moves between rests. Climb directly up the arête on its right side. Once standing on the third break, move a little right and mantelshelf on ironstone holds. Finish straight up. (The route was originally done with a jammed sling-knot for aid and a brief excursion into *The Niblick* – **The King** 6a(1 pt)).

★★★ 180 The Niblick 5b
A classic and varied route up the front face of the Block. Step off the wide flat boulder and go up a thin crack to the break; move left and layback into the square-cut niche above. A steep slab follows with an awkward wide crack to finish.

181 Pincenib 6b(NS)
An eliminate with some good moves up the face right of *The Niblick*.

Gain the first ledge easily, then pull onto the wall using the crescent-shaped flake (but without using the right edge). A tricky move then leads to a scoop and easier ground.

An easier alternative to Pincenib, *5c, is to climb the right edge itself which, despite the presence of the back wall of the passage, is a good route of some technical interest.*

★★ 182 Wellington's Nose 3b
A popular route which starts at the front end of the passage. Chimney up it until it is possible to step across onto the Block. Go straight up to the overhang and either go over it, or traverse right for two 2 metres to finish more easily up *Sabre Crack*. Another alternative, **Pince Nez** 4c, is a leftwards hand-traverse below the finishing crack of *The Niblick* that finishes over the front nose of the block as for *Sossblitz*.

The next seven routes are hidden in the passage behind the Block. On the left wall:

183 Lady Jane 5c
Gain the ledge a metre left of *Sabre Crack*, then climb the wall above with a peculiar mantelshelf move in the middle.

184 Sabre Crack 4b
The wide crack in the centre of the wall. Harder than it looks.

185 Caroline 5b
The wall just right of *Sabre Crack*.

186 Pete's Reach 5c
Two metres right of *Caroline*, and just before the passage narrows, is a small ironstone knob. Using this, move up onto the next ledge. Move left, mantelshelf, then layaway to the right and finish over the slight bulge.

187 Flower Power Jules 5b
Start at the end of the passage. Mantelshelf onto the ledge on the end wall then step left back onto the left wall. Follow this to the top trending slightly left.

On the back wall:

188 It May Be Green but It's Not a Teenage Mutant Ninja Turtle 6a(NS)
A direct line up the wall at the end of the passage. Gain the first ledge using the small crack on the left. Finish with two hard mantelshelves

On the right wall:

189 It Came From beneath the Slime 6a(NS)†
Start on the slimy wall left of the cave at the entrance of the passage. Using the massive pinch, reach out left for an ironstone knob. Gain a

standing position, then mantelshelf onto the ledge. Foot-traverse left or right to finish.

Back in the daylight:

190 Wellington Boot 6b(NS)
Climb the middle of the wall facing the Block making use of the thin crack and the ironstone holds above.

191 Kicks 6b(NS)
Climb the arête right of the last route on its left-hand side. The drilled holes on the top are not allowed.

★ 192 Belts and Braces 5b
Climb the buttress right of *Kicks* and left of the chimneys. Finish up the rounded groove on its right side.

193 Jetsam 3b
The left-hand chimney.

★ 194 Flotsam 2b
The right-hand chimney, and the better of the two.

Next comes a short slimy buttress.

195 Soft Cock 5c
Start in the middle of the buttress by a greasy foothold. Gain the ledge by either a hard mantelshelf or an undignified grovel. Trend left to finish just right of the arête.

196 Bootless Buzzard 5c
Just right of the last route. A long reach is needed to start after which a shuffle up and right leads to a bald finish just right of the arête. Shrouded by vegetation at present.

Round the corner to the right is a short steep wall.

197 Wildcat Wall 5c
Start at the left end of the wall by an oval pocket and go straight up to the ledge via a difficult mantelshelf.

198 Woodside Blossom 6a
The short slanting crack to the right is used to reach the break. Mantelshelf with great difficulty and then finish up the short wall above. This route is usually greasy and unclimbable.

★ 199 Deadwood Crack 4c
The shallow sandy crack leads awkwardly to the rounded ledge. Finish up the narrow groove. The overhang above and set back from this route provides a mildly strenuous boulder problem.

200 Tame Variant 2b
A popular climb which meanders up the the wide ledges at the right end of the wall. The crack formed by the jammed boulder on the right can also be climbed.

To the right is the isolated rock mass, the Squat Tower. There are bolt belays on top. Ascent and descent to set up the rope **must** *be by either soloing or jumping across the gully to the top of* Tame Variant. **Please do not abseil or lower off**.

201 Stag 5c
An awkward, unsatisfying route. Using good holds gain, and then climb, the blunt arête 2 metres left of *The Vice*. Finish with a mantelshelf.

★★ 202 The Vice 4c
A popular route. Start in the centre of the face and then climb the crack on well-worn holds. Traverse out right to finish.

★ 203 Toevice 6a
Climb the shallow, narrow crack 2 metres right of *The Vice*. Very tricky.

204 Handvice 6a
Climb the thin crack right again. Also very tricky.

205 Birch Nose 5b
Climb the right arête of the Squat Tower on its right-hand side.

The next climbs are on the side walls of the Squat Tower, next to a passage, which leads to the top of the crag:

206 Victoria 5c
Climb the bulging wall 2 metres right of *Birch Nose*. Finish between the two heather clumps.

207 The Clamp 5a
The centre of the short wall left of *Corridor Route*. The first holds are reached from the boulder on the right. A direct start is now much harder – 5c – due to ground erosion.

208 Corridor Route 4a
Start from the upper end of the stone steps and climb the passage face at the extreme right-hand end.

209 Rhapsody Inside a Satsuma 5b
Climb the arête right of *Corridor Route* on its right-hand side.

210 Quasimodo 4b
From the centre of the back wall of the Tower traverse left all the way round to the front of the boulder. Finish up *The Vice*.

On the right of the passage is an expanse of broken vegetated rock of little interest to climbers except perhaps for providing a good landing point after having leapt off the Squat Tower. Further right, on a wall by a large slabby boulder, are five routes:

211 Fat and Middle-Aged 6a
Gain the broad ledge on the left with some difficulty. Continue,

moving slightly right, up the obvious line of weakness. The hard start
can be avoided by chimneying up the gully on the left – 5b.

212 Knight's Gambit   5b
A balance move is made onto the first ledge 2 metres from the left
end of the wall; from here move up and then make an awkward step
up to the tree on the ledge. Finish up the crack.

213 Knight's Move   5c
Start as for *Knight's Gambit* but traverse right along the first break for
4 metres, where a long stretch is made to reach the next ledge.
Mantelshelf, then move delicately up right to a small pocket, from
where a further mantelshelf leads to an easy finish. A direct start is 6a.

★214 Skin Job   6b(NS)
Climb the wall 2 metres right of *Knight's Gambit*. Finish up the
light-coloured wall, using the obvious flake-crack.

215 Reach for the Sky   6a
Climb the blank wall left of *Set Square Arête*, starting 3 metres left of
that route and finishing straight up. Necessarily dynamic for most but
easier for the very tall.

★216 Set Square Arête   5b
A thought-provoking route directly up the arête opposite the large
boulder. From the broad ledge either finish easily up the top block or
walk off to the right. Please set-up the rope so that the karabiner is
below the level of the broad ledge.

Just right of the arête is:

217 Sandbag   5c
Balance onto the ledge, then stretch for the next break if you can.
Move 2 metres right and make an extremely difficult mantelshelf to
finish.

★★218 Sunshine Crack   4c
A good straightforward crack climb.

★219 The Knam   6a
Not an obvious enil. Climb the shallow recess 2 metres right of
Sunshine Crack. Make a hard move to get stood up on the ledge and
then a long reach up left for the next ledge. Continue straight up to
finish.

★220 The Mank   6a
An overhung scoop a few metres right of *The Knam* marks the line. A
move (or jump) is made to an obvious jug and the scoop gained.
Small holds beneath the overlap lead up to the ledge. Finish up the
groove.

★★ 221 Dr. Pepper 6b(NS)

A fine route up the improbable-looking wall right of *The Mank*. Not a route to be sneezed at.

★★ 222 Piecemeal Wall 5c

Starting from the right, gain, and then climb, the shallow crack in the bulge. Move right and up to the rounded ledge. Make a short traverse left and go up a scoop leading left to finish over the block above.

223 Karen's Kondom 6b

A sticky problem. The middle of the bulges right of *Piecemeal Wall*; finish direct.

★★ 224 The Chimney 2b

A good and popular climb. Follow the chimney easily (or perhaps with difficulty) to beneath the overhang; step left below this and continue up to the tree.

There is a variation finish to The Chimney – **Chimney and Traverse** 3a. *This traverses right along the broad ledge, past the finishing crack of* Reverse Traverse, *and then finishes up the top crack of* Two-Toed Sloth. *Please take great care when setting up the belay for this climb so as to avoid damaging the rock.*

225 Reverse Traverse 5c

Start just to the right of the chimney and go over the bulges following the vague grooves. From the broad ledge finish up the wide crack above.

226 Eric 6a

Find a way up the wall 2 to 3 metres left of *Two-Toed Sloth*, keeping right of the previous route. Move delicately onto the ledge and surmount the top overhang with some difficulty.

★ 227 Two-Toed Sloth 5a

Start just left of the passage by a large stalactite. An unusual but nice move is made to reach a jug on the first ledge; mantelshelf onto this, then meander up the slab to an easy finish up the wide crack above.

228 Soft Rock'er 5c

Start on the arête right of *Two-Toed Sloth*. Gain the ledge, then continue up the slab and over the bulge.

Just to the right is a gully, which leads very dirtily to the top of the rocks. On the right of this is:

229 Arustu 5c(NS)

Start just right of the gully. Climb up the scooped slab and then straight up the headwall to finish by the right-hand perched block. Would be good if it ever dried out, but it's usually unclimbable.

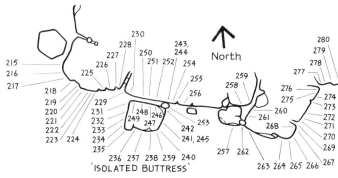

HARRISON'S ROCKS ~ SOUTH

230 Agent Orange 5a(NS)
Climb up to the right of the scooped slab, then move right to a line of
pockets that lead through the bulge 2 metres to the right of *Arustu*.
Pull over the bulge and finish up the slab left of the birch tree.

*The next feature is the Isolated Buttress, which gives some of the best
climbs at Harrison's. Access to the top is provided by the large jammed
boulder that spans the right end of the passage. Alternatively, there is
an obvious exposed step across the midpoint of the passage.* **Please
do not abseil or lower off.**

★★ **231 North-West Corner** 5c
Climb the arête on small positive holds to an awkward balance move
at two-thirds height. Finish in the depression right of the block or
straight over it.

A hybrid route – **Diagonal** 6a(NS) *– starts up* North-West Corner, *then
makes a strenuous finger-traverse across the second break of* Woolly
Bear *to join and finish as for* South-West Corner. *It is also possible to
climb the wall between* North-West Corner *and* Woolly Bear *at 6b(NS),
although the climb is not independent.*

★★ **232 Woolly Bear** 6c(NS)
Very technical and fingery climbing leads directly up the centre of the
wall to the traverse-ledge on *West Wall*. The crux can be avoided by
swinging right on the second break and going up just left of the arête
– 6b. Either finish up *West Wall* or step right and join *South-West
Corner*.

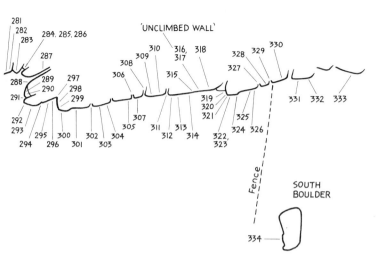

★★★ **233 West Wall** 5c

A classic trip. Climb the left edge of the wall to the big overhang.
Traverse left until half way across the wall then make a hard move up
to the large flake. Finish direct.

★★ **234 South-West Corner** 6a

Climb *West Wall* to below the overhang, then move round the arête
and gain the obvious undercuts up and to the left. Move back right to
finish. A finish can be made straight up from the undercuts, at the
same grade when dry.

★★★ **235 Isolated Buttress Climb** 4c

Start in the middle of the wall below the big overhang. Small holds
lead up and right to the rounded rib. Now either climb the rib, or the
wall just left of the rib, to a broad ledge. Finish up the crack above.
Alternatively, traverse right to finish more easily up the crack of
Birchden Wall – this gives a long and interesting climb requiring two
ropes.

*A barely independent eliminate takes the narrow wall immediately left
of* Edwards's Effort *–* **Edwards's Wall** *5c.*

★ **236 Edwards's Effort** 6a

Climb the niche in the front face and then continue up the flared, and often greasy, crack above. Finish by either traversing into *Diversion* or, much harder, directly up the blank-looking headwall – 6a(NS).

★ **237 Diversion** 5c

Start on the right side of the niche. Go straight up to the second break, then traverse right for a metre. A hard sequence of moves then leads up to a deep slanting hold high up on the wall above. Move right onto the large ledge and then finish up a crack just left of the *Birchden Wall* crack. Alternatively climb the blank-looking headwall above as for *Edwards's Effort* – 6a(NS).

★★★ **238 Birchden Wall** 5b

A classic route, which is high in its grade. Start up the shallow groove 2 metres left of the rounded arête. A tricky little move leads up to the fine wall above. Finish up the wide crack.

The narrow space between Birchden Wall *and* Birchden Corner *gives* – **Pan** 5c.

★★★ **239 Birchden Corner** 5c

Start on good holds beneath the arête. Go up for 3 metres, then pull left onto the front face. Continue up via a thin diagonal crack. Move a little right to finish.

★★ **240 Crowborough Corner** 5c

The crack just right of the rounded arête. At half-height pull blindly left onto the arête and finish delicately straight up. The arête itself has been climbed direct from bottom to top at 6a.

A route has been squeezed in between Crowborough Corner *and* Wailing Wall – **Mr Spaceman** 6a. *Start below the circular pocket and climb straight up.*

★★ **241 Wailing Wall** 5c

The layback crack in the centre of the wall is followed to its end, where a hard move is made to reach the main break; standing up on this can be very easy or very difficult!

There is an eliminate up the centre of the impending wall right of Wailing Wall, *the grade of which is increasing as the small holds gradually break off* – **Wailing Eliminate** 6b.

★ **242 Boysen's Arête** 6a

The short impending arête below the jammed boulder; go round this on the outside and up the bulging wall above. Short but fingery and technical.

★★★ **243 Boulder Bridge Route** 2b

Chimney up halfway along the passage. Sidle left (or right, depending on your orientation) to the jammed boulder and continue traversing, with some exposure, across the top of *Wailing Wall* to finish at *Crowborough Corner*. Alternatively, climb the main wall

Unclimbed Wall, 5b, Harrison's Rocks. Climber: Rebekah Smith.
Photo: Terry Tullis

Bulging Wall, 5c, Harrison's Rocks. Climber: Robin Mazinke. Photo: Ian Smith

behind the Buttress to the boulder bridge on good but often greasy holds – 3a.

★★ **244 High Traverse** 5c
Traverse round the Isolated Buttress in either direction at about the level of the jammed boulder. Various starts and finishes are possible. Belaying is difficult, but fun.

★ **245 Girdle Traverse** 5a
A low-level traverse of the Isolated Buttress starting at the foot of *Wailing Wall*. Hand-traverse left to *Birchden Corner* where a move up is made onto the front face; continue along and pass the rib of *Isolated Buttress Climb* with difficulty to join *West Wall*. Either follow that route, making an interesting and very long 5c climb, or jump off.

The next four routes are on the back wall of the Isolated Buttress and are graded assuming bridging methods are not used. They are described left-to-right as you look at them.

246 Powder Finger 6b
Climb the wall a metre or so right of *Boysen's Arête*. Go straight up all the way to the top. The last hard moves over the triangular block are often very greasy and can be avoided.

247 Bloody Fingers 6a
A direct line up the wall immediately right of the square niche.

248 Krypton Factor 6b(NS)†
Climb the wall a metre or so right of *Bloody Fingers*. Very hard to finish.

★ **249 Green Fingers** 5c
Start a metre left of *North-West Corner* and climb the steep wall on small holds. Finish left of the block at the top.

Still in the back passage but back on the main wall are:

250 Bad Finger 5c(NS)
Climb the lower and upper walls opposite *Bloody Fingers*. Usually an unpleasant route.

251 Plumb Line 5c(NS)
Climb directly up to, and then over, the small block that is poised above the passage – the block that serves as a launching pad for the jump across the gap. Watch out for people treading on your fingers!

252 Bolder Route 5b
The greasy wall directly opposite *Powder Finger*.

On the main wall to the right of the Isolated Buttress, and underneath the large boulder is:

253 Gall Stone 6a(NS)
Climb the short crack until progress is blocked by the large boulder.

Strenuously surmount the front face of the boulder and then finish precariously. Much harder for the tall.

254 Battle of the Bulge 6a
A technical route up the centre of the bulging wall between *Gall Stone* and *Jagger*.

255 Jagger 5b
A poor and usually slimy route. Shake (like Elvis, not Mick) up the shallow crack to the ledge; continue up the wall above using the tree.

256 Ear-ring 6a
Climb the wall a metre right of *Jagger* and without using the crack. Finish over the bulge just right of the tree.

Just up the slope to the right there is a descent route behind a large tree; to the right of this is a feature formed by a large boulder – the Big Cave.

257 Cave Wall Traverse 5b
Go up the green recess on the front of the boulder to its top; from here move right and follow *Smith's Traverse* but continue on past its finish to the arête and into *Crack and Cave*; carry on at the same level to finish by *Grant's Groove*.

★ **258 Big Cave Route 2** 2a
The left-hand crack on the back wall of the Cave.

★★ **259 Big Cave Route 1** 2b
A popular climb. The right-hand crack on the back wall is best climbed facing outwards! Finish through the hole at the back.

260 Rough Boy 5b
This climbs the left side of the right wall of the cave. Gain the break with difficulty, then trend slightly left to finish just left of the birch tree.

261 The Wallow 6a
Start about a metre right of *Rough Boy*. Climb the wall near its right edge on small holds and continue more or less directly up to the top. Easier for the tall.

★★ **262 Smith's Traverse** 2a
This is better than it looks and is an interesting climb for novices. From the top of the large boulder in front of the Big Cave, traverse right, along wide ledges, until past the overhang, then go easily up to the top.

On the main wall by the path again is:

263 Baldrick's Boulderdash 5b
A very direct line up the wall just left of *Forget-Me-Not*. Bridge up using the block to gain the first ledge, then go straight up and surmount the final overhang on good holds.

264 Forget-Me-Not 6a
The tenuous crack-line 2 metres right of the passage. Pull into the

crack and then follow the vague cracks until *Smith's Traverse* is reached. Finish over the bulge via the very thin crack.

265 Second Chance 6a
Climb the flared crack with great difficulty, either direct or by swinging in from the left. Continue straight up the wall to join *Smith's Traverse*.

⋆ **266 Last Chance** 5c
Climb the short crack just right of the previous route on good sharp holds. An awkward mantelshelf then leads to the horizontal break and the top.

⋆⋆ **267 Spider Wall** 5b
Start by a large pothole in the lower wall 2 metres left of the arête of *Cave Wall*. Climb straight up into a shallow niche; make a delicate move left onto the ledge and then finish easily.

⋆ **268 Cave Wall** 5b
The arête immediately left of *Crack and Cave*. Climb up on small holds to the horizontal break; surmount the bulge with difficulty to finish. It is possible to finish either to the left, by traversing onto *Spider Wall*, or slightly to the right.

⋆⋆ **269 Crack and Cave** 4a
A misnomer ever since vandals dislodged the boulder that formed the Cave. Nonetheless it remains a good and popular route. Climb the corner crack direct to easier ground and the top.

270 Grant's Wall 6a
Climb the wall 1½ metres right of *Crack and Cave* via the first of three indistinct grooves. At the ledge move a little left into the corner and then climb the overhang on good holds.

271 Tiptoe through the Lichen 6b(NS)
A direct line up the wall and bulge between the previous route and *Grant's Groove* using the second indistinct groove.

⋆ **272 Grant's Groove** 6a
The third groove. Although frequently greasy, this is a very good climb when dry.

⋆⋆ **273 Grant's Crack** 5a
The obvious crack in the centre of the wall. At its top move awkwardly left beneath the overhang to reach easier ground.

274 Thingamywobs 5b
The next thin greasy groove and the wall above. The face just left of the crack gives some eliminate 5c climbing – start up the crack.

275 Whatsaname 5b
The blind crack between *Thingy* and *Thingamywobs*.

276 Thingy 4b
Climb the short rounded nose at the right-hand end of the wall.

The next buttresses are very greasy, rounded and bulging but are broken by a number of wide cracks:

277 Little Cousin 5a
Two mantelshelves up the bulges a metre left of *Rum and Ribena*.

278 Rum and Ribena 4b
A wide crack leads to a commodious ledge. Another wide crack leads to the finish.

279 Purple Nasty 6b(NS)
Climb the bulge 1 metre right of *Rum and Ribena* with some awful contortions. Finish up the shallow groove.

280 Rum and Coke 5b
The next crack to the right. Move right at the break and then finish up the wide crack.

281 Bovver Boot 5c
Climb the pocketed wall 1 metre right of *Rum and Coke* and then step left to climb the upper wall left of the crack.

282 Cunning Stunts 5b
The product of a shining wit? The wall 3 metres left of *Scout Chimneys*. Start at a recessed vertical flake and go straight up to the yew tree.

283 Cabbage Patch Blues 5b
The bulging slimy wall between *Cunning Stunts* and *Scout Chimneys*. Suck your way up to a flat hold, then up and slightly right to the top. Hard for the short.

284 Scout Chimney Left 2a
This can either be climbed as a conventional chimney or through a hole at the back.

285 L.H.T. 5c(NS)
The small overhang between the *Scout Chimneys*.

286 Scout Chimney Right 1a
The straightforward chimney immediately left of the passage.

287 Back Passage 3a
A short wide crack in the right wall of the passage. It is much harder if the wall behind is not used.

288 Araldite Wall 5c
Just left of the right edge of the passage. Gain a ledge and then follow the shallow groove to finish. This is often wet and hence a bit epoxy.

289 Garden Slab Left 5a
Climb the left side of the slab following the line of least resistance.

290 Tiptoe Thru the Tulips 5b
An eliminate between the two original slab routes, with a finish over
the block at the top.

★ **291 Garden Slab Right** 5a
Delicate. Start from a block a metre left of *Biceps Buttress* and go
straight up trending right near the top. An interesting variation is to
start up this route, then traverse across the slab at half-height and
finish up *Garden Slab Left*.

292 Biceps Buttress 5c
The bulging arête where the wall changes direction is easy until the
finish, which is pretty awkward. A variation start can be made by
following *Muscle Crack* to the first break and then hand-traversing left
to the arête.

293 Finger Popper 6b(NS)
The wall and bulges a metre left of *Muscle Crack*, with a nasty hold
somewhere.

★ **294 Muscle Crack** 6a
Also known as The Graunch, which might tell you something! Small
holds left of the wide overhanging crack lead to a welcome rest – a
good place for second thoughts. The crack itself is every bit as
strenuous and thrutchy as it looks.

295 Crucifix 6a
Climb up the wall between *Muscle Crack* and *The Corner* slightly left
of centre.

296 Hector's House 6b(NS)
Start a metre or so left of *Corner* and go straight up to a hard finish.
Good value.

297 Corner 5c
Guess where this goes? Either start direct or as for *Hector's House*,
moving into the corner at about 3 metres. It is frequently wet and
unpleasant and 6a.

★ **298 Philippa** 6a
A good climb. Climb *Shodan* to the break, move left for a metre or
so, and then go over the bulges, either direct or trending right.

★ **299 Shodan** 5c
The overhanging wall to the left of *Half-Crown Corner* on crinkly
sharp holds. Go straight up to the first ledge, step right to the arête
and follow this to the top.

An eliminate route – **On the Edge** *6a – goes up just right of* Shodan,
moving into Philippa *to finish.*

★ **300 Half-Crown Corner** 5b
Start left of the angle of the buttress. Pull with difficulty into a niche,

then move up and right onto the wall; slightly easier climbing then leads to the top.

301 Wander at Leisure 5a
Several possibilities of about the same standard on the steep wall between *Half-Crown Corner* and *Birch Tree Crack*.

★302 Birch Tree Crack 3b
Follow the steep strenuous crack to the tree roots.

303 Birch Tree Variations 5c/6a
On the wall just right of the crack there is a stalactite at 3 metres, which can be gained from the left or the right. From there another hard move leads to the top. The grade depends on which holds you allow yourself.

304 Birch Tree Wall 4c
The wall 3 metres left of the polished stump trending slightly right to the top. Another less satisfactory climb starts a metre to the right – 4b.

Next is a wide crack containing an old polished tree stump giving an easy way down. The wall just to the right provides a 5c move using a big stalactite for the left hand.

★305 The Scoop 5c
Technical and delicate moves into and out of the scoop in the wall right of the stump. The right arête is awkward and 6a.

306 Easy Cleft Left 2a
Straightforward.

307 Pullover 5c
Start on the left or right and climb the undercut bulges to a strenuous mantelshelf in the centre. Finish up the little wall above with an interesting move. There is a 4c hand-traverse at half-height.

★308 Easy Cleft Right 3a
The chimney right of *Pullover*. Start in the small cave.

★309 Senarra 5a
Start in the middle of the wall; move up, then climb the wall on its left-hand side, trending a little right at the top to finish. Can be started further left.

★★310 Hell Wall 5a
A good and popular climb up the right-hand side of the wall. The start is the hardest part after which the difficulties ease.

★311 Charon's Chimney 3a
Straightforward and a good climb when dry. A name that Styx in the mind.

The next wall sports some fine open face climbs:

312 Baskerville 6a
A technical climb up the wall a metre right of the *Charon's Chimney*.
Holds in the chimney and on *Far Left* are out of bounds. No dogging
please.

★★ 313 Far Left 5c
Start 3 metres right of *Charon's Chimney* and go up to a break.
Move right and make thin moves up to the top. A climb for the well
read?

★★ 314 Elementary 5c
A good route. Climb the prominent crack-system until it peters out.
Finish slightly to the left of the final crack.

There is a barely independent eliminate which takes the wall immediately
right of Elementary, *using small layaway holds in the upper section –*
6c(NS).

315 Desperate Dan 6a
Start as for *Unclimbed Wall* but go straight up to the second break.
Move slightly right and, using a small undercut, gain the pocket hold
on *Unclimbed Wall Direct Finish*. Finish straight up with some thin
technical climbing. Easier for the tall.

★★★ 316 Unclimbed Wall 5b
An excellent and popular route. Start 2 metres left of two obvious
pot-holes in the face. Step up and move right, then use the potholes to
reach the break. Move right again and make a hard move to gain the
crack and ironstone holds above.

★ 317 Unclimbed Wall Variations:
A direct start to the two pot-holes is 5c. A better direct start straight up
to the finish is also 5c via a curving layaway. There is a fine technical
Direct Finish up the wall a metre left of the top crack of *Unclimbed*
Wall – 6a.

An eliminate, blinkers essential, takes the narrow piece of rock between
the direct start to Unclimbed Wall *and* Right Unclimbed *–* **Jingo**
Wobbly 6b. *It is necessary to do the adjacent routes beforehand to*
know which holds are in bounds.

★ 318 Right Unclimbed 6a
A technically satisfying but often frustrating problem on the wall left of
the chimney. Start at the top of the slab or on the wall lower down. A
thin diagonal crack first gives layaway holds and then provides a
crucial toe jam to enable a long reach to a pocket. Finish direct

The obvious chimney with the triangular slab at the base is the usual
descent route hereabouts – **Isometric Chimney** 1a. *The slab itself*
gives many good balance problems; try walking up it with no hands.

319 Sun Ray 5a
A poor route. From the first narrow part of the chimney climb the short
wall on the right.

320 Solstice 5c
Climb the steep wall immediately left of the arête.

★ **321 Bulging Wall/Zig Nose** 5c
Climb straight up the bulging arête on good holds.

★★★ **322 Zig-Zag Wall** 5a
Start just right of the arête and below a bulge at 3 metres; go up to
this, move right for almost 2 metres and then climb the cracks to the
break. Finish straight up or traverse back left to the nose and up this
to the top. It is possible to go up before the cracks are reached.

★ **323 Todd's Traverse (Boundary Wall Traverse)** 5a
Start up and move right on *Zig-Zag Wall*; keep traversing at this level
across *Rift* and *Witches Broomstick* to finish up *Neutral*. Tricky when
greasy.

*The starts of the following three climbs have become easier since the
building of 'The Beach' raised the ground.*

★ **324 Rift** 5c
A steep wall with a fingery undercut start, 3 metres right of the start of
Zig-Zag. Climb straight up the wall, past some good pinchgrips, to an
awkward finish.

A direct line just left of the next crack is 5c.

325 Witches Broomstick 5c
A crack with an undercut start.

326 Max 6a
The bulge and wall just right of *Witches Broomstick*. Hard to start.

327 Neutral 6a
The next crack to the right. Another difficult undercut start.

328 Stubble 6b
One metre right of *Neutral*. A difficult undercut start leads to the
easier wall above.

★ **329 Meat Cleaver** 6a(NS)
A chop route? The crack immediately left of the fence.

Outside the boundary fence and on private land are:

330 Holly Tree Chimney 2a
The wide chimney with a chockstone 12 metres right of the fence.

On a small buttress 10 metres right of Holly Tree Chimney *is:*

331 Nose and Groove 3b
Traverse in from the left, step up into the groove and climb it.

332 Golden Crack 4b
A variation start to the last route. Climb the crack and then traverse left into the groove.

Ten metres further on, and on the last sizeable buttress is:
333 Far South Wall 4b
Climb up the centre of the buttress.

334 South Boulder 4b
A fine slab with small holds. A step to the right enables one to pass the small overhang at half-height.

The Girdle Traverse

A girdle traverse has been made of the substantial part of Harrison's, giving over 500 metres of climbing. The original route started at *Far South Wall* (333) and finished at the foot of *Slab* (66) and is thus nearly 400 metres long. This was later extended and some of the walking sections eliminated, giving another 150 metres. In certain areas harder traverse lines were climbed as exploration proceeded. The worthwhile sections have already been described, while the whole route appears never to have been done in a single outing – yet.

High Rocks

High Rocks

OS Ref TQ 559 383

The Rocks are situated opposite the High Rocks Hotel, two miles west of Tunbridge Wells and two and a half miles east of Groombridge. From the centre of Tunbridge Wells take the Lewes road (A26); turn right at the second mini-roundabout and then first left. After about a mile the road makes a sharp S-bend over a railway bridge; immediately beyond this is the hotel and the entrance to the rocks. From Groombridge head south past the railway station and continue as the road bends round to the north-east. After about a mile a left fork leads to the hotel and the rocks. There is a large car-park just to the right of the entrance.

The Tunbridge Wells and Eridge Railway Preservation Society (TWERPS) intends to open a halt below and to the back of the hotel. This will make it possible, at various times of the year, to reach the rocks directly by rail from Eridge, Groombridge and Tunbridge Wells (for more details see page 9/10).

The outcrop is enclosed by high fences and lies within the gardens belonging to the High Rocks Hotel. They are open to the public for an admission fee of £2. There is a possibility that the season ticket scheme (recently suspended after three years of operation) will be re- introduced in the near future. Climbers are admitted to the grounds by permission of the Proprietor. Camping and bivouacing are not allowed at the rocks, and **abseiling and aid-climbing are prohibited.**

As the name implies these are the highest rocks in the area but, although their steepness gives an impression of even greater height, they never exceed 12 metres at any point. The rocks comprise a main wall some 400 metres long mainly facing north, and several isolated boulders, two of which reach to the full height of the crag. The rocks extend beyond the fence to the east but are less continuous and of poorer quality (see High Rocks Continuation Wall).

For most of its length the outcrop is heavily shaded by vegetation and as a result is slow to dry. However, the rhododendrons and trees make for a relaxed and intimate atmosphere during the summer, in complete contrast to the Bowles Bustle and the Harrison's Hordes. The tree cover was once even more extensive but the 1987 storms uprooted scores of mature trees and left many others damaged and dying.

When in condition, High Rocks is the best outcrop for high-grade climbing. The climbs are generally longer and more sustained than those at other outcrops and there is a much higher proportion of routes at 5c or above. These offer the expert a superb range of climbs unequalled in the South-East for their character and purity of line. Middle-grade climbers should not be discouraged, however, as there are sufficient good-quality climbs in their category, on the isolated boulders, and up the numerous chimneys and cracks.

High Rocks has been designated an SSSI. At one time English Nature suggested a climbing ban, although this threat was subsequently diffused by negotiation. However, it remains worried about the damage being done to the rocks by climbing, particularly to the isolated boulders. Whatever methods were used in the past to reach the summits of these boulders, only one is now acceptable – the first climber must solo up. Similarly, when you have finished on the boulder, the last climber must solo down – abseiling off and pulling the rope through is unacceptable because of the severe erosion that results.

English Nature is also worried about rope grooves destroying features such as polygonal markings. These are very common in areas such as Fontainebleau but rare in the South-East. Particular care should be taken in the area above *Infidel* to avoid making this situation any worse. The rocks are also home to a number of rare mosses and other plants, so please don't destroy any flora unnecessarily.

To minimise damage to the rock caused by moving and stretching ropes, it is essential. when top-roping, to use a non-stretch belay sling and to position the karabiner over the edge of the crag. If you see these instructions being ignored please make polite or stronger suggestions as to the correct procedure.

The entrance is opposite the Hotel, and this is in the Advertisement Wall *to* Mulligan's Wall *area – route numbers 100 to 125. To the right of the boundary fence at the left-hand end of the outcrop and beyond a gully is a block, the front left arête of which gives:*

1 Pure Arête   5b
The finishing holds often need to be dug out.

2 Peace on Earth   5c(NS)
Start as for *Pure Arête* but hand-traverse right at about two-thirds height towards the centre of the block. Go straight up when it feels right.

3 The Purvee   6b(NS)
A direct line up the centre of the wall. Leaving the ground is deceptively difficult.

★ **4 Lady of the Light-bulb**   5c(NS)
The right-hand arête. A long reach is needed at the top.

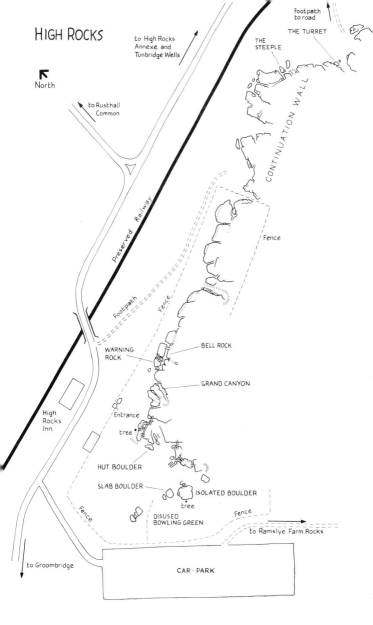

HIGH ROCKS

North

to High Rocks
Annexe and
Tunbridge Wells

to Rusthall
Common

Preserved Railway

Footpath

Fence

High
Rocks
Inn

WARNING
ROCK

BELL ROCK

GRAND CANYON

Entrance

tree

HUT BOULDER

SLAB BOULDER

ISOLATED BOULDER

tree

DISUSED
BOWLING GREEN

Fence

Fence

to Ramslye Farm Rocks

to Groombridge

CAR - PARK

THE STEEPLE

THE TURRET

footpath
to road

CONTINUATION WALL

Fence

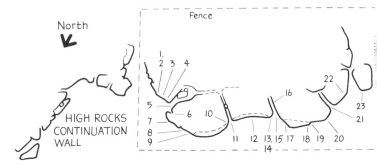

North

Fence

22

23
21

16

1,
2 3 4

5
6 10
7
8
9

11 12 13 15 17 18 19 20
14

HIGH ROCKS
CONTINUATION
WALL

HIGH ROCKS ~ EAST

5 Orion Arête 5c(NS)
The arête immediately left of *Orion Crack* and just right of the little
passage.

★★ **6 Orion Crack** 4c
Follow the shallow crack to a platform and then finish up the wall
above.

7 Scimitar 6a
Start at the steep crack 3 metres right of the previous route and go
straight up. Although the initial moves are usually greasy this is a
good climb when in condition.

8 Tubby Hayes is a Fats Waller 6b(NS)
The obvious line 2 metres right of *Scimitar*. The plant-filled groove at
the top is avoided by an excursion rightwards onto the headwall.

★★★ **9 The First Crack** 6b(NS)
Usually has the last laugh. The fine imposing crack about 10 metres
right of *Scimitar*. The first section, the crux, is a fiendishly hard
jamming crack – best left to connoisseurs with large rolls of sticky
tape. The middle section is slightly easier and leads to a finish straight
up the steep headwall.

★★ **10 Missing Link** 6b(NS)
Impressive and perhaps not possible for the short. Climb the arête just
left of *Anaconda Chimney* to the break at 4 metres. Traverse left to
the next arête and pull over the bulge to gain the upper wall; continue
straight up.

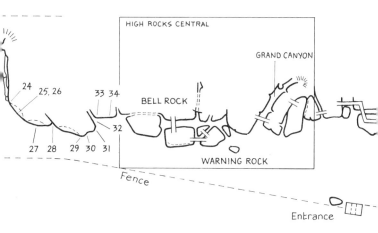

★★ 11 Anaconda Chimney 4a
A relatively pleasant chimney climb. The bottom section is best
climbed facing left. After the ledge at 3 metres the difficulties ease.

12 Bolt Route
The wall between the chimneys. A possible free climb so please don't
destroy the rock any further by aid climbing.

★ 13 Fungal Smear 6b(NS)†
Start as for *Boa-Constrictor Chimney*. At the first break move left and
climb the obvious ramp. A good climb when dry.

14 Rattlesnake II 6b(NS)
An eliminate but good climbing nonetheless. Start as for
Boa-Constrictor Chimney but at the first break swing onto the left
arête. Layback the arête to a tricky finish.

15 Boa-Constrictor Chimney 4b
Tight? From the ground just inside, go up the narrow front portion
facing left. At the top, traverse inwards across the wide part and exit
on the right.

At the back of the chimney is:

16 Boa by the Back 4a
Up the back facing right, to the top of a projecting bulge on the right
wall. Climb the narrow crack at the back to the chockstone; this is
hard until the chock is reached. Finish at the back.

17 Venom
An old peg route up the impressive crack 5 metres right of the chimney. Don't peg it please.

The next two routes start beside an odd-looking hole – the Needle's Eye:
18 Bone Machine 6c(NS)†
Move diagonally left up the absurdly overhanging wall; traverse left along the first break and then finish up *Venom*. Finishing up the arête looks feasible but has yet to be climbed.

★★ **19 Adder** 6a(NS)
Follow the impressive thin crack just right of the Needle's Eye. Previously an aid climb and usually very greasy.

The rocks now open up to form an amphitheatre, at the back of which is a flight of stairs leading to the top. Here are some of the most impressive and difficult climbs in the South-East.

★★★ **20 The Second Generation** 6b(NS)
A stupendous route which climbs the improbable-looking wall between *Adder* and *Cobra Chimney*. Start by stepping off the tree stump; follow the holds and finish up the square-cut arête on the left. Previously an artificial climb. Please don't aid it.

21 Cobra Chimney 4a
Wherever (if ever?) you climb this, it is too wide for comfort.

★★★ **22 Renascence** 6b(NS)
An excellent route which takes the rounded arête right of *Cobra Chimney*. Strenuous and sustained with the crux at the top.

On the small block left of the steps is:
23 Sorrow 5b
Climb straight up the front of the defaced buttress on good holds; mantelshelf to finish.

Just right of the steps is:
★★★ **24 Steps Crack** 5b
The fine-looking crack right of the passage. Exit left at the top. An early classic which still demands respect.

★★ **25 Chimaera** 7a(NS)†
Start in a cave right of *Steps Crack* and go strenuously up to the horizontal break. Hand-traverse left to the foot of a bottomless square-cut groove. Climb this by a series of strenuous contortions. The hardest climb in the South-East.

★★★ **26 Moving Staircase** 6b(NS)
Start as for *Chimaera* but at the first break move right onto the obvious ramp and follow this with escalating difficulty to finish up the steep slab above its end.

Rift, 5c, Harrison's Rocks. Climber: Jonathan Coe. Photo: Ian Smith

Marquita, 5c, High Rocks. Climber: Mike Vetterlein. Photo: Ian Smith

There is a 6b direct start to Moving Staircase, which starts 3 metres right of the ordinary route and finishes on the ramp.

Round the corner is a large concave wall bounded on the right by a chimney. This wall has no routes on its main face except for:

27 Pegasus 6b(NS)†
Climb the short crack in the centre of the buttress then traverse right along the obvious stalactites. Finish up the greasy arête.

28 Chockstone Chimney 2b
Facing right, climb a crack in the right wall; go outside the chockstone and into the recess in the right wall. Go up this and then step across to the second chockstone to an earthy exit left.

★★ **29 Judy** 6b(NS)
The centre of the massive overhanging wall. A desperate boulder-problem start on the right leads to an obvious traverse line into the niche. Exit up and then left to a semi-rest on a large flake.
Hand-traverse right and finish up the wide crack in the overhang. The route is easier and perhaps more enjoyable with a leg-up to start.

29A Punch 6c(NS)†
Start as for *Judy* but continue straight up – very reachy. From the break struggle awkwardly up the obvious flared crack.

★ **30 Telegram Sam** 6b(NS)
Climb the blunt arête right of *Judy* to the horizontal break. Finish up the slab above using the thin crack.

★ **31 Rag Trade** 6b(NS)
The arête down and left of *E Chimney*. It is possible, and perhaps more enjoyable, to avoid the hard start by a short traverse from the right – 6a(NS).

There are two short climbs on the left wall of E Chimney, a 6b(NS)† which starts 4 metres inside the chimney with a hard move to gain the sloping shelf, and a 5b, a metre further in and just left of an easy crack.

32 E Chimney 3a
Similar to *Cobra Chimney* but somewhat shorter.

An easy descent route is to be found at the back of the chimney.

33 Designer Label 6b
A technically interesting climb but more of a soiled second than catwalk material. Climb the right arête of *E Chimney* on its left side to start with and then on the front.

34 Recess Wall 3a
Climb the left-hand chimney, then traverse the wall leftwards along a broad ledge. Exit at the far end with an exposed step.

Back on the face by the path is:

★★ 35 Salad Days 6b(NS)
Climb the front face of the left arête of the buttress. At the first break move right and then climb the long thin flake. Step left at the next break to a loose and sandy finish.

★ 36 Leglock 6b(NS)
The crack right of *Salad Days* is gained from the right with difficulty. Follow it to near the top, where a move leftwards leads to the wide finishing crack. One may avoid the start by not doing the route, or by traversing in from *Cut Steps Crack* along a line of stalactites.

37 Crossing the Rubicon 6b(NS)
Start 3 metres right of *Leglock*. Using the small circular hold gain the line of stalactites. Move left onto a good ledge and then finish up the steep wall keeping just right of *Leglock*.

★ 38 Too Tall for Tim 6a(NS)
Right of *Crossing the Rubicon* is a vertical line of cut holds. Follow these to the first break and then continue straight up with an impossibly long reach for excessively short people.

★★ 39 Cut Steps Crack 5c(NS)
Start as for the previous route but at the first break traverse right to the nose. Lean across the wide passage and then climb the crack in the opposite wall (bridging is not allowed). Move left and climb the centre of the final block. Two ropes are needed to belay this 'adventurous route'.

★ 40 Too Hard for Dave 6b(NS)
The blunt arête right of *Too Tall for Tim* has a dynamic start and a finish which is far too hard – for Dave.

Right of Too Hard for Dave is the eastern entrance to Bell Rock Transverse Passage. The next 15 routes are to be found here – up the passage itself, on its walls, and in the numerous subsidiary chimneys and cracks. For those not wishing to sample its dank delights the next route on the front of the crag is Krankenkopf Crack (56).

41 Strangler 5a
In front of, and left of the slanting chimney, is a short crack. Climb this, then either move left to continue up the wide chimney or step right into the slanting chimney. It is possible – but unpleasant – to finish direct via the thin crack and earth bank at 6b(NS)†.

42 Deadwood Chimney 2b
Climb the slanting chimney making use of a crack in the right wall about 3 metres in. Traverse outwards at the top and finish either by an earthy exit on the left or by stepping across to the right, followed by a stomach-traverse over the chockstone. The whole chimney can also be climbed at the back with an exit through an earthy hole.

★ 43 Bell Rock Transverse Passage Route 1 5a
Chimney straight up the cleft to finish on the bridge. There are two
rest ledges on this impressive looking route.

44 Bell Rock Passage 4a
Climb straight up at the Transverse Passage end to a ledge on the left
wall. Finish either as a through route, or on the outside.

★ 45 Bell Rock Transverse Passage Route 2 5a
Similar to *Route 1* but narrower.

46 Spider's Chimney 3b
This is best done facing left.

47 Bell Rock Transverse Passage Route 3 4c
Climb the passage a metre right of *Spider's Chimney*. Avoid the
capping block at the top.

48 Giant's Stride 3a
Climb the chimney on the left at the Transverse Passage end; step
across to the right wall and go along a ledge high above the
Transverse Passage to the back corner of the Balcony. Finish up the
inside.

49 The Chute 4a
Climb the sandy and slimy lower crack facing left. Later a hand is
stretched across the Transverse Passage to enable the overhanging
chockstone to be passed. Finish easily above or step across to the
Balcony.

50 Labyrinth
An amazing route? Between *Deadwood Chimney* and the Balcony all
the chimneys and passages have a more or less continuous ledge
some 2 to 3 metres from the top. The route traverses this ledge and
can be started and finished anywhere. The grade is dependent on the
parts that are climbed.

*On the south-facing side of the Bell Rock Transverse Passage is a narrow
passage:*

51 Senile Walk 6b(NS)
The sharp arête left of the passage. Exit left under the capping block.

52 Warning Rock Chimney 2a
Walk up the passage to the highest point of the floor. Climb a sloping
ledge, facing right, to reach the Balcony and continue to the top on
the outside. It is possible to walk through the chimney and emerge
alongside *Henry the Ninth*.

★ 53 One of Our Chimneys is Missing 2b
Climb the chimney right of *Warning Rock Chimney* at the Transverse
Passage end. It is possible to walk through the chimney and emerge
at the front of the crag via *Smooth Chimney* and *Wye Chimney*.

54 Insinuation Crack 2b
The next chimney to the right. By squeezing through the chimney one can can pass through *Slab Chimney* and *Wye Chimney* and emerge at the front of the crag.

55 Hidden Arête 5b(NS)
The right arête of *Insinuation Crack*. Follow the arête to a ledge, move slightly right and finish with a hard mantelshelf.

Back on the main face is:

★★ **56 Krankenkopf Crack** 5b
A few metres right of the wide passage. Strenuous kranken on excellent jams in the steep crack leads quickly (or not at all) to the niche and a much easier wide crack to finish. This was one of Martin Boysen's 'Desert Island Climbs' so it must be good.

★ **57 Kraken** 6b(NS)
Start 3 metres right of *Krankenkopf Crack* with a jump for a good ledge. Move left and climb the blunt arête.

There is a hard and reachy direct start to the blunt arête of Kraken:
Kranked 6c(NS)†.

★★ **58 The Dragon** 6a
Climb the overhanging crack right of *Kraken* to a ledge. Move left and go up to an inverted scoop, which is used as an undercut; there is a good hold above and to the right of this. A powerful and technical route.

★ **59 Robin's Route** 6a
The bulging wall 4 metres right of the previous route gives thuggish climbing best left to the bumpy boys. Finish easily up the wide crack above. There is an equally Ramboesque start 2 metres left of the original – 6b.

★ **60 So What?** 6b(NS)
Start 3 metres right of *Robin's Route*. Climb the bulges to a poor sloping shelf. Using the obvious crescent-shaped undercut gain the ledge above. Finish precariously over the top bulge.

61 Wye Chimney 4a
Indeed? Start with a mantelshelf problem, with a hand on each wall, then wedge up to a ledge on the left wall. Back-and-foot up to a higher ledge on the same wall and then traverse outwards to finish just inside the huge block which crowns the chimney.

Inside, Wye Chimney *splits in two:*

62 Slab Chimney 2b
The left-hand chimney. Use holds on the left wall to gain a ledge. The slabby part above is surmounted by wedging, again on the left. From

the large ledge step across to the right wall and make an exposed stomach-traverse round the corner. Finish up the short crack.

63 Smooth Chimney 4a
Climb the right-hand chimney about a metre in. Finish on the bridge.

Three metres right of Wye Chimney *is:*

★ **64 Dysentery** 5c(NS)
Climb the thin overhanging crack and then move left along the ledge to the chimney. Follow the chimney for 3 metres and then traverse back right along a rounded ledge until a slanting crack is reached; climb this and then finish over a doubtful block on the left.

★★ **65 The Prang** 6a(NS)
Start round the corner from *Dysentery*. Jump for a high jug hold and then use a long slanting flake to gain a line of stalactites; follow these left to the nose and then for 2 metres more. Climb the wall by using a tiny flat edge and making a long reach for the next break. Finish up the pock-marked block.

There is an alternative start to The Prang *which starts 2 metres right of* Dysentery *and moves diagonally right onto the broad ledge –* **The Prangster** *6b(NS).*

★ **66 Lobster** 6a(NS)
An impressive line up the shallow groove in the Warning Rock. Claw your way up the crack until it peters out and then make a hard move to reach the break. This is usually greasy and hence hard to hold onto with one hand – it's easier and better if you clean the ledge first. Finish up the groove behind the small tree.

At the top of the next two routes are some rare polygonal rock formations of great scientific interest – see crag introduction. Please take great care with belays and ropes so as not to damage them – the belay sling for Infidel *can be run from the tree on the right with the karabiner positioned below the overhang.*

★★★ **67 Infidel** 6a
A climb of great difficulty and atmosphere – only added to by the accompanying inscription. Start up the inverted scoop just right of the corner and go up to the break. Move right, stand up with difficulty and make a frustratingly long reach for the next break. Go up to the roof and traverse off right.

★★ **68 Henry the Ninth** 5b
A good climb up the rib immediately left of the narrow chimney. Climb the rib, mainly on its left side. The upper part can be climbed either by laybacking or monkeying. Strenuous either way but nice.

69 Warning Rock Buttress 3b
A misnomer as the substance of the route is a chimney. Climb the

chimney to the level of the Balcony. Step up into the recess on the left wall and so to the top. It is possible to squeeze through the chimney and pass through *Warning Rock Chimney* into Bell Rock Transverse Passage.

70 Slowhand 6b(NS)
A strenuous and sustained climb up the overhanging buttress right of the chimney. Start in the cave about a metre in from the front. Move diagonally left onto the front face and finish straight up.

The next opening is the western end of Bell Rock Transverse Passage.

71 Balcony Direct 4b
Start just before the two walls of the passage meet overhead. Begin by bridging and finish with back-and-foot work facing the Balcony. Finish on this.

★ 72 Orca 5c(NS)
Start as for *Balcony Direct*. Climb straight up the impending wall to finish on the Balcony. Chimneying techniques are not allowed.

★★ 73 Jaws 5c
Start up the impending wall as for *Orca* but as soon as possible bridge out and make a hair-raising traverse towards the outside. Pull into the bottomless crack in the opposite wall and follow this to the tree. A gripping solo.

★★ 74 Boysen's Crack 6a
Narrow, earthy and often damp – nothing personal mind. The rounded crack 2 metres right of *Jaws*. Awkward jamming leads to a rounded, often dirty ledge and easier ground. Good when clean and dry.

75 Conchita 6a(NS)
The nose on the left of the entrance to the Grand Canyon is extremely awkward and technical. Start either direct or by traversing in from the left.

The next 17 routes lie on the walls of the Grand Canyon, the deepest and widest cleft at the rocks. Here is a concentration of classic crack climbs.

★ 76 Marquita 5c
The first crack on the left wall of Grand Canyon. A good jamming problem.

★ 77 Lucita 5c
Start 4 metres right of *Marquita* and traverse left into the S- shaped crack.

77A Mocasyn 6c(NS)†
Follow *Slant Eyes* to the fourth pocket. Using this, and a 'mono' above, reach up for the break in the centre of the wall (do not use the

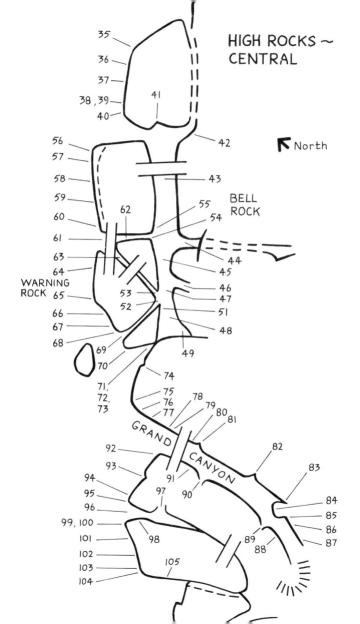

HIGH ROCKS ~
CENTRAL

35
36
37
38, 39
40
41
42

56
57
58
59
60
61
62
63
64
WARNING
ROCK
65
66
67
68
69
70
71,
72,
73

BELL
ROCK
55
54
44
45
46
47
51
48
49
53
52

43

North

74
75
76
77
78
79
80
81
82
83
84
85
86
87

GRAND
CANYON

92
93
94
95
96
99, 100
101
102
103
104
91
97
90
98
105
89
88
82
83
84
85
86
87

large break of *Slant Eyes* out to the right). Move left and then make an enormous reach for the ledge that runs out right from *Lucita*. Finish on tree roots.

78 Slant Eyes 5c

Start as for *Lucita* but then follow the obvious pockets diagonally right. Finish with a long reach for a tree stump.

79 The Gibbet 5b

The wide (hanging?) crack beneath the silver birch can only be recommended... to masochists.

★★ **80 Cool Bananas** 6c(NS)

The blunt arête and wall right of the bridge gives an intensely technical climb, requiring sustained concentration for success. Gain the horizontal break and then move up and right. Layback up the cracks above to a frustrating finish.

★★ **81 Effie** 5b

A fine and popular climb taking the split crack just past the bridge. Take the right fork until it is possible to reach across and move left. On the break hand-traverse left to finish near the bridge.

It is possible to traverse right along the top break of Effie *and finish, either up the delightful crack at 5b, or further right again by climbing the bulge below the large tree –* **P.M.A.** 6a(NS).

82 Mamba Crack 5b

A tedious, tiring tortuous trip, with an earthy finish to top it off nicely. It is best climbed facing left. Not a climb to 'remamba'.

83 Colorado Crack 2b

Face right and climb easily up to a ledge on the right wall.

84 Ockendon Slab 6a

Start on the arête right of *Colorado Crack*. Move delicately right and climb the slab to a problematic finish at the tree stump.

85 Rattlesnake 4b

A semi-layback start leads to a rake sloping up left into *Colorado Crack*. Finish up the wall above the rake.

86 Bright Eyes 5b

Climb the short wall right of the last route. Start at the right-hand end of the wall and trend diagonally left to the trees.

87 Short Chimney II 2a

A worthless non-route up the wide crack with tree roots at the back.

On the opposite side of the Grand Canyon is:

88 Issingdown 5a

First climbed in the rain? The first crack from the left is short and awkward.

89 Python Crack 5a
Is climbed facing right with the left leg in. An earthy traverse leads left at the top.

90 Beanstalk 5b
The wide crack right of *Python*. One fights it rather than climbs it.

91 Peapod 6b(NS)
The short flared groove immediately right of *Beanstalk*. At the top of the groove move right, rockover onto the ledge and then continue up the wall above. Finish up the earthy crack on the left.

★**92 Cheetah** 6b(NS)
The arête to the left of *Coronation Crack*. Two small undercuts are used to reach the ledge over the bulge; another hard move follows to stand up on this. Finish more easily up the fine arête above.

Back on the main wall is:

★★★**93 Coronation Crack** 5c(NS)
A classic jamming route following the striking diagonal crack in the steep smooth wall.

★★★**94 Krait Arête** 6b(NS)
A wonderful route up the blunt arête left of the old air-raid shelter. Start on the right then make a technical rockover move to get established on the arête, after which elegant friction and layaway moves culminate in a strenuous finale on jugs. Brilliant.

There is a poor variation finish to Krait Arête *which moves left after the rockover and climbs the pock-marked wall very close to the arête –* **Bad Blood** 6c(NS)†.

95 Shelter Arête 5c(NS)
Climb the flake-crack left of the air-raid shelter; move right and pull awkwardly onto the arête (crux). Continue up the front face of the arête and finish over the left wall of the passage. The hardest part is avoiding the opposite side of the chimney.

★**96 Shelter Chimney** 2b
Go straight up the chimney starting off the roof of the air-raid shelter.

97 Shelter Passage 4b
Chimney up the passage about halfway to the back. The smooth walls make this very strenuous.

98 The Oligarchy 6a(NS)
Start a metre right of the air-raid shelter. Climb the lower wall on small friable holds and finish with a strenuous layback up the arête on the right.

The steep walls round to the right feature a number of good routes, all based on the square-cut holes. The holes were originally cut to enable the attachment of an advertising hoarding which would be visible from the railway below.

99 Shelter Slabs   5b
Climb the short groove at the right-hand side of the slab, then traverse left to a ledge on the arête halfway up. Traverse left and finish up the chimney.

★★ **100 Advertisement Wall**   5b
Start as for *Shelter Slabs* but instead of traversing off into the chimney climb the left edge of the wall using the cut holes. Finish with a mantelshelf. The cut holes can be avoided totally, giving a nice 5c problem. A harder direct start can be made up the rounded nose at the left of the slabs – also 5c.

★★ **101 Engagement Wall**   6a
To the right of *Advertisement Wall*. Use the third and fourth holes from the left to reach the horizontal break. Finish strenuously slightly to the right.

★★ **102 Dyno-Sore**   6b(NS)
Climbs the right-hand-most pairs of cut holes, with a long reach to get off the first break followed by a massive leap for good holds on the next break. The finish is much easier.

103 Quirkus   4c
Start up the short crack then move right onto the arête and up. Use the tree if you like.

104 Genevieve   6a(NS)
Climb the right-hand arête of the block on its left-hand side – without of course using the tree.

105 Porg's Progress   6c(NS)†
A short desperate problem up the overlap halfway between the large tree and *Dirty Dick*. From the ledge finish easily up to the small tree.

106 Dirty Dick   4b
A layback crack in the corner.

107 Crypt Crack   4a
The short but awkward crack right of the last route. The chief difficulty occurs where it narrows and forces the climber outside.

108 Look Sharp   6b
A very technical eliminate, which involves laybacking the left arête of *Short Chimney*. This is becoming increasingly difficult as the initial holds wear away.

109 Short Chimney   2a
This can be done facing either way.

The next wall is riddled with square holes and has four hard routes:

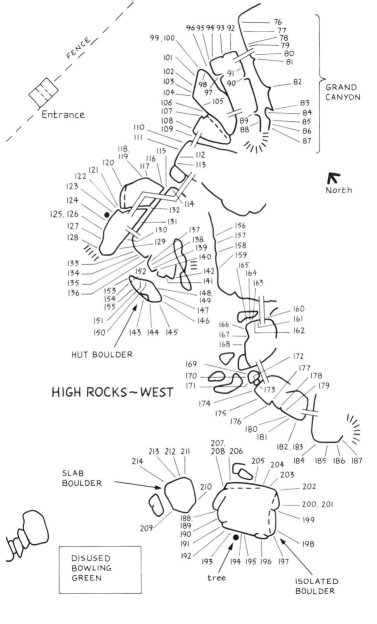

110 Natterjack 6b(NS)
Climb the left-hand side of the wall 2 metres right of *Short Chimney* using square-cut holes and small layaway ribs.

⋆**111 Death Cap** 6b(NS)
The centre of the wall. The crux is a baffling move just below the horizontal break at two-thirds height.

⋆**112 Mervin Direct** 6b(NS)
The right-hand side of the wall. Climb the line of square-cut holds, trending slightly right at the top.

113 Crack and Wall Front 6a
The short crack formed by the detached block followed by the arête above. A liberal use of the tree reduces the grade to 5a.

114 Hut Transverse Arête 5a
The greasy arête across the gap from *Crack and Wall Front*.

115 Hut Transverse Passage – Ordinary Route 2b
Climb straight up close to the entrance to *Brushwood Chimney*.

116 I'll Be Back 6c(NS)
Climb the arête at the entrance to Hut Transverse Passage on its right-hand side. Terminate on the rustic bridge.

⋆⋆**117 Educating Airlie** 6b(NS)
An intricate and highly technical route up the hanging crack just left of the front arête. Approach from the left.

⋆⋆⋆**118 Kinda Lingers** 6c(NS)
The front left arête of the block. A boulder problem start leads to the break. Climb the arête with difficulty on its right side to a climactic finish. The original start was via some perverse contortions on the right wall followed by a leftwards traverse – more 6c(NS). Both starts can be avoided by traversing in from the left – 6b(NS).

119 Celebration Hangover
An old, rarely ascended aid climb. Start as for the previous route and, using natural eyelets, bolts and pegs, go up for 3 metres until a traverse leads right to the next arête. From here bolts lead over the main overhang. Please **do not** put in any more aid points.

120 Roobarb 6b
Climb the middle of the wall beneath the big roof of *Celebration Hangover*. Traverse right at the roof and finish up the chimney. It is also possible to use a flake in the roof to bridge out to the oak tree –
All That Meat but Only Two Veg 6a(NS); doing this may increase the pitch of your voice.

121 Brushwood Chimney – Outside Route 3a
The chimney between the two oak trees; finish on the front side of the capstone.

Starting on the left side of the oak tree is:

★★ **122 Unforgettable** 6c(NS)
The front face of the left arête. Strenuous climbing on poor sandy holds leads to the horizontal break. Gain the arête above and continue directly to the top. Technical and sustained.

An alternative start to Unforgettable *which avoids the sandy rock is –* **Amnesia Variations** 5c(NS). *Start up* Brushwood Chimney *until an obvious traverse line and a big rockover leads out right onto the arête.*

★★ **123 Boonoonoonoos** 6b(NS)
Climb straight up to the main break keeping just left of, and without using, the tree. Follow the obvious holds rightwards, then back left to the break in the middle of the smooth wall. Make a long powerful move to reach a good hold on the break below the top. Finish easily.

★ **124 Firebird** 6a(NS)
The impending wall just right of the tree. Climb straight up on good holds to the horizontal ledge and continue up the wall above.

★★ **125 Mulligan's Wall** 5c
The obvious crack by the steps is climbed on good jams to a ledge below the top. Either move left and finish using the tree or finish direct – very thin and 6a.

★ **126 Bludgeon** 5c(NS)
Follow *Mulligan's Wall* to the ledge then traverse right and finish up *Firefly*.

127 Smoke 6b(NS)†
Climb the bulges right of *Mulligan's Wall* either by stepping off from the top of the flight of steps or (better) direct. Continue past the traverse of *Bludgeon* and finish right of the blunt arête.

128 Firefly 6b(NS)
A good route if you like this sort of thing. Gain, and desperately climb, the short shallow rounded crack 3 metres right of *Mulligan's Wall*; continue up the wall trending left to finish up a wider crack.

★★ **129 Celebration** 5c
The arête just beyond the top of the steps gives a very pleasant climb. Start at the boundary of smooth and honeycomb rock. Move left and go straight up to finish by some rhododendron bushes. It is possible to climb directly up the honeycomb rock – 6a(NS).

★ **130 Hut Transverse Passage – Rufrock Route** 3a
A straightforward chimney climb at the entrance near the steps.

131 Hut Transverse Passage – Central Route 3b
At the highest point of the floor. Smooth and strenuous.

132 Brushwood Chimney 2b

Start at the Hut Transverse Passage end and go straight up to finish through a hole between the top of the left wall and the capstone.

*The wall right of Hut Transverse Passage has some steep and impressive routes. There is also a good low-level traverse – **Lord** 6a.*

★★ **133 Tilley Lamp Crack** 6a(NS)

Climb the crack 2 metres right of the passage entrance. When it peters out a hard move is made (once you've seen the light) to gain the break and an awkward finish.

★★★ **134 Nemesis** 6b(NS)

The come-uppance for hubris? An excellent route taking the centre of the wall right of *Tilley Lamp Crack*. Precision pocket-pulling leads to a short diagonal crack and a very tricky move to reach the horizontal break; move a little right to finish with interest.

★★ **135 A Touch Too Much** 6b

The pocketed wall just left of *Viper Crack* is easier than *Nemesis* but still technically absorbing. Start as for *Nemesis* or (better) direct. The crux is passing the steep rounded ramp to reach the break and easy ground.

136 Viper Crack 5b

The wide crack bounding the right side of the wall. Often green and much harder than it looks.

137 Shattered 6b

The arête immediately right of *Viper Crack* is a powerful boulder problem.

138 Ponytail Pearson (and His Shorts of Doom) 6b(NS)

A highly technical proposition on the convex wall right of *Shattered*.

139 Jug of Flowers 6b(NS)

The square-cut pocket in the wall left of *Easy Crack* is gained either from the right, by starting just left of *Easy Crack* and using the obvious diagonal undercuts, or with more difficulty direct. Either way there is a hard move to get stood up in the pocket.

★ **140 Easy Crack** 2a

The wide crack in the main wall opposite Hut Boulder.

141 Mike's Left Knee 6a(NS)

Just left of *Bald Finish*. Go straight up to the obvious cut pocket. Finish direct beside a small sapling.

★ **142 Bald Finish** 5a

The rounded arête at the right end of the wall has a tricky finish – especially for the soloist.

The next series of climbs is on the Hut Boulder; between this and the main wall are the brick remains of the Sandstone Club Hut. There is a large, ancient bolt on top of the boulder. So as not to add to the already considerable erosion there are only two acceptable ways of reaching the bolt. One can either climb the tree which leans against the top of the rock between Pinchgrip *and* Pussyfoot, *or one can solo a route –* Crack Route *being the most suitable.*

Please descend by down-climbing on a slack rope, or soloing. The last person to leave the boulder must solo down. Do not abseil or lower off as the rock will be damaged when the rope is retrieved.

On no account should a rope be thrown over the boulder from either the top of the main wall or the ground. The last person to leave the top of the boulder must solo down – do not abseil or lower off.

★★ **143 Crack Route** 4c
A good climb. The obvious central crack in the front face is climbed on good holds to the ledge. Pull over the top on jugs.

★ **144 Pinchgrip** 5c
Fine technical climbing up the centre of the impending wall 2 metres right of *Crack Route*.

★★ **145 Pussyfoot** 5b
The right arête of the front face. Start in a small depression on the left; move right to the arête, using a short wide crack, and follow it to the top.

★ **146 Swing Face** 5b
The middle of the end face. Start at the wide cracks on the right, go up a little and move strenuously left to the middle. Continue directly to the top. There is a harder (5c) direct start.

★★ **147 Birthday Arête** 5b
The arête right of *Swing Face*, again starting by the wide cracks.

148 Sequins of Cosmic Turbulence 5c
Start as for *Roof Route* and climb the wall right of *Birthday Arête* without touching adjacent routes. Hard at about two-thirds height.

★ **149 Roof Route** 5a
The obvious left-to-right slanting crack on the back wall is followed strenuously to easier ground. Finish at the tree on the right or, harder, straight up.

150 Rockney 5c
Start a metre right of *Roof Route* by some square-cut holds and make some hard moves to gain the large pot-hole on the right. Exit right from this and then go straight up. An easier start can be made from the bricks 2 metres further right.

★ **151 Cough Drop** 5b
Start at a short flared crack and go up to the ledge; swing left and follow the rickety flakes to finish at the tree.

152 Rhino's Eyebrow 5a
Start as for the previous route but from the ledge make an ascending traverse right then back left on sloping mossy holds. Not very inspiring.

★ **153 Roofus** 6b(NS)
Climb the right-hand edge of the overhanging end of the boulder. At the obvious break swing left to the centre on jugs and surmount the overhang.

The original route on this piece of rock is **1d** 6a(NS), *which was omitted (accidentally?) from the 1963 guidebook. It climbs the right-hand edge of the boulder as for* Roofus *but at the break moves slightly right and finishes up the front face.*

154 Long Stretch 5c
The crack at the extreme left end of the front face of the boulder, just right of *Roofus*. The aptly named start is the crux.

★ **155 Bludnok Wall** 5c
Start 2 metres right of *Long Stretch* and just before the platform at the base of *Crack Route*. Gain the ledges at waist level; stand on the bulge and make a long reach for the next ledge. Finish by traversing leftwards and going up just before *Long Stretch* is reached – needs a direct finish.

There are several routes on the wall opposite Swing Face *and beyond some stone steps. The next four routes are rarely climbed as they are usually in very poor condition.*

156 Bush Arête 4b
On the extreme left of this section of the face, opposite *Swing Face*.

157 Open Groove 5b
Climb awkwardly up the obvious groove 3 metres right of *Bush Arête*.

158 Rhododendron Route 3b
On the main wall opposite *Swing Face*. A wet and unattractive route up the obvious square-cut shallow recess.

159 Seaman's Wall 5c(NS)
A horrible route climbed only by guidebook writers – honest. Climb directly up the green arête just right of the last route, by a series of slippery snatches.

Opposite Hut Boulder and round to the right of the last four routes there is a passage divided by a long low block. There are several routes on the blocks to the right of this passage:

Coronation Crack, 5c, High Rocks. Climber: Tim Daniells. Photo: Ian Smith

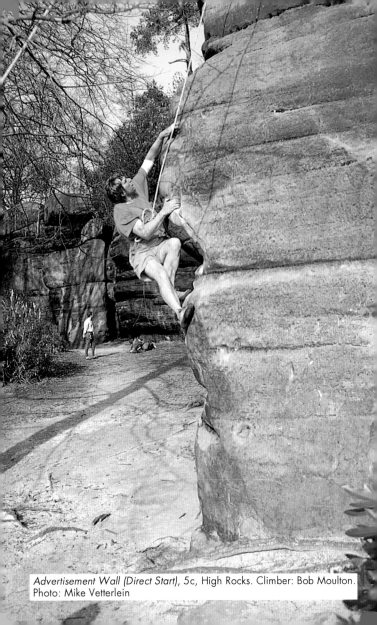

Advertisement Wall (Direct Start), 5c, High Rocks. Climber: Bob Moulton.
Photo: Mike Vetterlein

160 Solo 5a
The not-so-high but nonetheless strenuous crack around the corner from the extreme left end of the passage.

There is a good pumpy traverse starting round the corner to the left of Solo, crossing it and continuing rightwards to finish under the bridge.

161 Awkward Corner 5b
The extreme left edge of the wall has a hard finish.

162 Bow Crack 5a
Two metres right of the edge a crack begins at head-height. Follow this to a hard finish. An eliminate problem takes the wall just right on sharp holds – 6a.

163 Orrer Crack 5c
Climb the thin curved crack in the centre of the wall on sharp holds and an 'orribly painful jam.

164 Rum, Bum and Biscuits 6a
Truly the Navy Way? The wall immediately right of *Orrer Crack* has good sharp holds.

★ **165 Navy Way** 5c
The wall between *Orrer Crack* and the right arête of the wall. Start just left of the arête, climb the flakes and finish left of the bulge.

★★ **166 Odin's Wall** 5c
Just around the arête from *Navy Way*, between the arête and the S-shaped crack. Go straight up the wall on good holds to a hard finish. Watch out for Thor thingers.

167 Something Crack 6a(NS)
The S-shaped crack. It is difficult to keep out of *Odin's Wall*.

168 Whiff Whaff 6b(NS)
The vague cracklines 2 metres right of *Something Crack* gives a very technical problem. Formerly climbed using two jammed slings for aid (A2) but then as now only very rarely climbed.

Continuing rightwards round the corner, and on the front of the comparatively tall, narrow boulder left of the steps is:

169 Vingt-et-un 6a
The left arête of the block, climbed mainly on its left-hand side.

170 Profiterole 5c
Climb the centre of the front face avoiding holds on *Vingt-et-un* and *Degenerate*.

★ **171 Degenerate** 5a
Straight up the front right-hand arête. A nice little problem.

In the gully to the right is:

172 Barbed Wire Fence   5b
About 3 metres right of *Degenerate*, on the left wall of the gully, is a
short crack. Use this to gain the crescent-shaped edge and so to the
top.

173 Barbed Wire Kiss   6b(NS)†
The flakes on the right wall of the gully and to the right of the
off-width crack.

On the next wall there is a cluster of good but short routes:

174 The Gob   6c(NS)†
The slabby arête. Start on the left-hand side and finish direct on the
front face.

** 175 Honeycomb   6b
Start just left of the centre of the steep pocketed wall. Go straight up
for 2 metres; move 2 metres right and climb the steep wall with
increasing difficulty on friable holds. Sadly, there is a chipped hold
on the top. There is a harder direct start on the right.

An independent route, **Honeycomb Variant** 6b(NS), *starts just left of
the original and climbs the steep wall left of the blunt nose on very friable
pockets. Unfortunately there are some chipped holds at the top – no
more, please.*

* 176 Craig-y-blanco   6a
The steep arête right of *Honeycomb*. Strenuous with small sharp
friable holds.

177 Dagger Crack   6a
The thin curving crack; bear right at the top to a dirty finish.

178 Greasy Crack   5a
The very unpleasant crack right of *Dagger Crack*.

179 Wishful Thinking   5b or 6b
The wall with the inscription, just right of *Greasy Crack*. The easiest
way to do it is to run at it; a normal approach is very painful.

180 Woofus Wejects   6a(NS)
The doidy cwack just wight of the wall with whiting on it. A
twemendous awe-inspiwing woute.

181 Ides of March   6a(NS)
Climb the wall a metre or so right of *Woofus Wejects*.

182 Lunge'n'Shelf   6a(NS)
A short dynamic problem just left of *Puzzle Corner*; finish left of the
bridge but without using it.

183 Puzzle Corner   4c
At the far right-hand end of the wall. Go straight up the rounded
arête, which is unfortunately obstructed by the bridge.

A worthwhile traverse can be made starting at Honeycomb *and finishing at* Puzzle Corner. *To the right is a low block beside some stone steps.*

184 Marathon Man 6a
Start by a square block on the ledge under the overhang. Swing up to the break and move left to an awkward mantelshelf finish. Is it safe?

185 Beer Gut Shuffle 6b(NS)
Go over the small overhang at some weaknesses 2 metres right of *Marathon Man.*

186 The Diver 6a(NS)
The roof right of *Beer Gut Shuffle* using the obvious hole near the top.

187 P.E. Traverse 4a
Traverse awkwardly from right to left under the overhang, finishing round the corner and near the bridge.

Opposite, is the large Isolated Boulder on which there are many fine climbs. However a route has to be soloed in order to set up a top-rope. The best routes for this purpose are Ordinary Route *and* Simian Progress. *Some of the anchors on top of the Boulder are a long way from the edge so it is necessary to take up plenty of ropes and slings.* **If you have insufficient equipment then please don't attempt any of the climbs on the Boulder.**

Please descend by down-climbing on a slack rope, or soloing. The last person to leave the Boulder must solo down. Do not abseil or lower off as the rock will be damaged when the rope is retrieved. The best route to descend is Ordinary Route.

The last person to leave the top of the Boulder must solo down – do not abseil or lower off.

★ 188 Ordinary Route 4a
Opposite the easy-angled side of Slab Boulder. Climb up to the overhang and traverse right beneath it. Finish up the awkward wide crack.

189 Oven Ready Freddy 6a(NS)
Start easily as for *Ordinary Route* but move left along the long wide ledge. Climb with difficulty up the loose wall above to finish at the two small trees.

190 Plantagenet 6b(NS)†
Start a metre right of *Ordinary Route* and climb the blunt arête to the broad ledge. Surmount the roof at its left-hand end and finish up the easy slab.

191 Mysteries of the Orgasm 6b(NS)†
Start 2 metres left of the recess of *Devastator*. Climb the sandy bulge trending leftwards to the broad platform; finish direct.

192 Devastator 6a

Start just left of the large oak tree. Move up to the first break, traverse sandily left into a recess and go up to the small yew tree. Finish straight above this.

★193 Graveyard Groove 5c

Start as for *Devastator* but go straight up. A route with varied climbing and thus of some interest. Do not use the tree.

The next four routes right of the tree are all very strenuous, particularly their starts:

194 Tool Wall 6a(NS)

The wall between the tree and the crack of *Fork*. Move left at the top to finish near the tree (but without using it).

★★195 Fork 5c

The crack-system right of the tree without using it, the tree that is.

★★★196 Knife 5c

The best of the four. The crack to the right of *Fork* is slightly easier and has the same finish.

★★197 Dinner Plate 5c

An undercut start enables one to gain the crack, which is followed to the ledge. Finish up the wall above on good holds.

198 The Full Monty 6b

The undercut bulge just left of *Breakfast*, with a very difficult start. Finish direct much more easily.

199 Breakfast 5c

Climb the thin overhanging crack in the centre of the undercut face – a direct start to *Simian Progress*. When possible pull more easily left onto the sandy juggy nose and finish straight up, including the final overhang.

★★★200 Simian Progress 5a

A classic climb with an unusual start. Begin at the right-hand end of the undercut face either with a long stride from the small boulder, or with a long reach and pull up from the ground (5b). Monkey strenuously left on big holds to the foot of the main crack; finish up this.

★201 Simian Face 5b

Start as for *Simian Progress* but go straight up before the crack is reached, staying on the face all the way. More sustained than *Simian Progress*. A direct start is 5c.

★★202 Monkey Nut 5b

The overhanging arête to the right of the *Simian Face*. Start on the right of the arête, move left and continue straight up, finishing directly over the bulges at the top. A strenuous climb on large holds.

The next three routes start at the left-hand end of the enormous flake:

203 Monkey's Sphincter 6b(NS)
Climb onto the flake and then move left towards the arête on the sharp ironstone holds. Go straight up just before the arête is reached.

★**204 The Sphinx** 6a
Climb onto the flake, then climb straight up the overhanging wall on sharp ironstone holds. Strenuous and technical.

★★**205 Simian Mistake** 5c
Follow the flake rightwards until it peters out. Either finish straight up or, equally difficult, go diagonally right to the usual finish of *North Wall*. An alternative start is a 6b boulder problem 2 metres right.

★**206 Sputnik** 6a
The overhanging arête left of *North Wall*. Start on the boulder and finish straight up in the same line.

★★**207 North Wall** 5a
Climb the sharp flake-crack to the overhang, then traverse left to a short, wide crack and so to the top.

★★**208 The Helix** 5a
A very worthwhile traverse which is over 30 metres long. It starts at the foot of *North Wall* and winds its way anti-clockwise round the block:
1. Go up for 2 or 3 metres then pull right onto a broad grassy ledge. Follow this rightwards to a thread belay at its right-hand end.
2. Descend to the recess on *Ordinary Route* and then follow that route under the overhang to the foot of its finishing crack. Continue at the same level past a small yew tree to a belay on the large oak growing against the side of the rock.
3. Continue at the same level to the foot of the final crack of *Simian Progress*; belay (on a pre-placed sling dangling from the summit).
4. Either finish up *Simian Progress* or go further right and up *Simian Face*.
This is the original route. It is possible to complete the girdle of the boulder at sustained 5c.
5. Traverse at a high level across *Simian Face*, around the arête of *Monkey Nut* and on to join *Simian Mistake*. Descend to the top of the flake and then move right onto the finish of *North Wall*, which is then descended to the start.

The following routes are on the Slab Boulder, starting on the easy-angled face with two popular climbs:

★**209 Outside Edge Route** 3b
Go up the wall behind (and using) the tree, then delicately up the left edge of the slab. If the tree is not used the grade is 5a.

★ 210 Holly Route   2b
Start by a high mantelshelf at the right end of the slab and then go easily up the right edge of the boulder; follow the ridge leftwards to the top. Various other harder starts are possible round to the left.

There is also a 6a boulder-problem up the edge to the right of Holly Route.

On the impending front face are a number of short routes:

211 J.P.S.   6a
Takes the left arête of the front face; hard to finish.

212 Miss Embassy   5c
Start as for the next route but finish straight up using a sharp, upright ironstone hold.

★ 213 Z'Mutt   5b
Short but good. Start with difficulty in the centre of the overhanging wall; move right and do a hard mantelshelf to stand up; finish easily. A boulder problem direct start is possible at 6b. An easier start is to traverse in from *J.P.S.* along the first ledge.

★★ 214 Brenva   5c
A splendid little route up the leaning arête right of *Z'Mutt*. Move a little left towards the top. An alternative is to swing right at half-height and finish up a shallow crack – 5c.

A 6b problem has been done up the steep slab right of Brenva *to join* Outside Edge Route *a little above half-height. Hand-traverse the edge to the top.*

Fifty metres toward the road are four large but low boulders with many short problems at various grades – find out for yourself.

High Rocks Continuation Wall

OS Ref TQ 561 384

This outcrop is not an independent crag but is actually the continuation of High Rocks beyond the boundary fence to the east. Because of its different approaches and access situation it is now being treated separately, contrary to previous practice.

It can be reached by following a footpath which starts beside the railway bridge just east of the entrance to High Rocks. The path runs parallel to the boundary fence and eventually leads to the right-hand end of the crag. Alternatively go over the railway bridge and head towards Tunbridge Wells. Pass the road junction on the left and carry on for another 550 metres until a track on the right leads under a railway bridge and up to a gate and stile. Turn sharply right beyond the gate and carry on for another 300 metres. The left-hand end of the crag should then be visible through the trees on the left.

The Continuation Wall is markedly different in character to High Rocks, being lower, less continuous, and having a much smaller proportion of good routes. Here you'll find none of the awe-inspiring arêtes, impending walls and monolithic cracks of the main crag. Instead there is a range of short climbs in the easy and intermediate grades, thus making it a suitable place for the beginner. Like High Rocks it is heavily shaded by trees and can often be out of condition.

The outcrop lies within Friezland Wood and is a designated SSSI. The wood is owned by the Woodland Trust, a charity concerned solely with the conservation of Britain's native trees and woodlands. Although the wood is open to the public free of charge, the Trust has imposed a total climbing ban. The description of routes therefore is purely to serve as a record and does not imply that anyone has the right to climb here.

To minimise damage to the rock caused by moving and stretching ropes, it is essential, when top-roping, to use a non-stretch belay sling and to position the karabiner over the edge of the crag. If you see these instructions being ignored please make polite or stronger suggestions as to the correct procedure.

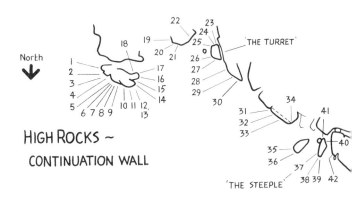

North ↓

HIGH ROCKS ~

CONTINUATION WALL

'THE TURRET'

'THE STEEPLE'

The first sizeable wall at the left-hand end has a large pot-hole at three metres; this can be entered and leads via a series of clefts to Limpet Crack and Bottle Chimney.

1 Yer Greet Narthern Basstud 5a
Start just left of the clean-cut arête and trend left past a flake and up to the bulge at the top. Finish over this with some difficulty.

2 Birthday Buttress 5a
The arête left of *Pot-hole Crack*. Start just to the left and move onto the arête when possible; finish direct.

3 Gentle Giant 6c(NS)†
A ferocious route up the line of old bolt-holes. An enormous reach and fingers of steel are prerequisites for success.

★ **4 Pot-hole Crack** 4b
The crack which sweeps up right of the hole. Straightforward except for the finish.

5 Travellin' Man 5c
Start just right of *Pot-hole Crack* and then move out rightwards onto the arête. Finish up the pleasant nose above. A hard route for the short.

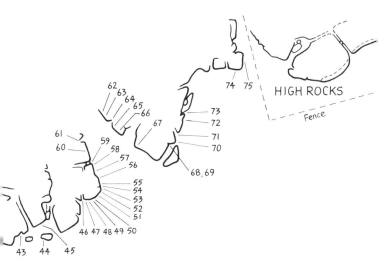

6 Gibbons Progress 6a
A steep route some 4 metres right of *Pot-hole Crack*. An undercut is used to leave the ground, after which one goes slightly left, through a scoop, to a difficult finish.

★**7 Co-Co** 5c
Start about a metre right of *Gibbons Progress* and climb straight up using the short vertical crack just to the left of the blunt arête.

8 Rake's Progress 5c
Either climb straight up 2 metres right of the previous route or trend more easily rightwards to finish near *Limpet Crack*.

★**9 Limpet Crack** 4a
Strenuous climbing leads to a rest ledge near the top and an easier finish.

10 Finger Wall 5b
Climb the wall 2 metres right of the last route on small holds.

11 Sombrero Wall 6a(NS)
The bulging arête below the finishing tree of *Stalactite Wall*. Start slightly to the left so as to avoid the eroded holds at the bottom.

★★**12 Stalactite Wall** 3b
From the foot of *Bottle Chimney* traverse diagonally left on good

holds to the arête. Finish slightly left of the top nose. A justifiably popular route.

13 Stalactite Wall Direct   5a

Start as for *Stalactite Wall* but at the large flake head straight up the wall.

14 Poacher Corner   5b

Start as for the previous climb but go straight up the arête.

15 Bottle Chimney   3b

A wide start leads to a tight finish, where the climber is forced outside the chimney.

16 Independence   6a

Start in the shallow scoop a metre right of *Bottle Chimney*. Climb this on poor holds, move slightly right and then pull over the bulge; finish straight up.

17 Jug Arête   3b

Immediately right of *Independence*.

18 Wobbler Wall   4c

The very short wall right of the arête.

The following problems are on a small boulder just before the more substantial Turret Face:

19 Yom Kippa   5b

An awkward little route up the middle of the left wall of the boulder; fast climbing seems to be the best approach.

20 Motza   5b

This takes a line over the bulges on the front of the boulder. The top moves are hard.

21 Green Slab   5b

The slab on the front of the boulder and right of the previous route. Go easily up to the second ledge and then finish with some difficulty.

22 Nosh   5a

Start at a large hole just round the corner from *Green Slab*. Either go straight up or move more easily right and then go up – 4c.

The next large buttress is the Turret, with five routes:

★ **23 Left Edge**   5b

The left side of the left face. A good climb with a hard finish.

★★ **24 Turret Face**   4b

Start a little right of the last route and go up, gradually moving right, to eventually finish on the front face. A more direct finish is 4c.

★ **25 Drunkard's Dilemma**   5c

Start below the overhanging arête right of *Turret Face*. Pull strenuously over the bulge using a good layback hold; move slightly left and then back right to finish as for *Turret Face*.

★ 26 Windy Wall 5a
Climb the thin crack in the front of the block. Traverse diagonally left along the ledges below the top to join and finish as for *Turret Face*.

There is a harder variation to Windy Wall *whichs swings left after the first ledges to gain a sloping ramp hold and then finishes direct on better holds –* **Nigg Nogg Variation** 5c.

27 Turret Wall 2b
The right-hand edge on the front face of the Turret. Much harder when greasy.

There are three routes on the boulder which adjoins the Turret:

28 Twinkle Toe Slab 5c
The steep slab just right of the Turret. A delicate climb on small mossy holds.

29 Limpet Wall 5b
The ledge to the right of the previous route is gained by a 'thoughtful move'. The crack above is not very useful as a source of holds.

30 Awkward 5b
Start up the right face of the boulder; move left to the edge and make a hard move to gain a small ledge on the arête.

Beyond the next bits of broken rock is a tree stump:

31 Rake Buttress 2b
An uninteresting climb but useful for beginners. Step off the tree stump and meander up to the nose above and then make a long reach for a tree root to finish.

32 Elephant's Umbrella 5c
Start under the yew tree right of the last route. Pull strenuously over the overhang, using holds to the right of the crack.

33 Parrot's Parasol 6a(NS)
A direct line 2 metres right of the yew tree.

34 Parrot's Wing 3a
Not a Budgies' Roundabout. A very short unsatisfactory crack.

On the boulder in the centre of the broad gully is:

35 Two Bit 4a
The front left-hand arête.

36 One Bit 3b
The front right arête. The middle of the front face is 5c.

The next feature is a steep-sided pinnacle on the slope in front of the main wall – the Steeple.

37 Steeple Direct 5a

Start on the left front arête; go straight up and then traverse right to the arête. Much more awkward than appearances suggest.

38 Obverse Route 4c

Start just to the right of the previous route. Climb up and out onto the left side face, and up this to an awkward finish.

39 I'm a Dutchman 4c

The front right arête of the Steeple.

40 Ordinary Route 2b

On the right-hand side of the Steeple and near the back. Straightforward and also the easiest way down.

41 Steeple Back 3b

The back left edge of the Steeple.

The next part of the main wall gives some short bitty climbs:

42 Two Mantelshelves and Cave 3a

An exceptionally contrived non-route. The mantelshelves are on two small broken boulders and the cave is the short finishing chimney on the main wall.

43 Barefoot Crack 5a

The start is tricky but the difficulty soon eases. Usually unpleasant. The wide crack to the left is 5b.

★**44 Scotland Slab** 1a

The line straight up the middle of the slab is ruined by the cut holds but as such is a useful beginners route. Can be climbed feet first or with no hands.

45 Stepped Buttress 2a

A straightforward series of barely worthwhile mantelshelf moves.

46 Midway Chimney 2b

A short chimney in the corner. The left-hand chimney is 2a.

47 Going to the Pub 5c

Is a much better idea, however good the route. Nevertheless, when it's shut, begin 2 metres right of the chimney and go straight up with some difficulty.

★**48 Camelot** 6a

Start 3 metres right of *Going to the Pub*. Climb the impending crack with difficulty and finish straight up the wall above.

49 Penis Door Slam 6b(NS)†

Strenuous climbing up the bulges a metre right of *Camelot*.

★**50 Lady of the Lake** 5b

The steep wall 3 metres right of *Camelot*; trend left at first and then back right.

51 Shalot 5b
The right-hand arête of the Midway block. Finish by a series of mantelshelves.

52 Midway Traverse 5a
A 12-metre leftwards traverse along an obvious line from the ledges left of *Tunnel Chimney* to *Midway Chimney*.

53 Whiplash 5b
The left arête of *Tunnel Chimney*.

54 Tunnel Chimney 2b
The strange leftward curve is difficult to negotiate.

55 Rubber Panty 5c(NS)
Not a little kinky. The green and lichenous arête right of the last route.

56 Taurus 5b
Start just left of *Hangman's Wall* and go up awkwardly leftwards.

57 Hangman's Wall 5c
This is climbed mainly in the crack.

58 Prickle Corner 5c
The awkward bulging arête to the left of *Icicle Passage*.

59 Icicle Passage 2a
Straightforward thrutching.

60 Green Gilbert 4c
The very mossy slab just right of the previous route. Harder than it looks.

61 Buzzard's Breakdown 2a
The short crack right of *Green Gilbert*. From the broad ledge step right and climb the enjoyable corner crack.

The next routes are on the low buttresses opposite Green Gilbert. *The most obvious feature is a chimney with a large chockstone at the top –* Capstone Chimney.

62 Nativity Relativity 5a(NS)
The groove 2 metres left of *Capstone Chimney*.

63 Increment Excrement 5c(NS)
The centre of the bulging face between the previous route and the chimney.

64 Capstone Chimney 2a
Finish inside or out.

65 Up the Junction 4b
The two grooves immediately right of the chimney; hard to start.

66 Down the Huntsman 5c(NS)
The right-hand arête of the buttress.

67 Seventh Heaven 5c(NS)
Start below a ramp across the wide gully from the previous route.

Gain the ramp, then use a heelhook and small undercuts to reach better holds above. Finish direct on jugs.

Next come some steep mossy slabs with no routes at all – probably best left that way so as to protect the flora. The next feature is a slab below a large yew tree, which provides some good boulder problems. Beyond this is:

68 Starboard Chimney   3a
The chimney behind the yew tree has a tricky undercut start.

69 Anchor Chain   4c
Cross the nose by broad ledges from *Starboard Chimney* to reach *Port Crack* above the constricted part.

★70 Battleship Nose   5b
The nose between *Starboard Chimney* and *Port Crack*; very hard to finish.

★71 Port Crack   4b
A steep clean-cut crack. The constricted middle portion forces the climber outside the crack. Higher up it is easier.

Beyond the next impressively steep and blank wall is:

72 Paul Skinback   5c
A smeggy route up the thin discontinuous corner crack.

73 Overboard   4b
Climb 3 metres up a crack to the oak, then move right onto a ledge and up.

The next climbs are about 30 metres further right, on a low block just left of the boundary fence.

74 Finger Fiend   5c
A short route 2 metres to the left of the right-hand arête. The name is a hint.

75 Demon Digit   4a
This short route is to be found round the corner from *Finger Fiend*, just right of the little chimney.

High Rocks Annexe   OS Ref TQ 562 385

This small outcrop faces High Rocks Continuation Wall across the valley, in a wood beside the Tunbridge Wells road. The approaches are as for High Rocks. The rocks, the true name of which is said to be Bristol Jacks, offer a small number of short climbs of reasonable quality. In places the rocks are overhung with dense vegetation and can become greasy. Because of this, spring and autumn are good times to climb; when there are few leaves on the trees and the sun has a chance to dry the rock.

The rocks are on private land and permission to climb must be obtained from the owner. His bungalow is behind and above the outcrop – in Tea Garden Lane. Permission is nearly always given to small, well behaved parties.

To minimise damage to the rock caused by moving and stretching ropes, it is essential, when top-roping, to use a non-stretch belay sling and to position the karabiner over the edge of the crag. If you see these instructions being ignored please make polite or stronger suggestions as to the correct procedure.

At the extreme left of the main wall is a face with a wide crack in its left-hand end and a yew tree on top. The first climb is on the green block some 10 metres to the left.

1 Bluebell 5a
Climb the short block starting on the right and finishing on the left. An exceptionally minor route.

On the buttress with the yew tree is, somewhat surprisingly:

2 Yew Tree Wall 3a
Go up the small buttress 2 metres left of the crack, moving right to follow the rock.

3 Yew Tree Crack 4b
The off-width crack, which was once described as a 'one-boot one-rubber climb'.

4 Shidid 6a
The rounded arête at the left-hand side of the slab. No excursions are allowed onto the next route.

5 Annexe Slab 5b
Climb the right-hand side of the slab trending rightwards.

The next four routes are on the small detached boulder right of the slab:

6 Titch Arête 5a
Gymnastic moves up the left edge of the boulder.

7 Meander 5a
Start a metre right of the left edge. Climb diagonally right to a
mantelshelf finish.

8 Twitch 6a
The blunt arête in the centre – small holds with a dynamic move in the
middle.

9 Arnold Thesanigger 6a
A powerful route up the blunt right-hand arête using the obvious
layaway.

To the right is a prominent nose, imaginatively called Nose One.

★ **10 Double Top** 6b
Start beneath an old yew and follow a line of improbable-looking
pockets directly to the tree trunk. Very thin and technical.

11 Ones Traverse 3a
Start left of *Nose One* and traverse across it and *Chimney Wall* into
the chimney. A strange, contrived route.

12 Rupert and His Chums 6a(NS)
The slab just left of *Nose One*, moving slightly left onto the small
ledge at two-thirds height.

★ **13 Nose One** 5b
Climb directly up the nose on sandy holds to a tricky finish. Moving
right at mid-height reduces the grade considerably.

14 Chimney Wall 4b
Immediately right of the last route; finish just left of the tree.

15 Chimney One 2a
A straightforward but thrutchy thing.

16 Spleen Slab 5a
Go delicately up the steep slab a metre right of *Chimney One*. The
footholds are poor but the handholds good.

17 Brain's Missing 5b
Quite possibly. The cracks 2 metres left of *Nose Two*.

18 Nose Two 4a
The outside edge of the short chimney.

19 Chimney Two 2a
An easy but not recommended way down.

20 Fahrenheit 5c(NS)
Start immediately right of *Chimney One*. Delicate moves lead slightly

Kinda Lingers, 6c(NS), High Rocks. Climber: Ian Stronghill. Photo: Luc Percival

Swing Face, 5b, High Rocks. Climber: Paul Hayes. Photo: Ian Smith

right to a cluster of holds; finish straight up using the curving crack at the top.

21 Thinner 5a
Straight up the nose left of *Nose Three*, to finish just left of the tree.

★ **22 Nose Three** 3b
Climb straight up the nose to a finish on tree roots.

23 Thug 6a
Pull strenuously over the bulge right of *Nose Three*. Finish up the easy groove, moving right at the top.

24 Valkyrie Wall 5c
Just right again. A technically interesting start leads to easier ground.

25 Chute and Chimney 3b
The chute leads awkwardly to the dirty chimney, which can also be gained more directly by laybacking.

26 Didshi 5c
Climb the wall immediately right of the last route on poor holds.

27 Gorilla Wall 5a
Step off the pedestal and follow the groove up to the left; move back right after a metre or so, and so to the top.

Continuing down the slope is a wall with some flutings in its lower part.

★ **28 Purgatory** 5a
Despite the name, a pleasant route. Climb straight up from the flutings on good holds.

★ **29 Augustus** 5b
The arête to the right is climbed without using holds on the face.

30 Corner Crack 3a
Dirty and uninteresting.

On the next wall is:

★ **31 The Entertainer** 6a
A good climb on small sharp holds. Start left of *Valhalla Wall* and trend left – going where the holds take you – to a hard finish.

32 Billy the Bong 5c(NS)
Start as for *The Entertainer* but instead of trending left continue straight up without using the right arête.

★★ **33 Valhalla Wall** 4c
The right-hand edge of the wall.

33A Fig Roll 5a
The arête right of *Valhalla Wall* using the obvious pinch.

To the right is a lower bulging wall and isolated block, giving some little problems.

HIGH ROCKS ANNEXE

34 Patrick's Wall 5b
Straight up the overhanging front of the block.

35 Dumpy 5a
The short nose left of the crack, with an earthy finish, is definitely not worthwhile.

36 Flatus Groove 1a
The wide crack between the block and the main wall leads to another earthy finish.

37 Quickset 3b
The nose right of the crack.

Up the broad slope and on the left-hand side is:

38 The Prow 3a
A short nose – perhaps better than a long one in this case.

On the opposite side of the broad slope is:

★ **39 Horizon Wall – Routes 1 and 2** 3b
Short face climbs on excellent holds giving brief but enjoyable climbing.

Back down the slope and further right is a large split buttress, upon which are four climbs:

40 Monolith Left Buttress 5a
Start immediately left of the crack and go straight up over the nose to

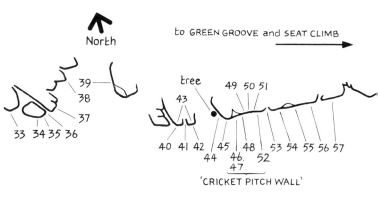

to GREEN GROOVE and SEAT CLIMB

'CRICKET PITCH WALL'

finish. The original finish traversed left and up over the letter 'T'. This is 4a.

41 Monolith Crack 3a
The wide crack can be climbed outside or, after a tight entry, inside.

42 Monolith Right Buttress 4a
Go straight up, with a mantelshelf to finish.

43 Monolith Girdle 2b
This route crosses the last three climbs halfway up.

Across the next slope is a large yew tree, behind which is:

44 Leg Break 5a
Go up behind the tree, then move right to the top. It is easier if the tree is used.

45 Nob Nose 5b
Climb directly up the nose right of *Leg Break*.

46 The Googly 3a
Start up the small crack in the left of the wall. Move left at 2 metres into a wide opening, which leads to the top. It is possible to start direct at 4a.

Immediately right of The Googly *is a steep wall called Cricket Pitch Wall. All the routes are good.*

★47 Run Out 5a
Traverse the wall at mid-height from *The Googly* to *Charon's Staircase* or vice versa.

★48 Off Stump 4c
Start as for *The Googly* but go straight up. Traverse right near the top to finish left of the yew tree.

★49 Middle and Off 5a
Start below the yew tree and go straight up.

★50 Middle Stump 5b
If you've had a nasty accident. Climb the centre of the face on small holds. More difficult than it looks.

★51 Leg Stump 5a
Better than losing middle. Start in the crack on the right of the wall and go straight up left of the tree.

52 Out 3b
The nose left of *Boundary Gully*.

53 Boundary Gully 2b
The crack right of Cricket Pitch Wall.

The rocks now become more broken, lower and, in places, vegetated, although they would provide some good problems if their condition ever improved. On the short bulging wall to the right are three routes:

54 IN 4b
The little bulges above the vague carved initials 'I.N.', and immediately right of *Boundary Gully*.

55 Eureka 3b
You'll be so pleased you've discovered this one! One metre right is a bulging wall; climb this to the shelf.

56 Charon's Staircase Hard Very Bellamy
A vegetated route for (bearded) enthusiasts only. Go straight up the right-hand side of the groove avoiding the small tree.

Further right is a mossy undercut boulder, which provides one route:

57 One Move 4b
The overgrown complex of cracks is more awkward than it looks.

Thirty metres further right is a buttress close to the road.

58 Green Groove 2b
Start on the left and go straight up the groove, which is not always green – honest.

59 Seat Climb 2b
Start in the centre and go straight up. The route is easier than it appears.

Stone Farm Rocks

OS Ref TQ 381 348

The rocks are situated 2¼ miles south-south-west of East Grinstead, and just to the south of a public bridleway which leads west from Stonehill House. They are owned by the Forestry Commission, who allow free access to climbers. The site is a designated SSSI.

An approach is best determined by consulting the map below. The track leading west from Stonehill House is a footpath only. Cars may be parked

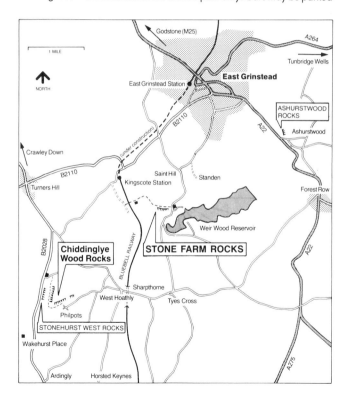

50 metres down the road towards the reservoir and should not be left to obstruct the entrance to the rocks.

A pleasant approach to the rocks can be made by a half-hour walk from Kingscote Station on the Bluebell Railway. Turn left outside the station and then left again along a minor road which runs parallel to the railway. Just before the entrance to Birch Farm Nursery turn left onto a bridleway. This leads through Mill Place Farm and eventually brings you out at the top of the outcrop. (At the time of writing this approach is not possible – see page 9/10.)

The outcrop is almost 200 metres in length and reaches a height of just over six metres at its highest point. It comprises a number of isolated boulders and rock faces in a picturesque setting on an open hillside facing south at an altitude of about 110 metres. In the valley below, the infant Medway feeds the Weir Wood Reservoir, which stretches from here to Forest Row and enhances the scenery considerably. The Forest Ridge rises beyond with Ashdown Forest in the south-east.

Its southern aspect, coupled with the comparative absence of overhanging trees, means that the rock is little vegetated and, hence, dries very quickly. It has also made the outcrop very popular, and at weekends it is often unpleasantly crowded. Even on weekdays it is not unusual to find all the easy routes monopolised by educational groups.

The quality of the rock is generally poor. At one time the phrase 'of Stone Farm texture and quality' was the byword for excellence in local sandstone. Sadly this is no longer the case as decades of abuse have taken their toll. In large areas the hardened surface of the rock has been worn away leaving only unconsolidated sand in its place. Footholds have been reduced from good flat-edges to useless sandy scoops, and this has meant that the bottoms of several of the popular routes have been worn completely smooth. The top of the crag has also suffered, and in many places there is a fragile fretwork of deep rope grooves.

To make things even worse, several of the described routes have **chipped holds**. Despite the fact that some good moves have been created **this vandalism cannot be tolerated**. The presence of stars on some of these routes is **not** meant as encouragement to chip holds. Give the rock, and those more able, a chance please.

All is not gloom, however, as recently the British Mountaineering Council (BMC), together with the local outdoor pursuits centres, have been assisting the landowners in the management of the rocks. Work has begun to repair the worst of the damage, by cementing-in the rope grooves, attempting to halt the subsidence at the foot of the crag, and treating worn holds with surface-consolidating chemicals. Also bolt belays are to be placed at the top of the crag in an attempt to minimise any further erosion. Please note that there is now a **total ban on abseiling**.

To minimise damage to the rock caused by moving and stretching ropes, it is essential, when top-roping, to use a non-stretch belay sling and to position the karabiner over the edge of the crag. If this advice is ignored there will eventually be no crag left at all. If you see these instructions being ignored please make polite or stronger suggestions as to the correct procedure.

The climbs are numbered starting at the end furthest from the road. Therefore, the entire outcrop is passed before the first listed climbs are reached. There are three small easy-angled buttresses in the trees about 20 metres beyond the main wall, the first of which gives:

1 Moss Wall 3b
The centre of the left-hand block. There are 4b problems on either side of this and a route up the centre of each of the other two blocks – both about 2b.

The first part of the main wall has a low block with a boulder on top. The next four routes are here:

2 Pyramid Route 4b
Step onto the ledge at the left end with difficulty; mantelshelf and then finish up the left side of the top block.

3 Kneeling Boulder 4b
Also difficult to start. Begin on the left and then move right to the centre. Reach over the overhang for good finishing holds. A direct start with a hard mantelshelf is 5c.

There is a 5b problem a metre right making use of good layaway pockets.

4 One Hold Route 3b
The short wall on the right has many good holds!

5 Obscene Gesture 3a
Climb the right arête of the wall, passing a two-finger undercut.

On the next wall is:

★**6 Medway Slab** 1b
Follow the narrow ramp which slants across the wall left of *Stone Farm Chimney*.

7 Footie 5c
Climb the steep wall immediately left of *Stone Farm Chimney* on layaway/undercut holds. A good sequence of moves but sadly it has been chipped.

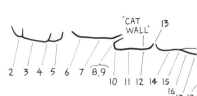

STONE FARM ROCKS ~ WEST

The wall below the ramp and left of Footie gives a couple of 6a problems.

★ **8 Stone Farm Chimney** 4a
The obvious chimney behind the buttress. The tight overhanging upper section is awkward. A classic route.

★ **9 Girdle Traverse** 5c
Start midway up *Stone Farm Chimney*. The hardest move is getting round onto the front – feet at mid-height. Continue across *Cat Wall*, *Pine Buttress*, *The Ramp* and *Slab Buttress* to eventually reach easy ground above the slab. From here *Garden Wall Traverse* may be reversed and a small but tricky boulder traversed to finish.

★ **10 Kathmandu** 6b
Start at the left end of the front face. Gain the first break, move up to an undercut on the right and then pull delicately onto the slab to finish.

The left arête of Kathmandu *has been climbed –* **Chalk'n'Cheese** *6a. Finish on the slab as for* Kathmandu.

11 Top Cat 6b
Climb straight up the wall a metre right of *Kathmandu*.

★ **12 Cat Wall** 6a
Start a metre left of *Stone Farm Crack*. Make a long reach for some good side-pulls and then move left up the overlap on good holds; trend right to finish a metre left of *Stone Farm Crack*.

There is an eliminate up the wall just left of Stone Farm Crack *–* **Sweet Carol** *5c or 6a depending on which holds you allow yourself.*

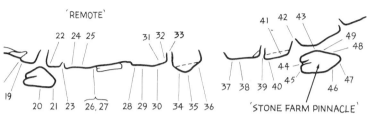

'REMOTE'

22 24 25   31 32 33   41   42   43   49
                                                48

44
                               45   47
                    37   38   39   40   46

19
20   21   23   26, 27   28 29 30   34 35 36   'STONE FARM PINNACLE'

★★ **13 Stone Farm Crack** 4b
Another old classic which takes the crack just left of the dead pine tree at the top. The finish is delicate.

★ **14 Pine Buttress** 5c
Between the two cracks. Pull onto the centre of the face either from the left or direct. Finish more easily to the right or, more sustained, straight up.

The right side of the face can be climbed at about 5c, depending on the holds used.

★ **15 Pine Crack** 3b
The crack just right of the last route. Harder than it looks.

16 The Ramp 2a
Climb the ramp that slopes from the foot of *Pine Crack* to the top of *Root Chimney*.

17 The Face 4a
Climb up to the 'face' that is carved in the rock, then move leftwards to finish on tree roots. It is also possible to finish on the right at 4b.

18 Root Chimney 1a
A very dirty and unpleasant route, climbed mainly on tree roots.

Between Root Chimney *and the yew tree is:*

19 Slab Buttress 4b
Start at the bottom left-hand corner and step up right. Tricky balance problems then lead to an easy finish. One can go straight up at 5a. The wall round to the left gives a barely independent problem, also 5a.

In front of the yew tree and set forward from the main wall is:

★ **20   Slab Direct**   4a
Climb straight up the centre of the slab, starting slightly to the left.

★ **21   Slab Arête**   2a
The easy-angled right edge. A tricky eliminate climbs up just left of the arête and without touching it – 5a.

22   Yew Arête   5b
The awkward arête above the slab and to the left of a second yew tree.

★ **23   Garden Wall Crack**   3a
The wide crack behind, and to the right of, the second yew tree.

★ **24   Remote**   4c
Start 1 metre right of the last route. Climb the steep slab to finish at the oak stump.

25   Control   5c
Climb the wall right of *Remote*, passing the undercuts at half-height with some very trusting moves. A good problem despite the chipped holds. Has been done without the offending holds.

There is a variation to Control, *which moves right at the undercuts and finishes with a hard rockover onto the obvious foothold at the top –* 6a(NS).

26   Garden Wall Traverse   3a
From the foot of the next route traverse left, gradually ascending. Step across *Garden Wall Crack* and continue along a narrow ledge to easy ground above the slab. A pleasant little diversion.

27   Holly Leaf Crack   1b
Follow the crack to the ledge and finish up the wall on the left. A number of problems have been done on the right side of the boulder.

Beyond the boulder is:

★ **28   Thin**   5c
Climb delicately up the blunt nose on the left-hand side of the slab. Start either on the left or more directly.

There is a good 5b problem up the short wall to the left of Thin, *moving right at the top to join that route.*

29   Chipperydoodah   6a
A technical but again heavily chipped route up the middle of the face. Move awkwardly left to join *Thin* near the top. A more direct finish is 6b, and avoids holds on *Thin* entirely.

★★ **30   Curling Crack**   4a
The jamming crack in the centre of the wall. Short but good.

★ **31 Illusion** 6b
The very thin and technical wall right of *Curling Crack*. Another chipped route.

32 Disillusion 5c(NS)
The arête right of *Illusion*. The jammed boulder is not allowed.

33 Inside or Out? 2b
Climb over the jammed boulder and finish up the gully. The boulder used to be at the top of the climb but thankfully one is no longer faced by the momentous decision suggested by the name.

On the next block is:

★ **34 Front Face** 5b
Climb the left edge of the block, trending right to the centre to finish. Poor holds.

35 Mania 6a
The undercut wall between *Front Face* and the next route. Hard to finish.

★★ **36 Undercut Wall** 4a
The right-hand side of the block. Pull over the overhang and then go straight to the top.

Beyond the wide gully is:

★ **37 Pinnacle Buttress Arête** 5b
Climb directly up the left edge of the block starting on its left-hand side and then moving onto the front face. It can be climbed entirely on the front face at 6a with some very iffy moves – soloists beware.

★★ **38 Pinnacle Buttress** 5b
Just to the right of the last route. Climb straight up the wall to the scoop and so to the top. Hard for the short. The scoop can be approached more easily from the right at 4a – this was how the route was originally done.

An eliminate, **Praying Mantles** *5b, has been climbed straight up about 2 metres left of* Easy Crack.

★ **39 Easy Crack** 2a
Between the two blocks.

40 Bare Necessities 6a
The rounded arête right of *Easy Crack*. Strenuous climbing on poor sandy holds.

41 Bare Essentials 5c
Climb the centre of the block left of Stone Farm Pinnacle, finishing towards the left. Despite the cut holds this is a good climb, especially when the topmost rope-grooves are avoided.

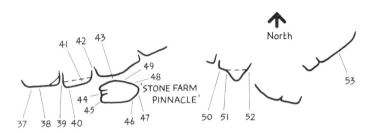

42 Pinnacle Chimney 2a
Behind the left end of the pinnacle. Straightforward.

Next is the prominent Stone Farm Pinnacle, which provides seven routes. There is a metal belay stake at the top; the easiest way up is Central Jordan.

43 Central Jordan 2a
The easy route to the top. Step across from the top of the main wall and then up.

★ 44 Key Wall 5a
The left face of the pinnacle. Climb the wall to the niche, then go up the wide crack above. One can also finish to the right of the niche at 5a.

★★ 45 Belle Vue Terrace 6a
Start a metre or so right of *Key Wall* and climb up to a large slot. Swing left and layback up to the break; move slightly right and make a hard move up and right to reach a slanting crack. Move back left and climb the slabby nose to finish. There is a direct start at 6b(NS).

46 Quoi Faire 6c
Start 2 metres left of the right edge. Pull up using a good hold and then swing a metre right along the break. Make an extremely powerful move to stand up and finish by moving back left a little.

47 Nose Direct 5c
High in the grade. Climb the nose at the right-hand end of the pinnacle starting with a long reach for small holds and finishing awkwardly. Pick your holds carefully. Starting on the right makes the climb 5b.

STONE FARM ROCKS ~ EAST

48 East Jordan Route 2b
Follow the line of large sandy holds up the back of the pinnacle.
Bridging is allowed at the start. Without bridging the climb is 4a.
49 Leisure Line 5c
The sandy wall between the Jordan routes.

*On the bulging boulder behind and right of Stone Farm Pinnacle are
three short climbs:* **Absent Friends** 6a, *which takes the blunt left-hand
arête;* **Arthur's Little Problem** 6b, *up the centre; and a 6a problem
to the right.*

*The next three routes are on a large boulder 10 metres to the right,
beyond some broken ground.*
50 Milestone Arête 4a
The rear left-hand arête. Stepping off the small boulder makes the
climb much easier.
51 Milestone Stride 4b
Climb the centre of the left side of the boulder on poor holds. There
seems to be little advantage in stepping off the small boulder.

The front arête of the block gives a difficult mantelshelf problem – 6a.
52 Concentration Cut 6a
Start round the corner from the previous route. Use the large pocket
and small crack to gain the top – harder for the short. Yet another
chipped route.

*More broken ground leads to another boulder. The next climbs are on
a low wall 10 metres further on. The original route here is:*

53 Traverse and Crack 2a
Start by traversing in from the right and then climb the pocketed
depression. A harder direct start is possible.

*There is an obvious line at the right end of the boulder (1a), and an
undercut crack on the left (3b), which is reached by continuing the
traverse of the original route. The small crack just left again is 5a, and
there are a couple more boulder problems left again at around 5b.*

On the next sizeable block is:

54 Open Chimney 3a
The shallow recess just left of the nose on the blunt arête. There is
another very short crack just to the left – 2b.

★★ 55 Bulging Corner 3b
Climb the obvious line of weakness on the front left-hand side of the
block.

A climb straight up the nose from the start of Bulging Corner *is*
Transparent Accelerating Banana 5b; *the name is longer than the
route. There is also a 5b problem starting a metre to the right and
finishing at the top of* Bulging Corner.

56 Bulging Wall 5b
Climb strenuously up the wall 2 to 3 metres right of *Bulging Corner.*

★ 57 Ashdown Wall 4b
Climb strenuously up the centre of the front face on sandy holds.

★ 58 Introductory Climb 2a
From the cleft at the far right-hand end of the block, traverse left
across the slab and finish up the crack in the centre of the face. This
can be started more directly at a shallow scoop, 2b, and finished
above this at 3a, or further right at 4a.

★ 59 Dinosaurs Don't Dyno 1a
Walk up the cut holds on the far right of the slab. A good beginners'
route.

★ 60 Gap Traverse 4a
Start on the wall right of the narrow cleft; move left and step across
the cleft at low-level. Continue along the easy ledges of the last route,
across *Ashdown Wall*, round to *Bulging Corner* and then onto easy
ground.

The initial wall of Gap Traverse *provides a number of pleasant little
problems – the central line is 3a.*

*The remainder of the routes are on the Inaccessible Boulder. This large
boulder has some fine routes over a range of difficulty. The easiest
approach to the top is by S.E. Corner Crack – a suitably long sling should
be used. Please don't make the rope grooves here worse by simply*

looping the rope over the buttress to belay. Descent should be by down climbing on a slack rope, with the last member of the party soloing down. **Do not abseil or lower off**. *The first route starts by the large boulder adjacent to the left face:*

★ **61 Guy's Route** 6c(NS)†
Climb the centre of the impending wall left of the triangular niche – mind your back! Stepping off the top of the large boulder reduces the grade considerably. Another variation is to move left from the niche of *Leaning Crack* – 6a.

★★ **62 Leaning Crack** 5a
Start left of the crack and climb into the triangular niche. Continue up the crack above. The start can be avoided by stepping off the boulder. The crack can be climbed to the niche at 5a.

63 Ducking Fesperate 6a
A spitty woonerism? Climb the steep wall a metre right of the crack. Stand up on the ledge with a hard balance move and then finish up the top slab with further interest.

★★ **64 S.W. Corner Scoop** 5a
Start 2 metres right of *Leaning Crack*. Some strenuous moves lead to the ledge, after which a move left enables the scoop to be gained.

★ **65 Primitive Groove** 4b
Climb strenuously up the centre of the front face on large holds, then go up the wide crack on the left.

66 Boulder Wall 6a
Various starts are possible – some of them difficult but all leading to a finish to the left of centre of the overhang. The overhang can also be climbed on its right side at 5b.

★ **67 S.E. Corner Crack** 4b
Start strenuously as for *Primitive Groove* but then traverse easily right to finish up the short crack in the bulge.

The lower wall below the S.E. Corner Crack *finish gives a number of boulder problems. The left side of the undercut nose is 5c, whilst its right side is 5b. There is a 5c mantelshelf just to the right and right again is:*

68 Balham Boot Boys 6b
Make an awkward mantelshelf onto the ledge left of *N.E. Corner*. Finish direct.

69 N.E. Corner 5a
Climb the rear right-hand arête starting from the boulder and then trending leftwards.

★★ **70 Diagonal Route** 5b
Start as for *N.E. Corner*. Make an ascending rightwards traverse,

crossing *Green Wall* and continuing in the same line to finish on the north-west arête. Difficult just after the start.

71 Simpering Savage 5b
The wall 2 metres right of the arête using the vandalised incut holds. It is possible to start further left and then move right into the line.

72 Green Wall 5a
A hard pull up the initial wall brings large flat holds to hand, or to foot if you climb upside down – take your pick. Trend left more easily to the top. It is also possible to finish direct (more 5a) or to the right at 4c.

★★ 73 Birdie Num-Nums 6b(NS)†
The rear left-hand arête of the pinnacle is a precarious proposition. Gain a standing position in the obvious pocket and then fall round onto the arête itself. Finish direct. The arête can also be reached by stepping off the large boulder – 5c.

74 Low-Level Girdle 6b
A very strenuous and sustained low-level girdle of the Inaccessible Boulder, though still not as yet across *Birdie Num-Nums*.

A Touch Too Much, 6b, High Rocks. Climber: Barry Knight.
Photo: Gary Wickham

Craig-y-blanco, 6a, High Rocks. Climber: David Atchison-Jones.
Photo: Ian Smith

Minor Outcrops

BASSETT'S FARM ROCKS   OS Ref TQ 491 414

This small outcrop consists of a steep smooth central wall and some lesser buttresses on either side. The central wall provides some good sustained climbs, and the crag is certainly worth a visit if only to do these.

The outcrop is located near Cowden, to the north of the main climbing area – see the map below. Approaching from the B2026 there is a sharp bend to the right just before Bassett's Farm itself is reached. There are two iron gates; climb over the first gate and follow the public footpath for 300 metres toward some trees, which initially conceal the crag from view. There is also a pleasant walk from Cowden Station. Follow a public footpath which runs parallel to the railway until Moat Farm is reached and then head east along the road towards Bassett's Farm.

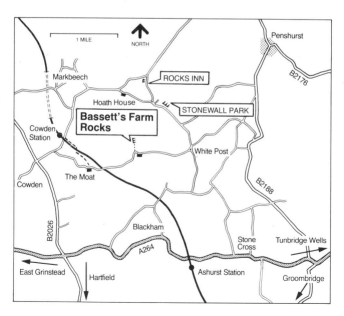

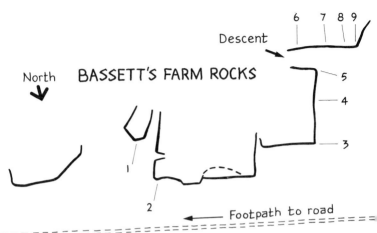

The outcrop is on private land, the owners of which are not known.

To minimise damage to the rock caused by moving and stretching ropes, it is essential, when top-roping, to use a non-stretch belay sling and to position the karabiner over the edge of the crag. If you see these instructions being ignored please make polite or stronger suggestions as to the correct procedure.

The first route is on a short, clean pillar.

1 Tim Nice but Dim Esquire 4b
Pleasant moves lead up to the holly tree.

2 Bertie 4c
The left-hand front face of the next buttress, again finishing at a holly.

Further right, and past some very unappetising rock, is a short wall set at right-angles to the main climbing area.

3 Chossy Arête 5c(NS)
The greasy left arête.

4 Tree Route 4c
Climb out of the cave to finish at the tree.

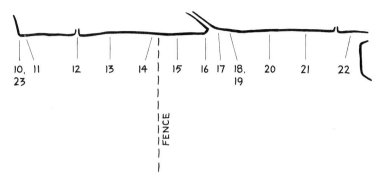

5 Silly Arête 5a
The right arête bears little resemblance to its Welsh namesake.

Right of Silly Arête is a descent gully. On the buttress to the right is:
6 Holly Tree Wall 5b
The left-hand side of the buttress, directly below the holly tree.
7 The Indian Face 5c(NS)
The centre of the buttress gives a strenuous climb on poor sandy holds.
8 Get Orf Moi Land 5a
The wall just left of the slabby arête.
9 Carpet Slab 4a
The slabby right-hand arête, which is usually very greasy.

Across from the wide earth-capped gully is the left-hand buttress.
10 Beyond Our Ken 5b(NS)
Climb the left arête initially on its left-hand side but then moving slightly right onto the front face near the top.
11 Ken's Wall 5c(NS)
Follow the thin crack on the left-hand side of the wall until it peters out. Traverse right until it is possible to reach the break above via an undercut in the niche; move back left then go straight up to an awkward mantelshelf finish.
12 Kenian Crack 4b
The obvious crack left of the central wall.
★★ 13 Dislocator 6a(NS)
Well-named. Climb painfully up the line of old bolt-holes to an

obvious peg in the upper wall (not an aid point). Either layaway right to finish, or traverse off left more easily.

★ **14 Karate Liz**   6c(NS)
Climb straight up to the left-hand side of the shallow scoop. Finish with a very long reach or a lunge. Very strenuous at the top and quite technical throughout.

★ **15 Dan's Wall**   6a(NS)
Go straight up to the right-hand side of the shallow scoop starting 2 metres left of *Excavator*.

★ **16 Excavator**   5c
The front face of the arête left of the gully.

After the next gully is the right-hand buttress and:

17 Foam Dome   5a
Sounds a bit rude. The wall right of the chimney. Finish in the obvious scoop.

18 Solution   5b
Start a metre right of the gully and go straight up.

19 Hypothesis   5b
Start as for *Solution* and then follow the left-to-right diagonal line to finish past the large stalactite on the next route.

20 Ian's Answer   5c
Start in the middle of the wall and climb straight up to finish past a large stalactite.

21 Final Solution?   5c(NS)†
Start a metre or so left of a short, dirty crack. Climb the steep wall trending left, then back right (don't touch *Ian's Answer*). Finish with a mantelshelf.

22 Docker's Armpit   4b
Climb the wall to the right of the dirty crack. Finish at the holly tree. A strong candidate for the worst route on sandstone.

★ **23 Girdle Traverse**   6a
A worthwhile expedition. Make the initial moves on *Beyond Our Ken* and then traverse right to the niche on *Ken's Wall*. Step into *Kenian Crack* and descend to the large ledge at 2 metres. Launch out across the central wall – very strenuous. Step across the gully onto the right-hand buttress, then either follow *Hypothesis* to the top or continue at a low level to reach the ground just beyond *Final Solution?*

CHIDDINGLYE WOOD ROCKS   OS Ref TQ 348 324

The rocks are situated one mile west-south-west of West Hoathly church, close to the B2028 between Turners Hill and Ardingly. They are on private land in their entirety and notices make prospective climbers aware of this. As far as is known, no climbers have been able to obtain

CHIDDINGLYE WOOD ROCKS

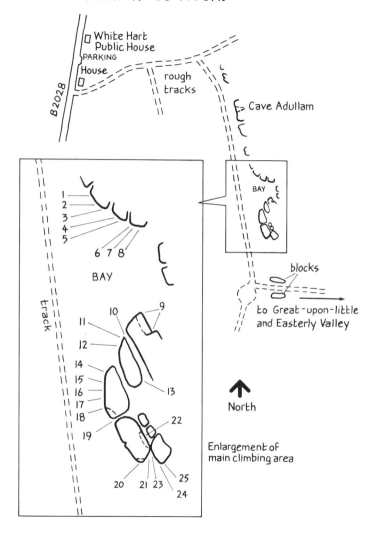

White Hart
Public House

PARKING

House

B2028

rough
tracks

Cave Adullam

BAY

1
2
3
4
5

6 7 8

BAY

blocks

to Great-upon-little
and Easterly Valley

track

10

9

11

12

13

14
15
16
17
18

19

22

North

Enlargement of
main climbing area

20 21 23 25

24

permission to climb here. The description of routes therefore is purely to serve as a record in case the access position should ever change.

In an attempt to preserve the rock features and the rare mosses and lichens, the site has been designated an SSSI. The owner of the outcrop has, with the support of English Nature, banned climbing – access is only available to groups with legitimate scientific interests who apply in writing beforehand. The one time dense covering of rhododendrons has been thoroughly cleared at the suggestion of English Nature to allow the mosses and lichens to flourish – rhododendrons are not native to England, having been introduced in Victorian times. Ironically, the clearance has meant that much virgin rock has been exposed, a high proportion of which is in excellent climbing condition.

The routes described are all in the westerly valley, which is in the grounds of Stonehurst. The rocks in the easterly valley (OS Ref TQ 351 322) extend into the grounds of Philpots and are extensive though discontinuous. These too have been cleared of vegetation and are no longer heavily shaded by trees. Consequently, the rock is in much better condition than previously.

Where the two outcrops meet there is a large boulder standing on a tiny plinth (accessible by jumping over from the adjacent crag). This is the famous Great-upon-Little. The valley below the boulder is said to be haunted by Gytrack, 'a gurt black ghost hound', though only a ginger tom has been seen lately; and, according to R.T. Hopkins's *Ghosts over England*, "here the just control of providence ceases and one comes under the powers of unseen presences which are inimical". There is an interesting Sacrificial Boulder just to the east of Great-upon-Little of about three metres in height. This has an easy-angled side with steps cut into it and, parallel to these, a narrow channel (for blood) leads down from the flat top. There is also said to be a Druid's Stone nearby.

To reach the westerly valley, park in a lay-by close to the Whitehart Public House on the B2028 and then follow a track into the estate – see the diagram. This eventually leads to some low rock walls. From here head right for about 200 metres until 'Cave Adullam' is reached. The first recorded climbs are about 200 metres right of this, where there is a wide open bay with three buttresses on the left-hand side.

On the first of the three buttresses is:

★★ **1 Amethyst** 5c
Climb the blunt arête to the left of the overhanging wall mainly on stalactite holds. When it's possible trend right to finish. The rock offers more friction than appearances suggest.

★★ 2 Harlequin 6b(NS)
Go easily up the crack just left of *First Visit* to a poor bridging rest.
Use the right-hand hold to go up and left over the overhang.

★ 3 First Visit 3b
Climb the buttress between the overhanging wall and the crack.

On the central buttress is:

4 Gascape 4c
Climb the left end of the central buttress; finish up the short ramp.

5 Warrior 5a
Start near the centre of the buttress, then move right and finish
awkwardly at the right-hand end. The finishing holds may require
excavating. There is a direct finish which goes straight up the middle
of the face to a hard finish – 6a(NS).

On the right-hand buttress is:

6 Doina da J'al 5c(NS)
Climb straight up the left-hand arête to an interesting finish.

★★ 7 Hound's Wall 4a
Climb the left side of the wall on good holds.

★★★ 8 Gytrack 4b
Start just right of the last route and go straight up the pock-marked
wall to its highest point. A good climb.

*The next routes are on some isolated blocks on the other side of the wide
bay, some 50 metres further right. There are no recorded climbs on the
low greasy boulders in between. On the first block with the obvious large
square-cut roof is:*

★ 9 R-Maker 5b
Start in the left-hand corner of the roof, move up and finger-traverse
rightwards to the nose. Finish straight up the thin wall. A direct start
can be done which avoids the initial traverse.

The next four routes are on the adjacent isolated block:

★★ 10 Spook 5a
Climb directly up the left side of the front arête, passing a small
rhododendron.

★ 11 Karen 5b
Start a metre or so right of the front arête and climb the thin wall,
finishing up the steep shallow groove.

★ 12 Stone's Route 5c
Climb the wall about a metre right of *Karen* passing the obvious
pinch and small sapling.

13 Sacrifice 4a
At the end of the passage. Climb the easy-angled arête. This route is

normally soloed to get to the belay; however, it is not always in condition.

On the front face of the next boulder is:

★★ **14 Gilt Edge** 5b(NS)
Climb the arête left of the curling crack.

15 Humphrey 4c(NS)
The curling crack. At the large ledge traverse right onto the next ledge, and so to the top.

16 Sandstone Bogey 5c(NS)
One metre right of *Humphrey*; finish as above.

17 Jennifer 5b(NS)
One metre right of the small crack; finish as above.

18 Cleanliness 5c(NS)
One metre right of the previous route and just before the buttress becomes undercut. Climb straight up via a large pocket to finish at a small rhododendron.

*A contrived climb, **Godliness** 5c(NS)†, starts as for the last route but traverses right, above the overhang, to finish on the right-hand arête.*

19 Chiddinglye Chimney 6a†
The obvious chimney. Desperately hard to start.

On the next block is:

★ **20 Herbal Abuse** 5a
Climb the steep bulging right arête on some excellent large holds.

★★ **21 Lord Chumley Pootings** 5b(NS)
The fine steep pocketed wall right of the last route and just left of an earth and bush filled gully.

The next route is on the back of the block. Crawl through the hole right of Lord Chumley Pootings; *stand up, and a metre to the left is:*

22 Back of Beyond 6a(NS)†
Climb straight up to the overlap, which is then climbed on small pockets; finish direct.

On the next block is:

23 Percy Pustule Went to Town 4c
Climb the steep slab right of the gully with an awkward long reach low down.

24 The Rough-legged Buzzard 6a(NS)†
Climb the triangular wall to the right of the previous route without using the arête on the right. The finish is quite tricky.

25 Three Cheers for Pooh 5a(NS)
Climb the arête to the right of the last route. Move right at the top
break and finish over the bulges.

*Working rightwards from here (see diagram) the easterly valley can be
found – see crag introduction.*

HAPPY VALLEY ROCKS   OS Ref TQ 565 392

This outcrop lies to the west of St. Pauls Church on Rusthall Common,
about a mile due west of the centre of Tunbridge Wells.

From Tunbridge Wells take the East Grinstead Road (A264) along the
north side of Tunbridge Wells Common. Pass the turning to Denny Bottom
on the right, then turn left into a cul-de-sac 200 metres further on. This
leads to the church and limited parking space (none on church days).
From the church continue walking in the same line as the road and
parallel to a wall. Follow the wall as it turns sharply left and continue for
about 150 metres until just before the path leads onto a metalled road.
The outcrop is about 50 metres right of here.

Other useful approaches include a path which leads eastwards from the
Beacon Hotel in Tea Garden Lane; and another which runs south from
opposite the cricket pitch on the A264. Both paths lead to the top of a
flight of steps between routes 3 and 4.

The outcrop comprises a low main wall, which never exceeds five metres
at any point – a good place for bouldering and soloing – and an
impressive pinnacle with a masonry plinth. The quality of the rock is
variable but much of it, including the pinnacle, is soft and sandy.

Most of the early development of the outcrop was carried out by the
JMCS in the late 1940s and early 1950s. Unfortunately the names of
their routes, and their exact location, have been lost. Most of the route
names, therefore, are of recent origin.

The outcrop has recently benefitted from some major tree-felling. At one
time heavily shaded and in poor condition, it is now almost completely
open. The clearance has also restored the whole area to its former scenic
splendour and there are now fine views over the surrounding
countryside.

**To minimise damage to the rock caused by moving and
stretching ropes, it is essential, when top-roping, to use a
non-stretch belay sling and to position the karabiner over
the edge of the crag. If you see these instructions being
ignored please make polite or stronger suggestions as to
the correct procedure.**

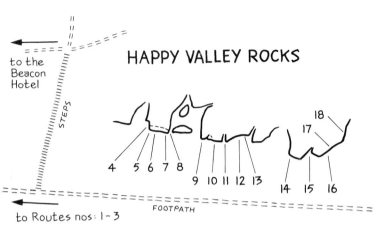

HAPPY VALLEY ROCKS

to the Beacon Hotel

STEPS

4 5 6 7 8 9 10 11 12 13 14 15 16 17 18

to Routes nos: 1-3

FOOTPATH

The first three routes are on a small buttress 60 metres left of the flight of steps:

1 Beacon Wall 4c
Climb the left-hand end of the buttress, finishing up the short groove.

★**2 Hidden Gem** 4c
The crack in the centre of the buttress.

3 Doug's Come-uppance 6a(NS)
Climb the line of slot-holds a metre or so right of *Hidden Gem*.

The next routes are on a buttress 60 metres right of the steps and just to the right of a short slab:

4 Stonefish 5a
Climb the gully wall of the buttress on crinkly holds.

5 Moray 4c
Climb the left-hand arête on its front face.

6 Red Snapper 5b
Climb the overhang a metre right of the arête, using the thin crack.

7 Going Turbot 5a
Pull over the overhang a metre right of *Red Snapper*, then finish up the leftward-slanting groove.

8 Kippers 2b
Climb the short crack and then the slabby wall on the left.

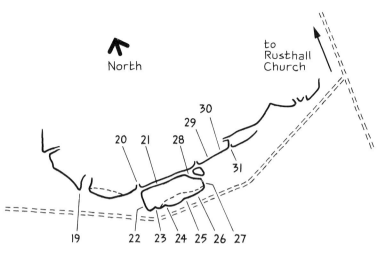

On the next sizeable buttress is:

9 Cleft 2b
The left-hand arête.

10 Pot-belly 4c
Climb the right-hand side of the buttress starting just right of the small roof.

11 Mist 2a
The short bramble-choked crack.

12 The Short Sharp Cock 2a
Follow the line of cut holds and then finish up the thin crack.

13 Master of Muck 5a
Start by the pictures cut in the rock and climb straight up between the two saplings. Finish with a mantelshelf.

On the next block is:

★ **14 The Buzzard Years** 4a
The crack just right of the arête.

15 Corner Crack 4a
The corner crack.

16 Rotpunkt 4c
Start just to the right of the small slab on the arête and climb straight up.

17 The Deadly Lampshade 3a
The short crack-system right of *Rotpunkt*.
18 Malcolm McPherson's a Very Strange Person 1a
The short crack to the right again.

The next route is on a buttress about 15 metres to the right:
19 Two Step 5c(NS)
Start at the toe of the buttress and climb the slabby arête to the ledge on the right. Finish up the short slab.
20 NS (Not Skinnered) 5c
The off-width crack in the main wall opposite the left-hand end of the pinnacle. Move slightly right at the top of the crack and climb the short headwall, including the top block. Low in the grade.
21 The Chimney 3a
Climb the narrow passage between the pinnacle and the main wall about half-way back.
22 Thoroughly Kentish 5c(NS)
The west face of the pinnacle.

On the front face of the pinnacle are three cracks:
23 Eckpfeiler 6a(NS)
The indistinct left-hand crack.
24 Brouillard 6a(NS)
The central crack.
25 Frêney 6a(NS)
The right-hand crack. Very friable rock.
26 Sandstone Safari 6a(NS)
The overhanging wall right of Frêney. Better than it looks.
27 Chalybeate 5c
The east face of the pinnacle.
28 From Behind 5b
Step onto the wedged block at the start of the chimney between the pinnacle and the rest of the crag. Climb the scooped wall on the left without recourse to the other side of the chimney. Much harder for the short.

The next routes are on the main wall to the right of the pinnacle. On the left-hand side is a rhododendron near the top.
29 Rhody-O 5c(NS)
Start below the aforementioned vegetable and climb straight up passing the plant on the right. A 'quality route'.
30 Route Minor 4c
The centre of the wall. Start up the cut holds and finish up the short crack.

31 Undercut Rib 4b
The short rib on the extreme right.

PENNS ROCKS

These rocks comprise three separate outcrops, of which two – Jockey's Wood Rocks and Penns House Rocks – have recorded routes. The other outcrop, Rocks Wood, is low and of lesser interest to the climber (see Other Outcrops). The outcrops lie within a designated SSSI.

All the outcrops are on private land in the grounds of Penns in the Rocks, and climbing is not allowed. The description of routes is purely to serve as a record and does not imply that anyone has the right to climb here. In the past limited access for very small groups was granted – hence the new routes that have appeared since the last guidebook.

The rocks are situated 1½ miles west of Eridge Station and 2¼ miles south-south-west of Groombridge. From Groombridge take the B2110 south out of the village; after half a mile turn left onto the B2188 and follow this for about 1¼ miles until you reach a crossroads. The drive leading to Penns in the Rocks is 200 metres further on, on the left-hand side. Approaching along the drive the first outcrop you reach is Jockey's Wood Rocks. This is well-hidden by trees to the right of the track about 400 metres in.

JOCKEY'S WOOD ROCKS   OS Ref TQ 516 347
This crag is parallel to, and 150 metres right of, the drive that leads into the estate. The main part of the outcrop consists of two buttresses separated by a wide gully. The right-hand buttress is the better of the two, being about eight metres high and composed of good quality rock.

The first route is on the left-hand buttress:

1 The Ice Cream Garden 5c(NS)
Start 2 metres left of the shallow groove in the centre of the buttress by some large jugs. Climb straight up the wall and finish with a mantelshelf up to the tree roots.

2 Winch Me Up Scottie 6a(NS)
The wall between the previous route and the shallow groove without using either.

3 Rodomontade 5b
The thin crack and shallow groove lead to a tree and the top.

★ **4 Identity Crisis** 6b(NS)†
Start just left of the arête. Gain the break and then swing left and reach up for some obvious sloping diagonal holds. Somehow pull over the bulge using these to reach easier ground above.

★ **5 Dying for a Tomtit** 5b
A pleasant climb up the right arête of the block.

Jockey's Wood Rocks

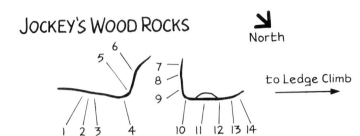

North

to Ledge Climb

★ **6 Clenched Buttocks** 5c(NS)
The thin discontinuous cracks on the left wall of the gully.

Across the gully is the more impressive right-hand buttress.

7 Jockey Shorts 5b(NS)†
Start 7 metres left of the arête. At the first break move left then back right to a finish on tree roots above a small roof.

8 Why Fronts? 5c(NS)
Start 3 metres left of the arête by a curving horizontal crack. Climb straight up the wall and finish by moving left into the scoop.

★★ **9 Huntsmans' Wall** 5c
Start 2 metres left of the arête. Climb directly up the steep thin wall, trending right to finish.

★☆ **10 Jockey's Wall** 5b
Start immediately left of the arête and continue by trending right to a large diagonal break, which leads to a large recess on the front.

The wall to the right provides some difficult boulder problems and an eliminate – **Andy the Bearded One** *5b(NS)†. This follows Woodpecker Crack to the first break, hand-traverses left for about a metre, and then climbs the wall direct to the recess.*

★ **11 Woodpecker Crack** 5b
The obvious steep crack below the recess.

12 Tartan Custard 5c
Start as for the last route. Move right at the rounded flake and then climb delicately up the wall to finish at the recess.

★★★ **13 Pie an' Ear-ring** 5c
Start 2 metres right of *Woodpecker Crack*. Take a direct line up the

short crack, the slab and the impending wall above. A very enjoyable climb with surprisingly good holds.

14 The Last of the Pie an' Ears 6a(NS)
Start in the niche just right of the last route. Pull onto the slab and climb this to the impending wall. Finish up the shallow scoop.

★ **15 Panty Girdle** 5a
A left-to-right girdle traverse of the right-hand buttress at one-third height. Follow the obvious break across the gully wall and out across the front face.

★★ **16 Playtex Girdle** 5c(NS)
Another traverse but this time at two-thirds height with the feet on the handholds of the previous route. Start as for *Why Fronts?*; traverse rightwards past a hard section on the front face (don't step up) and finish in the gully on the right.

Ten metres to the right is another buttress.

17 Ledge Climb 3a
A pleasant climb up the short nose.

PENNS HOUSE ROCKS   OS Ref TQ 520 346
These are a fine group of large boulders close to the house. The easiest way to get to them is to follow the drive until fairly close to the house and then head off right across some fields. The rocks are at the top of a large field and are partially obscured by a line of planted trees. They offer good quality climbs of reasonable length, in an idyllic setting. The rock is generally in excellent condition, especially in those areas that are regularly cleared of bushy vegetation by the landowner. Some of the climbs are hard to set up because of a lack of suitable anchors on the summits, and it's therefore essential to bring plenty of ropes and slings.

The first climbs are on two large boulders close to the fence. On the boulder nearest to the gate is:

1 One Up the Rectum Don't Affect'em 5b
The crack right of the tree. Continue up over the bulges above. Alternatively, step left and avoid half the climb.

★ **2 Crusaders** 5c(NS)
Start up a groove just left of *Streetlife*; move up to the obvious undercut and use this to reach good holds directly above.

★★ **3 Streetlife** 5c(NS)
The arête left of *Midweek Chimney* is very strenuous and awkward.

4 Midweek Chimney 2a
The obvious chimney on the left side of the boulders.

On the second boulder is:

5 Carry on Up the Tower 5b(NS)
Start on the bulge just right of *Midweek Chimney*. Move up and slightly right to the ledge and then climb the right arête of the chimney.

6 Pullover 5a
Start as for the last route but at the ledge move right and thrutch up the wide crack above – a previous guide suggested bridging up this crack!

★ **7 Recess Chimney** 4b
Bridge up the big recess and go up through a hole in the back. Entertaining.

8 Cretin 6a(NS)
Start as for *Recess Chimney* but then bridge out backwards in a cretin-like manner. Swing round and finish on the left.

★ **9 Going Turbo** 6a(NS)
This is the 'holdless' right arête of *Recess Chimney*. Gain a (once rather large) hold a metre right of the arête and then go for the top.

★★ **10 Cowgirl in the Sand** 5c(NS)
Climb the wall a metre left of *Split's Groove* using an obvious broken undercut.

★ **11 Split's Groove** 4b
The left-hand groove.

12 Spook's Groove 4c
The right-hand groove.

13 Rocket Man 5a
The arête right of *Spook's Groove*.

14 All Quiet on the Western Front 5c(NS)
This climbs the arête at the left end of the back side of the boulder, finishing on the obvious flakes. Hard to start.

Further east, and across a wide passage, are three more large boulders, on the first of which is:

★★★ **15 Upwards Scoop** 5a
The fine open groove on the left edge. Go delicately up on good holds. Finish slightly to the right. Hard to start for the short.

★★ **16 Stone Ape** 6a(NS)†
Climbs the wall just left of the right edge. Gain a standing position on the first ledge and reach up for the break running leftwards from the arête; use this to reach the top break and then move leftwards to finish up the crack. Don't use the right arête as this is part of:

★★ **17 The Juggler** 4b
Climb the short crack and then continue straight up.

18 Déjà Vu 6a
Climb the wall left of the overhanging crack and finish straight up.

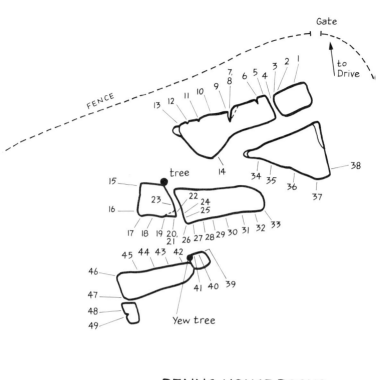

PENNS HOUSE ROCKS

North →

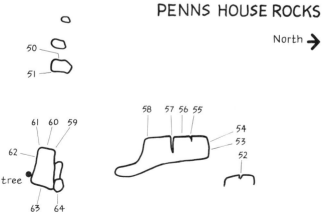

★ **19 Trapeze Crack** 5b
Climb the overhanging crack and then trend slightly right to finish with a mantelshelf.

20 The Contortionist 5c
A hand-traverse from the right-hand side of the overhang enables one to pull over the second overhang at a point just right of the last route.

21 Electric Rainbow 5c
The obvious mid-height traverse from right to left. Start as for *The Contortionist* and finish in the groove just left of *The Juggler*.

22 Circus Act 6a(NS)†
The overhanging right-hand arête.

23 Descent Gully 2a
A convenient means of ascent and descent.

On the second boulder is:

24 Blue Helmet 5b
Climb the short wall using the two flakes.

25 Doug's Dilemma 4b
The groove just left of the arête.

26 The Gamekeeper 5c
The blunt arête.

27 The Lion Tamer 4a
Climb the scoop right of the arête on large layaways.

28 Woodlice Crack 5b(NS)†
The corner and groove capped by a small overhang.

29 Cut and Blow Job 4a†
The grooves 1 metre right of *Woodlice Crack*.

30 The Trivial Trappist 5c(NS)
The diagonal crack just right of the last route.

31 Over the Rainbow 6a(NS)†
Mantelshelf onto the ledge and then climb the flakes just left of the crack.

32 Pigs on the Wing 5c(NS)
The inverted Y-shaped crack.

33 Golden Nose 6a(NS)†
The right-hand arête.

On the third boulder is:

34 Bertie Bothways 4a
The crack at the left-hand end.

35 One Out, All Out 5c†
The thin wall with the two obvious layaway holds.

36 One Flew over the Buzzard's Nest 3b
The obvious ramp at the right-hand end of the wall.

37 Arnold Anyways 5b(NS)
The wall and discontinuous flakes between the birch tree and the arête.

★**38 Attack of the Killer Pigs** 6a(NS)
Immediately right of the arête. Finish up the obvious crack.

Going further east, on a boulder with a large yew tree in it, there are nine routes:

39 Parba Nangbat 5b
The wag bill at the left-hand end.

40 The Clown 3b
The short groove.

41 The Acrobat 3b
A short problem just left of the tree.

42 The Fire-Eater 5c
Climb the series of layaway holds just right of the tree.

43 Dynamo Deltoid 6a
Layback the grooves a metre or so right of *The Fire-Eater*.

44 The Ring Master 5a
Climb the large flake-crack 4 metres right of the tree.

45 Lunar Music Suite 5b
Pull into the next short groove from the left.

46 Station Master Leroy Winston 5a
The short arête right again and behind the tree.

47 Auxiliary Arête 4a
Round to the right is another short arête.

On the small boulder to the right is:

48 Beef Curtains 5b
The wall between the left arête and the central crack; hard to start.

★**49 The Bearded Clam** 4b
The central crack.

In the area to the right are three isolated pinnacles, the first two of which are small and have perched blocks on top. On the third pinnacle is:

50 Turfed Off 4a
Climb the crack and then finish direct.

51 Quentin's Crisps 4c
The face round to the right of *Turfed Off* using the crack.

Nearer to the house, and across a wide clear area, are some low, but steep and clean, boulders. On the most northerly boulder is:

52 Shorter than the A3 2b
The obvious crack.

The next boulder is L-shaped, and on its shorter side is:
53 Swingtime 6a(NS)†
Climb the short, slanting crack at the left-hand end of the wall. Finish direct.
54 Handfuls of Dirt 6b(NS)†
Bridge up the shallow groove and then finish slightly left on solid earth holds.

On the longer side is:
★**55 Going Straight** 4c†
The flake-crack 4 metres right of the arête.
★**56 A.W.O.L.** 6a(NS)†
The dog-leg crack right of the last route.
★**57 Jackson Hole** 2b
The chimney in the centre of the face; finish through the hole at the back.
★**58 Cowardly Custard** 4c
The flaky cracks immediately left of the right-hand arête; finish slightly right.

On the next (and last) boulder is:
59 Garlic Chives 5a†
The left-hand arête.
60 Sex Buzzards 5a
The crack system right of *Garlic Chives*.
61 The Jungle Book 5a
The right-hand arête.
62 Aladdin and the Ramp 5a
Follow the ramp leftwards to a finish on the arête as for the previous route.
63 Spermatozoa 6a(NS)
A tricky little climb up the sperm-shaped feature on the back wall.
64 Brittle Arête 5a
The well named arête to the right.

RAMSLYE FARM ROCKS   OS Ref TQ 568 379
These rocks are situated 1½ miles south-west of Tunbridge Wells and 400 metres north-west of Strawberry Hill. The quickest approach is from Strawberry Hill on the A26 but the rocks can also be approached by a 10-minute walk along a footpath leading eastwards from High Rocks. The path starts from the car-park at the right-hand end of High Rocks and

runs next to the new fence, continuing straight on into the wood where the fence turns left.

The outcrop, although very close to a public footpath, is on private land. The description of routes therefore is purely to serve as a record and does not imply that the public has the right of access to the outcrop, or the right to climb.

The outcrop is in two sections: the right-hand section, which rises to a height of 6 metres, and lies overgrown and neglected behind farm buildings; and the more open, but lower, left-hand section. The rock is sound and in reasonable condition.

As there are few trees on top of the crag, setting up a belay can present problems. A second rope to act as a long sling is therefore essential.

To minimise damage to the rock caused by moving and stretching ropes, it is essential, when top-roping, to use a non-stretch belay sling and to position the karabiner over the edge of the crag. If you see these instructions being ignored please make polite or stronger suggestions as to the correct procedure.

The first climb is on the small slab to the left of a large fallen tree.

1 Lichenous Language 5b
Climb the short, mossy slab on its right-hand side.

On the next buttress to the right is:

2 Stinging Nettle 4b†
Climb the short wall left of a dirty corner-crack, via the obvious pockets, and without using the tree at the top.

The routes described next are all on the clean slabby wall adjacent to a large oak tree. Starting just to the left of the tree is:

3 Tumble 4b
Go straight up the blunt arête after an awkward start.

4 Tequila Mockingbird 6a
The boulder problem arête right of *Tumble*.

★ **5 Thin Wall** 5b
Climb straight up the line of layaways and flakes in the centre of the wall.

★ **6 Cut Holds** 3b
Start on cut holds just left of the big overlap. Finish up the slab almost anywhere.

7 Overlap Centre 5a
The easiest line is to start as for *Undercut* and then to move left onto

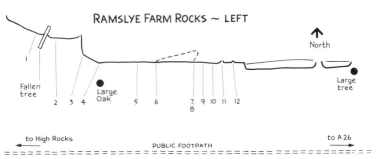

RAMSLYE FARM ROCKS ~ LEFT

↑
North

I

Fallen
tree

2   3   4

Large
Oak

5   6   7 9 10 11   12
                8

Large
tree

← to High Rocks

PUBLIC FOOTPATH

to A 26 →

the arête. A harder direct line can be done by starting at the centre of the overlap.

8   Undercut 3b
The obvious diagonal line beneath the big overlap.

9   Short Wall 4a
Take a direct line just right of the end of the overlap.

10   Slapper 5a
Climb the wall to the left of *Jamber* using the good flakes. Bushwhack off left to finish.

11   Jamber 2a
The extremely short crack at the right-hand end of the wall.

12   Grandad Goes Bird Watching 1b
One of the best and most impressive routes on sandstone, an experience not to be missed. The 3-metre crack just right of *Jamber*.

Seventy metres right and immediately behind the farm buildings is, you guessed it, the right-hand section. The base is currently very overgrown with head-high nettles, so bring a scythe. The first feature is a blank-looking slab; to the right of this is:

13   Forgotten Climb 4c†
Start below the right-hand end of the slab. Climb over the overhang and continue up the leftward-slanting groove above. Finish on grass.

14   Squirter 5b(NS)
Start to the right of the small roof. Climb up and left to finish in the shallow groove right of the previous route.

★ **15   Doing the Dirty** 5c(NS)
Start 2 metres right of *Squirter* and climb up past the two square holes.

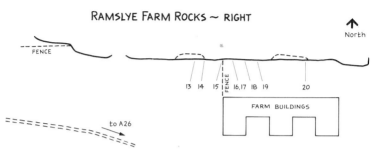

RAMSLYE FARM ROCKS ~ RIGHT

↑
North

FENCE

13 14 15 FENCE 16,17 18 19   20

to A26

FARM BUILDINGS

★16 Headhunter 5c(NS)
The thin crack just right of the barbed-wire fence.

17 Hanging Crack 5c(NS)
Climb *Headhunter* for 3 metres and then traverse right to the bottom of the hanging crack; finish up this.

18 Equinox 6a(NS)
Start a metre right of *Headhunter*. Go up to the small square pot-hole and then move right, to the bottom of the hanging crack of the previous route. Traverse for another metre or so and then finish straight up the steep headwall.

19 Phoenix 6b(NS)
A direct start to *Equinox*. Start 3 metres right of *Equinox* and climb straight up to the horizontal break via the undercut flakes and ribs. Finish as for *Equinox*.

20 Chez Moi 5c(NS)
Start at the right-hand end of the buttress. Traverse left past a thin crack. Go up a little, move left and then finish as for *Equinox*.

UNDER ROCKES   OS Ref TQ 556 264

Under Rockes is a pleasant secluded outcrop consisting primarily of a fine steep wall which provides a number of good hard routes. There are also a few good climbs in the easier grades. The rock can be in condition all the year round but is probably at its best in spring and autumn when there are few leaves on the trees.

The outcrop and its approaches are on private land, the owners of which are not known.

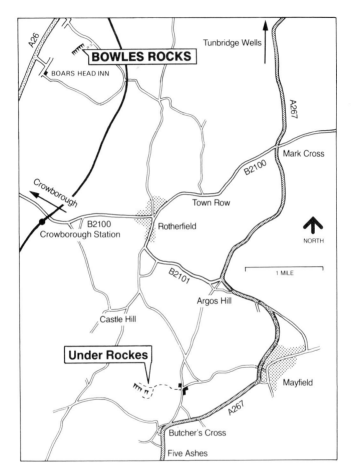

Under Rockes, the most southerly of the Southern Sandstone venues, lies just over 2 miles south of Rotherfield. The map shows how to get there – going south from Rotherfield follow the signs to Heathfield and Five Ashes until a large house on the left is reached. There is a small road signposted to Mayfield by the house. To avoid conflict with the residents please **do not** park in front of the house. There is a lay-by slightly further down the road.

A footpath starts almost opposite the house and soon leads to a much wider track. This runs between the fields for about 400 metres until the remains of an iron gate is reached. The track continues but deteriorates after this, so just before the gate step over the fence into the field on the right. Carry on in the same direction along the edge of the field and parallel to the track. Go over a fence into another field and then head diagonally right to a line of trees that stops well before the fence on the left. Follow the trees for about 150 metres and then step left over the fence. This brings you out at the top of the crag in the vicinity of *Dark Crack*. Alternatively, at the line of trees pass into the next field. Drop down the slope and cross over a wooden fence into a wood. The rocks are another 50 metres further on.

To minimise damage to the rock caused by moving and stretching ropes, it is essential, when top-roping, to use a non-stretch belay sling and to position the karabiner over the edge of the crag. If you see these instructions being ignored please make polite or stronger suggestions as to the correct procedure.

The first two routes are on a short wall to the left of the main wall:

1 Assault 5c
Climb the wall just left of, and without using, the descending tree roots.

2 Battery Wall 4a
A direct line 2 metres left of *Wide Crack*.

3 Wide Crack 2a
The crack bounding the left-hand side of the main wall.

The main wall has five lines of large, square-cut pot-holes running vertically, all of which form good hard routes.

3A Birthday Buttress 6a(NS)†
An eliminate between *Wide Crack* and *The Thirteenth Light*. Awkward to finish.

4 The Thirteenth Light 6a(NS)
The left-hand-most set of pot-holes. Reach left for layaway holds at the top.

** **5 Lionheart** 6a(NS)
The line of pot-holes second from left. High in the grade.

* **6 Over the Hill** 6a(NS)
An eliminate between *Lionheart* and *Uganda Wall*, avoiding the pot-holes entirely.

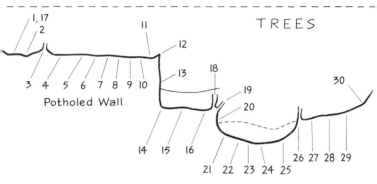

★★★ 7 Uganda Wall 5c
The central line of pot-holes.

★ 8 Magic Pebble 6a(NS)
A line straight up between the pot-holes of *Uganda Wall* and *Fireball*.

★★ 9 Fireball 5c
The line of pot-holes second from right. Similar to *Uganda Wall*.

★ 10 Dogs of War 6a(NS)
Yet another direct line between the pot-holes.

★ 11 In One Hole... 6a(NS)
The right-hand set of pot-holes. Exit leftwards from the last hole.

★★★ 12 Central Crack 5c
An excellent route up the steep corner bounding the right-hand side of
the main wall. It is also possible to climb the corner entirely by
bridging, without using the crack at the back or the pot-holes – 6a.

12A The Apex 6a(NS)†
A high-level girdle of the pot-holed wall. Climb *Wide Crack* to the
ramp of *The Thirteenth Light*. Traverse rightwards roughly at the level
of the old roof-line. Finish up *Central Crack*.

★ 13 The Touch 5c
A pleasant climb on the wall right of *Central Crack*. Climb directly up
the centre of the wall. Finish up the top arête as for *Evening Arête*.

*An eliminate with an imaginative(?) name has been climbed up the wall
to the right of the lower section of* The Touch – **The Alien Succumbs**

FIELD

North

Fence

UNDER ROCKES

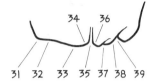

34   36

31   32   33   35 37 38 39

to the Macho Intergalactic Funkativity of the Funkblasters
5c.

★★ **14 Evening Arête** 5b
A bit of a leveller. Climb the arête on its right side to the large ledge and then continue in the same line up the mossy wall above. The route is 4c if one traverses off right along the large ledge.

★ **15 Hear No Evil** 5a
Climb up just left of the centre of the slab with a long reach near the bottom. Finish where you like. An eliminate line just to the right is 5b.

16 Speak No Evil 4b
The right-hand end of the slab, passing a big pocket low down.

★★ **17 Girdle Traverse** 5b
It is possible to make a very worthwhile low-level girdle traverse, from *Assault* (1) to *Speak No Evil* (16). The traverse can be continued to *Dark Crack* (26) at 6a, and then completed by finishing up *Peregrine* (28).

To the right of Speak No Evil *are two cracks:*

18 Channelsea Crack 2b
The left-hand crack.

19 Outfall Crack 6a(NS)†
The right-hand crack. A vicious overhanging off-width. Bridging across *Channelsea Crack* is not allowed.

20 What the Buck   6a(NS)
Climb directly up the wall below the oak tree.

21 Rapunzel   5c(NS)
Start at the blunt arête. Climb diagonally rightwards to a
problematical finish up to the strange-looking tree stump.

22 Bow Locks   5c(NS)
Start right of *Rapunzel* and go straight up via the short crack.

23 Mastercard   6b(NS)
A steep route which takes a direct line up to the left-hand side of the
strange tree. Start by the horseshoe carved in the rock.

★ **24 Meridian**   6b
The bulging, overhung arête directly below the right-hand side of the
strange tree. Start on the right by climbing up to, and then traversing
in from, the large stalactite. Pull powerfully onto the right side of the
arête where the breaks peter out. Very friable rock. A direct start is
also 6b.

25 Funnel Web   6b(NS)
Start as for *Meridian* but continue straight up past the large stalactite
at mid-height. Spoilt by the quality of the rock.

★★ **26 Dark Crack**   5c
The overhanging crack. Very difficult in the middle section and
generally harder than it looks.

27 One Up All Up, Except Mat   6a(NS)
Climb the blunt arête right of *Dark Crack* up to the huge stalactites.
Continue over the bulge with difficulty to finish at the small tree.

28 Peregrine   5b
Start as for the last route but then climb the wall diagonally
rightwards to finish just right of the holly bush.

29 Kestrel   5c(NS)
Start to the right of *Peregrine*. Climb straight up to the large stalactite,
then finish slightly to the right.

30 Merlin   4a
Start beneath the tree right of the previous route and climb straight up.

*Thirty metres further right and over an earth hump there is a smaller
easy-angled outcrop.*

31 The Waltzing Buzzard   5c(NS)
Climb the slab at the left-hand edge of the buttress. Finish on the front
face of the short arête at the top.

★ **32 Trouble with Rubble**   5b
Climb up the centre of the slab directly below the odd-looking dead
tree.

A metre right of Trouble with Rubble *is a 4b problem which uses the large pocket just below the top break. A metre right again is another short route which climbs directly out of the shallow niche* – 5b.

33 Departure Slab 4a
The short slab just right of the shallow niche.

34 Manteloid 5c
The nose just left of *Thorny Crack*. Start in the small cave and then head up past the obvious vertical slot.

35 Thorny Crack 1b
The easy crack. Choked with brambles at present.

36 Lamplight 5a
The left edge of the slab.

37 No Ghosts 5b
Climb straight up the centre of the slab mainly on pockets.

38 Wind and Wuthering 5c
An eliminate up the slab a metre left of *Roger's Wall*.

39 Roger's Wall 3a
On the right is a rightwards-slanting crack; follow this to the top.

Other Outcrops

The purpose of this chapter is to record all known (or even hinted at) rock in the South-East. The list is certainly not comprehensive, as can be seen by scouring the 1:25000 OS Maps of the area, and it is hoped that further details and outcrops will be added in the future. For more details of the authors referred to, see the bibliography on page 268.

ASHURSTWOOD ROCKS   OS Ref TQ 415 370
This outcrop is about 1 1/2 miles south-east of East Grinstead and runs roughly parallel to the A22 Forest Row road. It can be reached by taking the left-hand of two roads immediately opposite the car-park of the Three Crowns public house. After about 200 metres the road ends at a small industrial estate. From here a public footpath leads leftwards to the rocks.

The rocks are extensive but low – seldom reaching more than 5 metres in height. The rock is generally of poor quality and is heavily vegetated. Furthermore, the outcrop lies on private land and the area is a designated SSSI. Climbing is not allowed.

BALCOMBE MILL ROCKS   OS Ref TQ 317 305
These rocks lie about half a mile east of Balcombe, beside the road west of a small lake. The outcrop begins at a bend in the road where some shattered rocks occur in an ex-quarry. Further on the rocks are very close to the road immediately behind some farm buildings. A flight of steps carries a public footpath over the crag, which continues beyond into private land. The total length of this section is about 25 metres and its height about five metres.

The crag is on strictly private land and is signposted as such. Should access be possible there would appear to be four or five routes on two reasonably clean buttresses, although they are overgrown at the top. Elsewhere the rock tends to be lichenous.

BLOOMER'S VALLEY ROCKS   OS Ref TQ 337 318
A quarter of a mile west of the Turners Hill to Ardingly road (B2028), in the grounds of Wakehurst Place. An extensive natural outcrop, almost 1000 metres long, but too low and carrying too much vegetation for the climber. Also known as Long Wood Rocks. See also Wakehurst Place Rocks.

BLUNDS HOLE ROCKS   OS Ref TQ 412 368
A small outcrop on private land on the opposite side of the A22 from Ashurstwood Rocks. It can be reached by following the public footpath

which leads west from the road junction. It comprises a number of small buttresses in a picturesque location overlooking the eastern end of Weir Wood Reservoir. The rock is comparatively clean and free from vegetation. A pinnacle and adjacent buttress facing the field appear to offer the best chance of a route or two.

BOARSHEAD ROCKS   OS Ref TQ 538 328
These rocks are situated close to the Boarshead Inn on the Tunbridge Wells to Crowborough road. They can be easily seen from the Sussex Border Path. They comprise, in the main, a number of isolated blocks, one of which, the Loaf of Bread Rock, is close to 8 metres high. There are also numerous low walls. The entire outcrop is on private land, the most impressive parts being in the gardens of Chapel Cottage and Long House. Climbing is not possible.

CHIDDINGLYE FARM ROCKS   OS Ref TQ 350 329
A low, partially quarried, outcrop on the south side of the drive leading to Chiddinglye Farm. On private land and signposted as such.

THE CHIDDING STONE   OS Ref TQ 501 451
This is situated in the village of Chiddingstone on National Trust land. It can be approached by a short public footpath which starts from the south side of the main street, almost opposite the church. The Stone is a small boulder some three and a half metres high; a walk on one side, rather tricky on all the others.

CLAY'S WOOD ROCKS   OS Ref TQ 583 280
On private land three quarters of a mile north-north-west of Mayfield Church. A super Bulls Hollow, being also an ex-quarry, but lower, dirtier, and more(!) quaggy. Some slight possibility and much room for improvement.

CODMORE HILL FARM ROCKS   OS Ref SU 051 202
Of academic interest only due to its location some 20 miles west of all the other recorded inland climbing. A disused quarry immediately south of the minor road running due west from Codmore Hill, and just before (Codmore) Hill Farm.

Details of the climbing here first appeared in print in the 1963 guide: 'This little practice crag, an ex-quarry which was unearthed by local school parties, gives about six routes of 15 feet or so...'.

The rock is not sandstone as we know it (Jim), consisting of coarse grit and pebbles and being friable.

The quarry is used as a car-park for vehicles and agricultural plant. Much of it has been infilled with agricultural waste. It seems likely that the latter has covered up the pre-1963 climbing, but even so it is hard to imagine the climbing being much good due to the poor rock.

COOPER'S GREEN ROCKS   OS Ref TQ 475 233

A number of small buttresses situated in the centre of a triangle of roads. They are all in private gardens and completely inaccessible. Also known as Warren Rocks and Maresfield Rocks.

DENNY BOTTOM ROCKS   OS Ref TQ 568 395

These rocks are on Rusthall Common, a mile west of Tunbridge Wells and very close to Bulls Hollow Rocks.

There are numerous boulders and short rock walls adjoining the village, which give many scrambles and short climbs. Notable are the isolated rock called Denny Bottom Pinnacle, which is situated in someone's front garden (the East Face is 4b, the South Crack 5c), and the famous Toad Rock, which is fenced-off.

FURNACE FARM ROCKS   OS Ref TQ 449 400

A small outcrop on private land immediately north of a road that runs due east from Cowden, and about 200 metres east of Furnace Pond. It is 5 metres high and has several large caves at its base. Nearby is Mill Wood Quarry, a small rock exposure adjacent to a public bridleway (OS Ref TQ 442 398).

GLEN ANDRED ROCKS   OS Ref TQ 530 358

Nearly a mile south-south-west of Groombridge Station. These rocks, which are on private land, face Harrison's Rocks across the valley and are conspicuous therefrom. Here the early OS maps show an Eagle's Rock and a Ward's Rock. Sandstone is also exposed in the railway cutting nearby.

HERMITAGE ROCKS   OS Ref TQ 496 251

These rocks are located 1 1/4 miles north of Buxted Station and just south of the junction of two footpaths.

The outcrop is some 300 metres in length and 6 to 8 metres high. Its character is unusual in that the tops of the buttresses form large domes, somewhat reminiscent of the sandstone boulders of Fontainebleau. Because of negligible tree cover the outcrop is in good condition and the rock is light-coloured and lichen-free. The rock quality varies from reasonably sound to extremely poor.

The climbs range from wide middle-grade cracks to steep technical walls with thin slab finishes. Most of the obvious lines have already been done.

The rocks are on private land belonging to The Hermitage. The left-hand third of the outcrop forms the backdrop to a formal garden; it is here that the hermitage is to be found – a series of chambers hewn in the solid

Undercut Wall, 4a, Stone Farm Rocks. Climber: Teresa Hill. Photo: Ian Smith

Uganda Wall, 5c, Under Rockes. Climber: Brian Kavanagh. Photo: Ian Smith

rock. The right-hand section is in some paddocks and overlooked by stables.

Even if the access position were to change, it is hoped that these rocks would be left in their unspoilt condition so that future generations could see what all the outcrops were once like.

HOATH HOUSE ROCKS
OS Ref TQ 491 427

This lies about a mile north-east of Cowden Station, on the north side of the road and opposite Hoath House. The house itself is an extremely unusual building — well worth a quick look.

The outcrop rises straight from the road and consists of a 7- metre high vertical wall, the first two of which are utterly rotten. There is a steep 5a crack in the centre of the left-hand portion, and scope for a couple more routes. Top-roping is potentially dangerous here, as the belayer would have to stand in the road.

A little further to the east, up the hillside and on the same side of the road, are a few small, clean buttresses about four metres high. The buttress on the extreme left sports what is probably the largest stalactite/mite in the South-East.

HOMESTALL HOUSE QUARRY
OS Ref TQ 425 374

This small outcrop lies to the north of Ashurstwood, in a private garden on the west side of the road that leads from the village to the A264. It is about 6 metres high, rotten and in need of gardening, and might offer a rock-starved climber a route or two.

LAKE WOOD ROCKS
See Uckfield Rocks.

LAMPOOL FARM ROCKS
OS Ref TQ 465 255

Some low boulders in a garden on the opposite side of the B2026 from Lampool Farm, and visible from an adjacent footpath.

Close to Lampool Farm Rocks is a man-made cave, of which Courtney-Bryson said: "Speleologists and those who delight in throwing light on the dark places of the bowels of the earth, when tired of delving into the endless underground tunnels near Godstone or testing the acoustic properties of Chiselhurst Caves or the humidity of Dover Castle passages, should explore the rather curious three-roomed rock cave situated in the field on the left of the lane running through Maresfield Park, just before it debouches at the fork in the main road south of Lampool Farm. It is a snug little cave, where there is barely room to swing a mountaineer." This is now inaccessible.

LANGTON GREEN ROCKS

OS Ref TQ 542 392

At the west end of the village, north of the Groombridge road. A low sandy wall, completely overgrown, and of no climbing interest.

LEYSWOOD HOUSE ROCKS

OS Ref TQ 528 351

This outcrop is located on a private (and exclusive) housing estate on the opposite side of the valley to Harrison's Rocks. Rocks Wood is nearby and is part of the same outcrop. The rocks reach a height of 7 metres and consist of a number of clean, attractive-looking buttresses arranged around a large, grassy amphitheatre; and several deep passages, reminiscent of High Rocks. Climbing is not possible at present.

LONG WOOD ROCKS

See Bloomer's Valley Rocks.

MARESFIELD ROCKS

See Cooper's Green Rocks.

PEMBURY QUARRY

OS Ref TQ 613 413

A small outcrop on a disused road close to Pembury Hospital. A few micro-climbs may be possible.

PENNS LAKE ROCKS

OS Ref TQ 517 345

A collection of small, clean boulders close to a footpath that runs parallel to, and to the east of, the B2128, and just south of Jockey's Wood Rocks. About 100 metres to the north-east is another outcrop composed of several small, heavily vegetated buttresses (TQ 518 346).

PHILPOTS ROCKS

Another name for the rocks in the easterly valley of Chiddinglye Wood – see Minor Outcrops section.

REDLEAF HOUSE ROCKS

OS Ref TQ 523 455

Nearly half a mile south-south-east of Penshurst Station, on the southern edge of a wood facing Redleaf House, is a crag on private land. The outcrop is about 15 metres in length and 5 metres in height. It is mainly overhanging and very undercut at its base. If access were possible a couple of short uninteresting routes may be climbable on horizontal features. This outcrop is probably best left to the sheep that shelter under it.

REYNOLDS LANE QUARRY

OS Ref TQ 577 409

This is to be found on the outskirts of Tunbridge Wells on the north side of Reynolds Lane and just to the east of a sharp bend in the road. It is a quarried wall about 6 metres high and 75 metres in length and apparantly in fine condition. Unfortunately it is excessively private, enclosed by two barbed-wire fences. Squirrels' Rocks is nearby.

ROCKROBIN QUARRY
OS Ref TQ 626 333

The quarry is ¼ mile north-east of Wadhurst Station on land so private that just to get a glimpse of it is something of an achievement. It reaches a height of about 10 metres and is composed of an attractive sandy-coloured rock, which is in suprisingly good condition, considering the lush vegetation at the base of the crag. Quarrying ceased at the outbreak of World War 2 and the rock has probably weathered sufficiently since then to make climbing possible. If the access position should ever change there is scope for at least 20 steep wall climbs.

ROCKS ESTATE
See Uckfield Rocks.

ROCKS INN
OS Ref TQ 497 430

These rocks lie on private land close to The Rocks Inn in the hamlet of Hoath Corner. From the inn walk south and turn left at a fork in the road. The rocks are on the right-hand side, 100 metres further on, and seeningly on private ground behind some allotments.

The outcrop rises to just over 6 metres and comprises a fine collection of cracks and chimneys. Despite being partially shaded by trees, the rock is in fairly good condition.

The most prominent feature of the left-hand side of the outcrop is a thin dog-leg crack. To the left of this is a 5a corner-crack, whilst to the right are three routes: a wide chimney formed by a flake (4c); a sandy crack (5c,NS), finishing in the same place; and, immediately to the right, a corner-crack with an earthy finish. Across a wide slope, and past a narrow gully containing a tree, are three more routes: a 5b up the right arête of the gully; a 5b crack finishing at a tree; and a wide crack in a green recess (4b).

ROCKS WOOD
OS Ref TQ 524 351

There are a few low rock walls scattered about in this wood, some of which exceed 5 metres in height. There is also a fine isolated block – Penns Approach Pinnacle. The bridle paths in the wood are open to the public, but climbing is not permitted. The rocks extend into the grounds of the Leyswood estate; in fact Rocks Wood and Leyswood Rocks are two parts of the same outcrop.

ROCKY WOOD
OS Ref TQ 445 205

This outcrop is located on the western edge of a wood overlooking the River Ouse, about a mile south of the village of Piltdown. The best approach is to follow a public footpath eastwards from Sharpsbridge Farm until a bridge over the river is reached. From here the rocks can be seen some 100 metres away, and in the same line as the footpath. The section from the bridge to the rocks lies on private land and includes a second river crossing. The rocks themselves are 3 to 5 metres high and heavily vegetated.

ROWHILL WOOD ROCKS   OS Ref TQ 303 292
Half a mile south-south-west of Balcombe Station. There are a few small buttresses in a private wood immediately below the road on the east side.

SANDFIELD HOUSE QUARRY   OS Ref TQ 485 413
This quarry is located about ½ mile south-east of Cowden Station, on private farm land overlooking the railway line. The public footpath between the station and Sandfields Farm approaches to within 50 metres of the quarry.

The quarry reaches a height of about 7 metres and is capped by an unstable earth slope. The rock is well weathered, of sound quality and, despite the dense thicket at the bottom, is generally dry. The possibilities are: two good cracks, if someone bothers to clean them up; and at least two face climbs on small holds.

The most interesting feature of the quarry is the wall to the left of the left-hand crack. This is almost entirely devoid of features and is the smoothest wall in the South-East.

SANDHOLE WOOD QUARRY   OS Ref TQ 336 298
A quarter of a mile west of Ardingly on the north side of the Balcombe road. Provides the passing motorist with a few climbs of three to four metres, at least two of which have been done.

SANDSTONE QUARRIES
A number of sandstone quarries were listed in the 1969 guide, none of which were considered suitable for climbing for various reasons; principally, insufficient weathering. This position hasn't changed since then, but the list is included for completeness: (1) near Rotherfield (TQ 567 294) now a garden; (2) Selsfield House (1½ miles north-west of West Hoathly church) TQ 348 341, also a garden; (3) Rock Cottage (TQ 372 226) on the west side of the road in the grounds of Rock Lodge Vineyard; (4) Rocks Farm (TQ 517 284) marked on the 1-inch OS map; (5) TQ 356 312, opposite Hook Farm Quarry; (6) near Pennybridge Farm (TQ 599 281) on the east side of the road; (7) near Calkin's Mill Farm (TQ 602 281) on the east side of the road; (8) on the east side of the road between Eridge Station and Park Corner (TQ 543 350); (9) in Hawksden Park Wood (TQ 611 262); (10) at Bestbeech Hill (TQ 619 315) north-east of the crossroad; (11) immediately north of Balcombe Station (TQ 307 303); (12) near Saint Hill (TQ 383 360) north of the road; (13) near Little Strudgate Farm (TQ 330 324); (14) on the north

side of the footpath between Harrison's Rocks and Park Corner (TQ 535 353).

SHAGSWELL WOOD ROCKS   OS Ref TQ 364 332
A small rock exposure in a garden in West Hoathly village. It can be seen from the footpath which runs along the west side of Shagswell Wood.

SQUIRRELS' ROCKS   OS Ref TQ 578 407
A natural outcrop in the garden of a private house in Reynolds Lane on the outskirts of Tunbridge Wells. It is about 40 metres long, 5 metres high and is capped with a turf-dome. Reynolds Lane quarry is nearby.

STANDEN HOUSE ROCKS   OS Ref TQ 389 357
An old quarry within the grounds of Standen House, a National Trust property close to Saint Hill Green. It is about 70 metres long, 6 metres high, and is heavily overgrown at the top. If climbing was possible, there would be scope for about ten or so routes, mainly following crack lines.

STONEHURST WEST ROCKS   OS Ref TQ 345 323
This outcrop lies just below the Turners Hill to Haywards Heath road (B2028) and faces Chiddinglye Wood Rocks across the valley. A public footpath leading from the B2028 to Philpots House crosses the outcrop at an unimpressive part. Finer rock exposures occur both north and south of here, but all of it is private and completely inaccessible.

STONE MILL ROCKS   OS Ref TQ 544 264
There are one or two buttresses in an inaccessible position on a hillside above the infant River Uck. Under Rockes is nearby.

STONEWALL PARK ROCKS   OS Ref TQ 500 424
A fine outcrop just below the road to the south-east of the hamlet of Chiddingstone Hoath. The outcrop is on strictly private land and a plethora of signs make this abundantly clear.

The rock is in good condition except in the few places where it is shaded by trees. The rock quality is reasonably good although the bases of the buttresses tend to be a bit friable.

If access were ever possible the outcrop would provide up to 20 climbs of between 5 and 6 metres in length, mainly on open faces.

STRIDEWOOD SHAW ROCKS   OS Ref TQ 492 418
These are situated about a mile west of Cowden Station. Four public footpaths converge on the outcrop: two from the Bassett's Farm area, one from the station, and one from Hoath Corner. The rocks extend for about 500 metres but, as they are low, broken and excessively vegetated, they are of little interest to the climber.

TEA GARDEN COOMBE ROCKS   OS Ref TQ 559 386

Two outcrops facing each other across a narrow valley. The first, and smaller of the two, faces west and comprises a number of low buttresses of good-quality rock; a few short climbs have been done.

The second, facing east, reaches a height of 10 metres and is much more imposing. The main feature is a wickedly overhanging crack rising out of a large cave. This provides the (reputed) three-star route **Lapcka** 5c(NS). The wall to the left of the large cave is almost blank and has probably been quarried at some time in the distant past. To the left again are several good-quality buttresses. All the obvious lines, both on these and on the lesser ones at the right-hand end of the outcrop, have been climbed.

Both outcrops are on private land behind some houses. Climbing is not possible.

TILGATE WOOD ROCKS   OS Ref TQ 330 309 & 331 312

A series of low isolated buttresses in dense woodland on the west side of Ardingly Reservoir and facing Wakehurst Place across the valley. On private ground, but not excessively so. One or two short climbs have already been done and there is scope for a few more.

TOAD ROCK

See Denny Bottom Rocks.

UCKFIELD ROCKS

This outcrop lies about ½ mile to the west of Uckfield, on either side of a minor road that leads to the hamlet of Shortbridge. It is split into three distinct sections:

1. Lake Wood Rocks   OS Ref TQ 464 217

This picturesque section of the outcrop lies to the north of the road and consists of an impressive 8-metre buttress rising straight out of the lake; and several others, lesser and more vegetated, in the surrounding woodland. Other things of interest include a grotto-cum-boathouse carved out of the sandstone, and two tunnels: one cut through the rear of the main buttress and the other, partially blocked at present, burrowing underneath the road into Rocks Estate.

The wood is owned by the Woodland Trust, who, although allowing free public access, have imposed a climbing ban. Despite this, some climbs have been done. There is a 5b at the left-hand end of the main buttress; and on the wall to the right of the tunnel are two routes: a 6b(NS)† up the offset groove and crack-line, and a 5a(NS) up the blunt arête and thin crack to the right.

2. Rocks Estate   OS Ref TQ 463 216
This lies to the south of the road, seemingly on common land. It comprises
a number of low, sandy buttresses of little interest to the climber, although
some short climbs and scrambles have been done.

3. White Cottage Rocks   OS Ref TQ 469 218
A low wall, wet and vegetated, forming the back wall to a number of
private gardens on a modern housing-estate.

WAKEHURST PLACE ROCKS   OS Ref TQ 336 312
These rocks lie within the grounds of Wakehurst Place, a National Trust
property managed by the Royal Botanic Gardens, Kew. They are located
1½ miles north of Ardingly, on the west side of the road to Turners Hill
(B2028). They comprise a number of low isolated boulders on an open
hillside overlooking Ardingly Reservoir. See also Bloomer's Valley Rocks.

WARREN ROCKS
See Cooper's Green Rocks.

WELLINGTON ROCKS   OS Ref TQ 579 393
Close to Wellington Hotel on the north side of Tunbridge Wells Common.
A childrens' playground suitable for the initiation of beginners of the
youngest age group. There are one or two odd rock walls also along
the top edge of the Common, but no real climbing prospects.

WEST HOATHLY NORTH ROCKS   OS Ref TQ 358 332
Half a mile north-north-west of West Hoathly church. A small outcrop on
private land immediately below the road from West Hoathly to Turners
Hill, on its north side. The rocks are out in the open and face north across
a field. Mentioned optimistically at one time, the outcrop has only yielded
one route so far, **Icicle Crack** 4b, just right of the big overhang.
Prospects for further development are limited.

WHITE COTTAGE ROCKS
See Uckfield Rocks.

WHITESTONE HOUSE ROCKS   OS Ref TQ 363 307
This is to be found on the road that leads from West Hoathly to
Highbrook, ¼ mile north of Highbrook church. It comprises a low
quarried wall, which faces east across the road, and a higher, natural
wall, facing west behind the first. A climb or two might just be possible
on the latter if it were not so private.

WICKEN'S FARM QUARRY   OS Ref TQ 484 415
This is a small quarry situated half a mile east-south-east of Cowden
Station and 50 metres south-east of Wicken's Farm. Sandfield House
Quarry is close by.

It is 6 metres high and in very poor condition. The 'one climb' mentioned by Courtney-Bryson in his 1936 guide would seem to be a vile open corner, which is plastered with moss, has no footholds, and only one handhold – a large and dangerously unstable flake.

Lost Outcrops

The six outcrops in this chapter are ones that have been described in previous editions of the guidebook, but which the present author has been unable to locate. Included are the most informative/interesting descriptions of the outcrops and their last known grid-references. For more details of the authors referred to see the bibliography on page 268.

BUDLETT'S GREEN ROCKS   *(OS Ref TQ 47 23 – S.W. Corner)*
'Three-quarters of a mile south-south-east of Maresfield Church. Courtney-Bryson draws attention to rocks here but they are very elusive'. (Pyatt, 1956)

BUXTED ROCKS   *(OS Ref TQ 48 23 & 49 23)*
'Lucas speaks of rocks beside the road to Maresfield and Uckfield, but they seem to be rather elusive'. (Pyatt, 1956)

EAST GRINSTEAD ROCKS   *(OS Ref TQ)*
'This title serves to introduce a quotation from Lucas. The rocks in question have not been identified: "The most beautiful rocks in Sussex and perhaps in England are those near East Grinstead which Mr. Hanbury has converted into a garden and made colourful...planting it with all the most equisite and all the most vigorous of those plants that prefer a precarious footing to the security of a deep rich soil, many of them brought hither from the ends of the earth. In this precipitous paradise pious horticulturists scramble like goats, expressing as they pass recognition and emotion in long Latin names."

Though probably of little use to the climber, the scenic attractions of this outcrop, wherever it may be, would appear to be considerable'. (Pyatt, 1956)

ROCKS LANE-BUXTED   *(OS Ref S. edges of squares TQ 48 25 &*
49 25)
'One and an eighth miles north-north-west of Buxted Station. The only rocks actually discovered so far are the very miniature samples on the south side of the road at its east end – only suitable for very young aspirants. However, suggestive names like 'Rocks Wood', 'the Rocks', etc, are found on the 1:25000 OS map, which also shows some rock lines on private ground. In Topley (1875) there is a woodcut of an outcrop said to be near Rocks Farm, Buxted. Rocks Farm was the name formerly given to the house near the east end of the lane, now called

'The Rocks', and it is most likely that he was referring to Hermitage Rocks which are close by. If not, there is an outcrop here awaiting rediscovery'. (Pyatt, 1956)

ROCK WOOD-MARESFIELD   (OS Ref TQ 470 259)
'One and an eighth miles north-north-east of Maresfield. A low natural outcrop of no climbing interest'. (Pyatt, 1956)

SHEFFIELD FOREST ROCKS   (OS Ref TQ 41 25 & 41 26)
'Mantell writes of "A fine lake overhung with sandstone rock near the seat of the Earl of Sheffield in the parish of Fletching". A local inhabitant we consulted said that the rocks there are "as high as that house" indicating one of a size which would make them the highest rocks in this part of the country. Those we did find were only some ten feet high, so that all the indications point to a magnificent outcrop here awaiting discovery'. (Pyatt, 1956).

'Recently, a 25-foot buttress has materialised on the valley slope east of the lake, with a couple of possibilities for the climber, but the lofty outcrop referred to above remains as elusive as ever'. (Holliwell 1968)

Other Rock

CHALK QUARRIES
The North and South Downs and the other lesser chalk ridges are gashed at intervals by quarry workings – great and small, some active and some disused. A certain amount of climbing has been done in some of these on chalk of varying quality, requiring various specialised techniques as per the Chalk Sea Cliffs. In all cases the rock is extremely unstable and great care is required. Warlingham Quarry (OS Ref TQ 337 594) has provided a 25-metre climb, **Sandinista,** up the obvious crack in the back right-hand side of the quarry (S Shimitzu, D Cook).

WHITE ROCKS   OS Ref TQ 560 530
Some development has been recorded at White Rocks, One Tree Hill, south-east of Sevenoaks. This 8-metre outcrop lies on National Trust property and as a bird-nesting site is best avoided during spring and summer. The 'rock' is "rag with a small proportion of interbedded sand and hassock". The western, left-hand quarter of the outcrop has recently collapsed, leaving an avalanche cone of debris on the have been climbed – due to loss of holds, the climbs tend to change after each ascent.

The Sea-Cliffs of South East England

Introduction

WARNING
Chalk and the Hastings Sandstone/Clay are unstable and dangerous rocks. Most of the climbs are considerably harder undertakings than the grade alone indicates. Experience of, and the ability to handle, serious and dangerous situations are at a premium.

THE ROCK
The chalk ridges of the Weald are terminated abruptly by the sea, giving the characteristic 'white cliffs' of England. The South Downs end in the line of chalk cliffs stretching from Brighton, past the Seven Sisters and Beachy Head, to Eastbourne, whilst the North Downs give the chalk cliffs of the Dover area. In exactly the same way as the chalk, the sandstone ridges in the centre of the Weald are terminated abruptly at the south coast between Bexhill and Pett Level (5 miles east-north-east of Hastings), but here the sandstone is intermingled with clay and mud to provide a variety of different types of climbing experience.

Chalk does not form a long-lived vertical cliff as it is too soft. It needs the erosion of the waves to retain its verticality. The rock's softness varies: in the St Margaret's Bay area (Kingsdown to Dover) the chalk is soft enough to allow effective use of front-pointing ice techniques. At Beachy Head, however, a more blocky chalk structure prevails and the chalk is climbed as conventional rock.

ENVIRONMENTAL ISSUES
Due to the transitory nature of their surface the cliffs support relatively little vegetation. The cliffs west of Beachy Head have special conservation status because of their outstanding geological (chalk faces) exposures. They are also noted for their important coastal bird populations and the unusual plant communities found in the chalk

grassland on the cliff tops and the clumped areas of chalk rubble at the base of the cliff.

The marks left by ice-style climbing on chalk is causing concern in some people's minds. However, the numbers climbing chalk are relatively few and any damage is insignificant given the continuous rockfalls (as witnessed by the litany of collapsed routes mentioned in the text – not that any of these rockfalls have ever been attributed to climbers!). In fact the impact of climbers on the appearance of these cliffs is as nothing when compared to their impact on the sandstone outcrops and further afield.

NEW CLIMBS
Please send details of new climbs to Chris Mellor: ITI, 4 Barnfield Avenue, Shirley, Croydon, Surrey, CRO 8SE. Telephone number: 0181 654 5846.

EQUIPMENT AND GRADING
The grade of a climb will indicate whether it is climbed as a quasi-ice climb with crampons and axe or as a rock climb with rock boots and standard rack supplemented by a selection of rock and ice-pegs.

One obvious note of caution is that since chalk is not a very hard rock, anything smaller than an *8 Rock* sunk 6" into a crack is merely cosmetic protection. The preferred method of protection with ice pegs are wart-hogs driven in with a lump hammer. Some of the rock-style routes rely on these for protection as well, but large nuts and *Friends* should also be carried. Hanging from tools to place and remove gear is not considered unethical – you will find you need all the support you can get! As on any sea cliff, be wary of fixed gear and bear in mind the pounding that it has received to get there in the first place. Please refrain from using rebar protection and leaving it in place: it is an eyesore and could be very dangerous to anyone who fell onto it.

The climbs have not had many repeat ascents and erosion is constant. This means that the grades are approximate. Ice-style climbs are given ice grades from I to VI, with individual pitch gradings where known. Second and subsequent ascents of ice-style routes are often easier than first ascents as ice-screw and ice pick holes often already exist to both show the way and save effort.

Rock-style climbs are given an adjectival grade from Severe to Extremely Severe and, where possible, a technical grading from 4a to 6a. The old Extremely Severe grade is used in preference to E grades to reflect the serious nature of the climbing involved and the need for judgement. An Extremely Severe grade means at least E3 and in the case of the 'big three' on the walls of Beachy Head itself up to E5. Climbs that have had only one known ascent are indicated by a † symbol. Routes known to have suffered from major rockfalls are given a † † symbol, whereas those that are known to have fallen down completely are referred to in passing in the text and are not described in full.

SAFETY & RESCUE
The one certain way of causing access problems with sea-cliff climbing is if climbers put public safety at risk. For example, tourists walk along the foreshore from Dover to Kingsdown and climbers should be extremely careful not to put them at risk. If climbers get into trouble, rescue is effected via the police and coastguard services. The coastguards at the Dover Maritime Rescue Co-ordinating Centre (MRCC) should be phoned before **and** after climbing attempts on any of the sea cliffs described in this guide on 01304(Dover) 210008. Calls are logged in and a failure to report back could trigger a rescue operation. Give your name and where you will be climbing. It also helps to tell them what colour helmet and jacket you will be wearing to aid your identification from any shipping or helicopter sightings. It may seem obvious, but do not flash torches out to sea unless you are in trouble.

Access to almost every route described involves walking along tidal beaches. Check the tide times; it is not always possible to wade out.

ACCESS
A large portion of the cliffs and cliff-tops are owned by the National Trust. In the past local wardens have raised some concerns about climbing. Currently the situation is viewed as acceptable. However, if anyone approaches you, be polite, and find out the reasons for their concern and who they represent. Report any access problems to the BMC.

Historical

Perhaps surprisingly, the chalk cliffs were amongst the first in Britain to receive attention from the climber. The late 19th century Alpinists were well aware of the challenges available and regarded these cliffs as a training ground for their Alpine exploits. A F Mummery was active in the St Margaret's Bay area, where he encountered 'amongst the hardest *mauvais pas* with which I am acquainted', and Edward Whymper, perhaps the best known Alpinist of the period, also climbed occasionally on the cliffs. However, all of these early explorations kept to the steep grass and chalk slopes or the more reliable chalk below the high-tide level. It is unfortunate that no records remain of the exact achievements of the era.

A tremendous change in attitude came in the 1890s in the form of Aleister Crowley. Crowley was a leading Alpinist of the day but was shunned by the Alpine Club and took a positive delight in the bizarre. Supposedly indulgent of some notoriously perverse activities, his climbs on chalk were generally considered as just a further example of his eccentricity. On reflection his achievements are now seen to be truly remarkable for their time. As early as 1894 he climbed *Etheldreda's Pinnacle* and the even more spectacular *Devil's Chimney*, which collapsed in the 1950s (there is a photograph of Crowley's ascent in *Climbing and Walking in South-East England*). Etheldreda's Pinnacle still retains a VS grading. Still more impressive was his attempt on the soaring crack (now named after him) in the main face adjacent to the pinnacle. Although unsuccessful in his efforts, which resulted in him being rescued by the coastguard from two-thirds height, the standard of climbing to reach his high point was probably the most difficult then achieved in Britain. Crowley's enthusiasm was not blunted by the derision of the Alpine Club and he undoubtedly thrived on the criticism, producing many unreported and sadly untraceable routes.

No activity following Crowley's efforts was reported until 1969, when Tom Patey and John Cleare proved famously unsuccessful in their attempt to reach the base of Etheldreda's Pinnacle. This event undoubtedly consolidated the opinions of most climbers who considered the cliffs to be too loose and dangerous to provide any worthwhile climbing. It was nearly 90 years after Crowley's example when a small group of climbers began a more enthusiastic appraisal of this exciting area.

1979 saw Arnis Strapcans re-ascend Etheldreda's Pinnacle by a new route, and in 1980 the crack which provided the scene of Crowley's epic rescue was finally climbed by Mick Fowler, Mike Morrison and Brian Wyvill.

1981 was to prove a crucial year. In January a revolutionary precedent was set when Fowler, Chris Watts and Andy Meyers made the first true ascent of the White Cliffs of Dover. Their ascent of *Dry Ice* was noteworthy not because of extreme difficulty but because it was the first clear demonstration that ice axes and crampons could be used effectively on steep pure chalk. Unfortunately, the ascent was plagued by a determined rescue effort mounted by the coastguard and the police, which culminated in the appearance of a BBC TV crew and a feature on the national news. This publicity had a detrimental affect on further developments for two years, as climbers were reluctant to risk the wrath of the coastguard.

Throughout the rest of 1981 and 1982 Fowler transferred his attentions to the many fine lines at Beachy Head. One of his trips, in November 1982, saw the first appearance of a future key figure on the South-East sea-cliff scene, Phil Thornhill. On the same day that Fowler climbed *Vaginoff* and the first pitches up the stupendous crack in the sheer wall of Beachy Head itself, Thornhill was introduced to chalk climbing by Steve Lewis. In December, Fowler, together with Morrison and Watts, completed *Monster Crack*, and Thornhill went on to Dover, where after a brief apprenticeship of 'solo non-achievement and tidal epics' he made solo ascents of *Escape Hatch* and *Dover Patrol* (now fallen down but 'one of the best routes in the area' in the old guide).

Over the next year Thornhill was to amaze his contemporaries and become renowned for his remarkable persistence and daunting solo exploits. Frequently enduring solitary winter weekends alone and enjoying numerous night-time epics (both on and off the crag), he rekindled interest in the Dover area. The first four months of 1983 saw Thornhill spearheading frantic activity on the cliffs between St Margaret's Bay and Dover harbour. In January he joined forces with Fowler and Meyers to climb *The Birds* and *The Tube*. The former has now fallen down: on the first ascent the brick pillar that can be seen at the front of the cave was 3 metres inside the cliff. Before it was blocked, the cave could be approached by a tunnel linking it to the now bricked-up entrance in front of the beach huts. During their explorations the first ascensionists encountered many dead birds on the tunnel floor, but without head-torches they emerged in daylight to discover the birds stuck in their crampons. The 4-month period culminated with Thornhill's ascent of *The Ferryman* with Crag Jones and *Great White Fright* with Fowler and Watts, two of the first routes to be given the grade VI (Fowler's *Dry Throat* was an earlier VI, which has since fallen down). Fowler followed with *Channel Holes*, another grade VI, later in the year.

The latter part of 1983 saw Thornhill's attention move to other cliffs in the South-East. Almost always climbing roped-solo he produced two routes at Saltdean and several horrors on the sandstone cliffs at Hastings,

The Fortress, VI, Dover. Climber: Jon Lincoln. Photo: Mick Fowler

Sunday Sport, XS, Beachy Head. Climber: Francis Ramsay.
Photo: Mick Fowler

where the only climb was Fowler's lead of the 40-metre 'conventional sandstone' HVS, *Railway Crack*. The highlight of Thornhill's activities was the 1250-metre six-day traverse of *Reasons to be Fearful*, climbed with Anthony Saunders and completed in January 1984, '...our monster traverse, probably the silliest route on the silliest cliff ever climbed.' (Phil Thornhill *On The Edge 14*).

Thereafter Thornhill's interest waned somewhat and the flood of new routes slowed to a trickle in 1985 and 1986. This was really a period of consolidation with interest spreading and several new faces acquainting themselves with the cliffs by repeating the existing lines. By 1987 a brief interim guide had been written and the time was ripe for another new route boom. The year started with Fowler, Watts and Akil Chaudry climbing *Yorkie* on the Seven Sisters cliffs, which is still the only climb on those extensive cliffs. At Dover, Mark Lynden accompanied Fowler on *The Fog* before adding several fine lines of his own: *The Fortress* with Noel Craine, and *The South Face of Kent* with John Sylvester being particularly fine. Duncan Tunstall added several lines and Simon Ballantine teamed up with Andy Perkins to climb the horrifically overhanging *Dukes of Hazard*, still the only route on the cliffs between Dover and Folkestone. Thornhill returned to put up *The Furious Tax Collector*, yet another of his routes that was to collapse.

After a lessening of interest in 1988 and 1989, new activity was generated by the 1989 Southern Sandstone guide, which included a chalk section written by Fowler. 1990 saw Frank Ramsay, who in the spring of the previous year with Andy Popp had made the second ascent of Monster Crack, emerge as a major pioneer in the area. He also made a rope-solo second ascent of Yorkie, with a fall on the very loose top pitch. In March Fowler, Ramsay and Steve Sustad alternated leads on *Sunday Sport*, a very big extreme at Beachy Head to the west of the lighthouse, 140 metres long and with 6a climbing. A few days later Fowler and Saunders climbed *Demolition Men* up a spectacular 30-metre pinnacle formed by a large landslide east of Etheldreda's Pinnacle during the previous winter (which also demolished two more of Thornhill's 1983 routes) – their ascent was well-timed as the pinnacle was demolished the following week by the Council with a ball-and-chain. Ramsay and Doug Smith put up *Flying Doctor*, a grade VI, at Dover in the same month. Ramsay and Fowler returned to the big walls of Beachy Head in November and climbed *Passion Flake*, whilst in the same area Andy Wielochowski climbed *The Ghost*, which he gave the thought-provoking grade of E1 4c.

Fowler did four new routes in 1991 and the year saw the arrival of Dave Wills, who partnered Fowler on *Mr Angry*. Danuska Rycerz and Duncan Hornby also appeared in the 1991 new route listings putting up more routes in 1992. Also that year, Wills and Hornby completed *Space Odyssey*, a notable grade VI at Dover. Trevor Brady and Adrian Trendall put up *White Man in Hammersmith Palais* in January 1992, repeated eight or nine other routes and then put up four hard new climbs in 1993. Their activities culminated in *Jive Chalkin'*: their ascent featured broken picks as well as a chopped rope, and they graded it VI+ with a serious top pitch (within two years the route had fallen down). Also in 1993 Fowler put up *Some Like it Hot* with Jones at Dover on a very warm day in July. In October Wills climbed *Rampant Erosion* with Matt Kingsley: the 'ramp' fell off alongside Wills as he was climbing the headwall, just missing Kingsley.

Saltdean had seen little if any activity since Thornhill's two routes there in 1983. Two routes were put up in 1992: *Prunes* and *Exlax*. Wielochowski added several lines to the cliff, such as *The Bill*, *Jailhouse Rock* and *Lime Wall*, between December 1993 and May 1994, and continued with a further three in early 1995, including the three-star *The Greenhouse Effect*.

Sea-cliff climbing in the South-East is now coming of age with 15 years having passed since the start of the 'modern' phase. Although the numbers are small, and will probably continue to be so, new climbers continue to come forward to accept the challenges. The scope for development is almost unlimited with large sections of unclimbed chalk, and then there's Hastings....

Margate

MARGATE   OS Ref TR 347 708
The cliffs here are too small to give any important routes, but two climbs have been recorded. Between Birchington and Westgate is a stretch of low cliffs with a concrete walkway at its base. At low tide an obvious deep chimney can be seen with a distinctive overhang formed by a horizontal layer of chalk.

1 Margate Chimney   15 metres   Difficult
Climb the chimney direct.

2 Tiny White Tremble   15 metres   IV
Climb the groove-line just left of the chimney.
P Thornhill 1983

RAMSGATE   OS Ref TR 389 652
Several short routes were top-roped on the cliffs above the ferry terminal
by Chris Adye, Duncan Hornby and Stephen Jones in September 1990.
These convenient routes with *in-situ* belays on the park railings above
provided some interest for Sunday strollers. However, the police were
called and the offenders were asked to move to a more discrete crag
above the beach. It would seem sensible to stay away from the chalk
directly above roads or footpaths.

Dover   OS Ref TR 380 470 to 340 421

Come on, sir; here's the place: stand still. How fearful
And dizzy 'tis to cast one's eyes so low!
The crows and choughs that wing the midway air
Show scarce so gross as beetles; half way down
Hangs one that gathers sampire, dreadful trade!
Methinks he seems no bigger than his head.
The fishermen that walk upon the beach
Appear like mice, and yond tall anchoring bark
Dimish'd to her cock, her cock a bouy
Almost too small for sight. The murmuring surge,
That on th'unnumber'd idle pebbles chafes,
Cannot be heard so high. I'll look no more,
Lest my brain turn, and the deficient sight
Topple down headlong.

King Lear Act IV Scene VI

The climbs lie on the 4-mile stretch of cliffs from Kingsdown to Dover,
which is broken only by the beach at St Margaret's at Cliffe. The climbing
is described from north-east to south-west (right to left).The distances
given along the foot of the cliffs are at best estimates and should not be
relied upon too greatly. As will be seen from the text, rockfalls are a
constant feature of these cliffs, and there is no guarantee that any
particular climb described below will exist at the time of reading. One
by-product of the rockfalls can be that the piles of debris at the foot of

the cliff are useful as identifying features, but these too are liable to be swept away by the sea and their presence or otherwise should not be relied upon. All of the cliffs in this area are to a greater or lesser extent tidal.

KINGSDOWN TO ST MARGARET'S
The most easterly routes lie on the Kingsdown to St Margaret's Bay cliffs. Approaching via the firing range at Kingsdown, after approximately 700 metres, an obvious feature is a very smooth east-facing, brown, slabby, wall. About 250 metres east of this is a distinctive small cave at 9 metres.

1 French Tickler 48 metres V/VI
A deceptively difficult route. Start directly below the small cave.
1   9 metres.   Climb to the cave with no special difficulty.
2   18 metres.   Move left for 6 metres and surmount the overhanging wall at its steepest point.
3   21 metres.   A serious pitch. Ascend steeply right to reach grass tufts and proceed direct on precarious ground to the top. A hawthorn bush provides a convenient belay.
M Fowler, C Watts (AL), 8 January 1984

★★ 2 The Great Escape 37 metres III
An excellent route being both straightforward and safe – for chalk. Start 100 metres west of an obvious headland that stands out below the high water mark. Its base is impassable 4 hours either side of high tide. An obvious rubble gully can be seen at the top of the cliff; the route starts below and to the left of this. Surmount the bulge in the corner and climb across the slab finishing up the gully.
M Kingsley, D Hornby, 29 February 1992

3 Rampant Erosion 55 metres V†
This climbs an obvious narrow ramp formed by a right-facing corner that trends leftwards. It is a deceptive route and starts by a small hole below a small vegetated bay.
1   9 metres.   Climb up to the bay and belay well to the right.
2   46 metres.   Climb the ramp to a steep finish, moving right in the last 3 metres.
D Wills, M Kingsley, 10 October 1993

Three hundred metres west of the previous route and half a mile east of St Margaret's Bay is a poor route which takes a line up the most easterly of two grass slopes capped by a 9-metre rock wall:

4 Oily Bird 85 metres IV†
Start at the bottom left-hand corner of the grass slope.

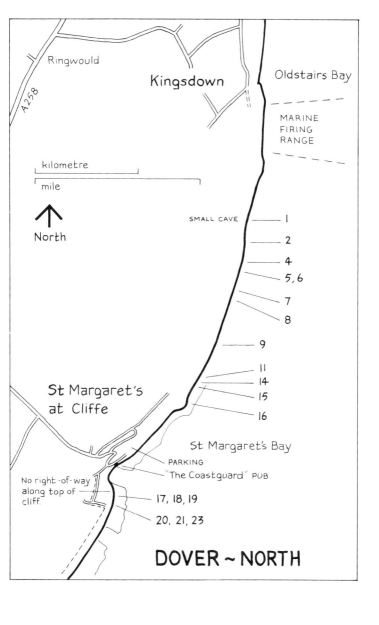

Ringwould

A258

Kingsdown

Oldstairs Bay

MARINE
FIRING
RANGE

kilometre

mile

↑
North

SMALL CAVE — 1

— 2

— 4

5, 6

7

8

9

11

14

15

16

St Margaret's
at Cliffe

St Margaret's Bay

PARKING

"The Coastguard" PUB

No right-of-way
along top of
cliff.

17, 18, 19

20, 21, 23

DOVER ~ NORTH

1 70 metres. Ascend chalk for 8 metres to gain the grass, which is followed diagonally rightwards, choosing the easiest line, to reach the highest point.
2 15 metres. Move up left on tufty grass for 8 metres, then climb directly to the top just right of a line of disintegrating flakes.
M Fowler, P Thornhill, 13 January 1983

5 Even Better than the Real Thing 75 metres V
A direct approach to the 'tube' of *The Real White Cliffs Experience*. Start at the chalk scar which forms a break in the lower overhangs.
1 15 metres. Move up and make a hard step right and continue right until you can move up and gain a ramp. Move up left to belay below overhangs at the base of a jammed block.
2 30 metres. Climb the right side of the jammed block then traverse left to a corner and up to a good foot-ledge. Move up mixed ground and a slab to belay at the base of the tube.
3 30 metres. Climb the tube to a stake belay.
T Brady, A Trendall, 16 January 1993.

★**6 The Real White Cliffs Experience** 118 metres IV†
A significantly better and cleaner route than appearances would suggest. The man-made 'tube' high on the cliff west of *Oily Bird* provides the aim of this route.
1 44 metres. Climb up good chalk and then trend right, staying as low as possible.
2 44 metres. Continue in a rising line to belay at the base of the tube.
3 30 metres. Climb the tube to a stake belay.
D Hornby, D Barlow (VL) J Lay, 16 February 1992

Continuing west along the beach, a prominent feature is a very fine groove in the arête 700 metres east of St Margaret's Bay. It is unusual in that the upper section sports an obvious crack. Another, less obvious groove lies 30 metres east along the seaward face. The following route takes the less obvious groove:

7 Houdini 64 metres VI
A fine, serious climb which is rather dangerous as pitch 2 still boasts some loose rock, which has a tendency to land on the second. Start slightly right of the line of the groove on a large grassy ledge at 9 metres.
1 21 metres. Ascend relatively easy ground followed by an overhanging wall, which gives access to a left-trending ramp leading to the foot of the corner.
2 43 metres. Climb the corner to the top. The interest is sustained but a loose 9-metre section at mid-height provides the crux. A fine

pitch.
M Fowler, D Hamilton, 14 January 1989

★ **8 The Time Warp** *77* metres V
This climb takes the obvious groove mentioned above.
1   34 metres.   Climb for 12 metres to beneath a clean-cut roof; traverse right, round the roof, and ascend to a good stance.
2   43 metres.   Climb easily up the scoop, trending slightly left. After 21 metres the wall steepens to vertical and becomes loose. Climb up into the corner for 3 metres and then traverse left out of the corner to finish up the face.
S Ballantine, B Murphy (AL), 1 November 1987

★★ **9 Into the Groove** *76* metres V
A fine route. Start directly below the groove.
1   37 metres.   Ascend rightwards on conglomerate rock and vegetation and then back left on a fine clean chalk ramp to belay at the base of the groove.
2   30 metres.   Climb the steep (overhanging in places) groove to an easing of the angle at 21 metres. A further 9 metres of looser ground leads to a surprisingly good ledge on the right arête.
3   9 metres.   Move back into the groove, which is climbed first on the left wall then on the right to the top.
M Fowler, M Lynden (AL), 21 December 1986

10 The Corner Shop *75* metres V†
This takes the corner high in the cliff 30 metres right of *More Neck...*
1   21 metres.   As for that route.
2   30 metres.   Trend right across grass to the foot of the corner.
3   24 metres.   Climb the corner, trending right 5 metres below the top to finish on the right arête.
D Donovan, P Waters, November 1994. *Only the top pitch was climbed after an approach by abseil.*

★ **11 More Neck than Simon Ballantine** *70* metres IV/V
Approximately 100 metres further towards St Margaret's Bay is an arête bounded on its right-hand side by a grey slab in its lower third. Start in the centre of the grey slab.
1   21 metres.   Climb directly up the slab.
2   49 metres.   Move up leftwards and follow the increasingly loose right-hand side of the arête to the top. It is possible to split the pitch by belaying some 9 metres from the top at the point where the loose material ends.
S Ballantine, M Nicholson 4 November 1984 (final moves top-roped in the dark). D Tunstall, A Wood 21 September 1986 (without top-rope).

12 Brain Dead 73 metres V†

The corner left of the previous route.

1 49 metres. Climb the slab directly below the corner. A good pitch.

2 24 metres. Climb the corner by its left wall to avoid loose chalk.

D Donovan, G Owen, 19 February 1994

Left (west) of More Neck... is a steep face shaped like an isosceles triangle. The next route attacks this face, starting right of the centre line. On the left of the face is a slabby area.

13 White Sail 71 metres V†

1 37 metres. Ascend straight up for about 18 metres, and then go left to belay on a ledge on an arête.

2 34 metres. Go around the arête and then ascend its left side to the top, climbing in balance all the way.

Pitch 1: R Mear, 1988. Pitch 2: R Mear and a Polish party, June 1988

14 Loose Living 70 metres III†

This route climbs the rubble and grass slope to the left of the above route.

1 15 metres. Climb directly up the mudslide, surmount the grassy bulge and belay on the right. No protection.

2 20 metres. Move up the groove to belay where it steepens.

3 35 metres. Climb the corner to the top.

Variation

1a 20 metres. Follow pitch 1 for 5 metres, then traverse right onto the slab under the vertical wall. Move up and back left, climb up the left edge of the wall and move around the arête to belay as above.

D Hornby, D Rycerz, 9 February 1992. *The original start was covered by a mudslide around 1993/94.* Starts as described: G Whittaker, C Holder; M Kingsley, S Jones.

15 La Cicciolina 75 metres III†

A line to the left of *Loose Living* and similarly unpleasant.

1 40 metres. Climb the ramp and surmount a grassy cornice (problematical). Belay up on the slab.

2 35 metres. Climb the flaky, steepening, vegetated slab to the top. Belay in bushes.

D Rycerz, M Kingsley, December 1992

The following route is entered for historical reasons only, as climbing in this area could seriously endanger future access to the cliffs in general. On the first ascent a lot of debris was dislodged onto the garage of one of the houses which housed the owner's Rolls-Royce.

16 Rich Bitch 46 metres IV†

Above the houses at the east end of the St Margaret's Bay car-park is a slab with an obvious TV aerial at the top. Climb the slab to the aerial.

J Lay, A Fanshawe, 7 November 1984

ST MARGARET'S BAY TO DOVER

The climbs at the eastern end are best approached from the car-park at St Margaret's. The climbs from *The Fortress* (route No 37) onwards are closer to the Dover end of the cliff, and these can be approached by descending the zigzag steps at Langdon Bay. The top of the steps is a 30-minute walk from Dover – discretion is advised with parking cars as climbers have been prevented from climbing by various officials. The walk leads from the National Trust car-park across or around a hummocky dip to the top of the steps at the top of the zigzag path. The path ends some 5 metres above the beach at an entrance into the cliff that leads to three look-out posts. As at April 1995 a new-looking fixed ladder and an older knotted hawser were in place to assist the final descent to the beach, but these should not be relied upon and an abseil may be necessary. It should be possible to regain the ledge with the use of combined tactics or ice gear at a reasonable level of difficulty if necessary. Access to the foreshore is not possible through the ferry port terminal.

From the Coastguard Pub at St Margaret's Bay walk 150 metres west along the beach to reach the pile of rocks which formed the now-collapsed routes of Catwalk and The Birds. Just around the corner is a man-made cave and brick pillar at 15 metres, where The Birds used to belay, although these may not survive much longer (and their collapse could well affect the top pitch of Dry Ice). Above and to the left is the prominent grey ramp-line of Dry Ice.

When topping out on any of the routes in the first 100 metres along the beach, be discrete. If you arrive in open fields, follow the path that goes inland of the cliffside properties and then back to the car-park. If you are finishing between the beach and Mr Angry keep a very low profile. Do not enter the gardens. Follow the line of the old coast path down to the right. You will have to negotiate brambles, barbed wire and a fence panel across the path, and should emerge at the steps above the pill box. It need hardly be added that there is no right-of-way.

17 Life Begins at 30 39 metres IV

Start by a big block 5 metres left of the cave.

1 24 metres. Climb the scoops, exiting left at the top to belay on *Dry Ice*.

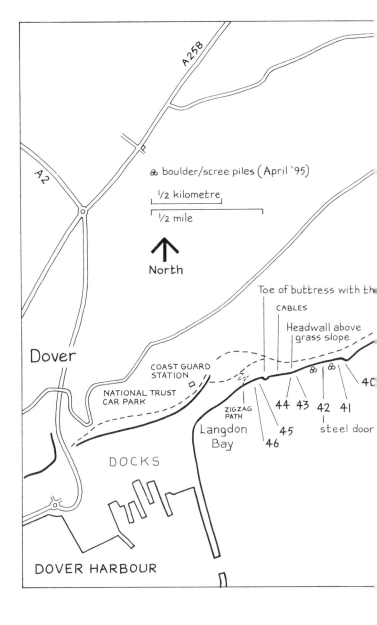

A258

A2

⚘ boulder/scree piles (April `95)

½ kilometre

½ mile

↑ North

Toe of buttress with th

CABLES

Headwall above grass slope

Dover

COAST GUARD STATION

NATIONAL TRUST CAR PARK

ZIGZAG PATH

Langdon Bay

DOCKS

44 43 42 41 40

45

46

steel door

DOVER HARBOUR

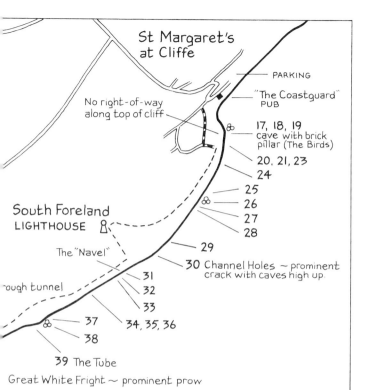

St Margaret's
at Cliffe

PARKING

"The Coastguard" PUB

No right-of-way
along top of cliff

17, 18, 19
cave with brick
pillar (The Birds)

20, 21, 23
24

25
26
27
28

South Foreland
LIGHTHOUSE

The "Navel"

29

30 Channel Holes ~ prominent
crack with caves high up.

31
32
33

34, 35, 36

rough tunnel

37
38

39 The Tube

Great White Fright ~ prominent prow

just above beach

DOVER ~ MAIN AREA

2 15 metres. Finish as for *Dry Ice*.
C Adye, D Rycerz, 20 January 1991

★★ 18 The Plank 42 metres V†
The previous route is bordered on the left by an overhanging arête
offering a sporting challenge.
1 21 metres. Start directly below the arête and climb the left-hand
side, which emerges onto the slab after 12 metres. Move up left to
belay on *Dry Ice*.
2 21 metres. Follow *Dry Ice* to the narrow traverse. Climb up into a
shallow niche, move up left passing a small roof, then finish
rightwards up a vague ramp.
D Hornby, D Wills (AL), 15 December 1991 & 1 February 1992

★★ 19 Dry Ice 54 metres III
The original route of the cliffs is justifiably popular and provides an
excellent introduction to the area, although it is harder now than it
used to be due the bucket footholds on the traverse having been worn
away. Start at the foot of the prominent grey ramp-line slanting from
left to right 6 metres left of the previous route.
1 24 metres. Pull over a short bulge to gain the ramp. Climb the
left-bounding corner for 15 metres before traversing right to a good
stance.
2 30 metres. Follow a rising traverse to where the ramp narrows,
continuing rightwards to reach an obvious exit onto the grass. Belay
stake.
M Fowler, C Watts (AL), A Meyers, 4 January 1981

20 Sound Effects 43 metres IV/VI
The obvious ramp-line just left of *Dry Ice* with a loose exit. Climb the
ramp easily to a desperate finish direct up the short headwall. An
alternative easier finish, *The Inevitable Plastic Inflatable Finish*, takes a
line just right of the original on the headwall and reduces the overall
grade to IV.
M Lynden, K Slevin, D McDonald, M Moss, 8 March 1987.
Alternative finish: Leeds University Group, 1987

21 Mr Angry 45 metres V
To the left of *Sound Effects* is an orange-coloured cave. Start 5 metres
west of the cave at a steep shallow corner.
1 30 metres. Follow the corner to reach a terrace and belay on the
right.
2 15 metres. Step right and climb a corner-flake, finishing to the
right at the top.
M Fowler, D Wills (AL), 20 January 1991

★**22 Old Red Eyes** 54 metres V

Start 20 metres west of *Mr Angry*, at a prominent groove starting from a small cave on the beach, the left wall of which is reddish in colour.

1 24 metres. Climb the left wall of the groove until it fades away into steeper rock.

2 30 metres. Traverse left and move up the second groove. Follow this to loose vertical walls and move 5 metres right before ascending these to the top.

M Fowler, J Lincoln (AL) 18 October 1987

23 Vulgar Armadillo 54 metres V

Start 20 metres west of *Old Red Eyes* at a left-slanting line of weakness leading into an open groove/corner.

1 24 metres. Climb up leftwards into the corner and follow this to a difficult pull onto a ledge. Traverse this to a stance at the right-hand end of the overhanging wall above.

2 30 metres. Climb straight up then trend left to the foot of the finishing groove. Climb this, exiting right at the top.

M Fowler, S Sustad (AL), 21 January 1991

24 Careless Chalk Costs Lives 60 metres VI†

Start just over 100 metres west of *Sound Effects*.

1 30 metres. Go up a short wall into a corner and continue up this until a loose move left is followed by a pull up onto a wall. Go over to the right and up the wall to a ledge (possible belay). Climb up the flaky wall to belay on a very steep slab.

2 30 metres. Move left and climb a short wall, then move up and right on poor chalk to hard moves up and left to gain a slab/ramp. Climb this leftwards and ascend direct to the top, where there is a twin stake belay.

T Brady, A Trendall (AL) 30/31 January 1993

The next obvious feature used to be a grassy groove/gully climbed by Lunchtime Gully. This has now fallen down leaving a smooth slide with a large scree pile at the bottom. The White Knight used to take the slab and vertical headwall to the right of where the gully used to be. Desperate Dan takes the slab immediately right of the slip and The Chalker Spur is to the right of that.

25 The Chalker Spur 61 metres V†

Start to the right of *Desperate Dan*.

1 46 metres. Move up detritus and, at 6 metres, climb up and right onto a 'buttress'. Follow this direct to the headwall.

2 15 metres. Climb the headwall.

T Brady, A Trendall (AL), 24 January 1993

26 Desperate Dan *57* metres V
1 15 metres. Scramble up the detritus, moving right to belay at the foot of the groove in the slab.
2 30 metres. Follow the groove to belay below the headwall.
3 12 metres. The headwall provides an interesting finish.
Variation
3a From the belay trend right to the obvious crackline, which provides a sporting finish.
D Rycerz, D Hornby, 2 & 16 June 1991 *pitch 3 was originally done with aid*. Pitch 3a: G Whittaker, C Holder, 31 January 1993

★★**27 The Kiss** *61* metres V/VI††
This route is vaguely distinguishable as a very large 'X' with its centre halfway up the cliff. Start just left of the scree at the bottom right arm of the 'X'. The top pitch has lost what used to be an 'absorbing cornice finish'.
1 43 metres. Climb up leftwards to the centre of the 'X'. Ascend 6 metres on the right-hand ramp above to a belay.
2 18 metres. Climb the loose ramp above to the headwall.
D Tunstall, M Fowler (AL), J Lincoln, 11 December 1988

★★**28 Great Exploit** *60* metres V
Twenty metres west of *The Kiss* is a long slab bordered on the left by a steep rightward-trending ramp-line which begins with a short wall. A varied and interesting route.
1 18 metres. Climb the wall with difficulty and make a rising traverse left to belay at the foot of the tufty ramp-line.
2 24 metres. Delightful climbing takes the steep right-trending ramp. Belay below a prominent flake at the top of the ramp.
3 18 metres. Make a slightly rising traverse right for 12 metres and finish delicately up a vague groove.
M Fowler, A Saunders (AL), 22 December 1991

29 The Flying Doctor *78* metres VI
Five hundred metres west of *The Kiss*, past a grassy section of cliff, and 150 metres east of *Channel Holes*, is a rounded buttress with a prominent loose-looking left-facing groove at the top in its centre. Start below the centre of the buttress at the right-hand end of a grassy ledge at 2 metres. A superb route.
1 30 metres. Move onto the ledge and climb directly up via a shallow groove to a flinty scoop. Exit onto a slab and belay at the top of this on a good ledge in a short corner.
2 24 metres. Step out left and climb straight up steeply to a slab. Climb to its top and traverse right for 5 metres to an uncomfortable belay below a very steep, grey, blocky wall.
3 24 metres. Traverse right to below the steep groove and climb its

steep wall until 9 metres from the top, when the actual groove is climbed. Although loose-looking, this pitch is fairly solid.
D Smith, F Ramsay (VL), 10 March 1990

★★★ **30 Channel Holes** 78 metres VI
Three hundred and fifty metres west of *The Kiss* is a prominent rightward-trending crackline ending in a series of caves near the top of the cliff. Stepping back from the foot of the cliff, it can be seen that the crack forks at about 60 metres to form a letter 'Y'. This excellent route takes the right-hand fork. Start 9 metres right of the foot of the fault-line at a leftward-leaning corner.
1 30 metres. Climb the left wall of the corner for 9 metres and move diagonally left between small bulges to gain the fault-line after 20 metres. Continue up the fault-line to belay on a small grassy ledge.
2 12 metres. Climb the slabby ramp to a small overhang and continue, to belay in a constricted cave.
3 24 metres. Continue in the same line to a large cave at 21 metres. Pull over the overhang to a smaller cave.
4 12 metres. Surmount the overhang above to gain a ledge. Move right for 2 metres before taking a direct line up the loose material forming the final wall.
Variation
Left-hand Finish 30 metres V
Belay just below the fork of the 'Y'. Climb the chimney that forms the left fork to the top.
M Fowler, C Watts (AL), N Bankhead, 25 September 1983. Left-hand Finish: F Ramsay, D Smith, 21 January 1990

About 400 metres west of Channel Holes is a very smooth wall easily identified by a prominent shallow cave (the Navel) at 27 metres.

★★★ **31 South Face of Kent** 82 metres VI
An excellent and very sustained route, which climbs the shallow groove snaking its way up one of Dover's most impressive walls. Start by a short groove, with an overhang low down, below the grass slopes right of the wall. The start is marked by a small 'S'.
1 27 metres. Climb to the left of the overhang onto a grassy ramp and then straight up to the cave of the Navel. It is advisable to carry a ⅔ metre stake to belay in the cave.
2 34 metres. Exit from the cave on the left and then trend up and left to gain the shallow groove. Follow this until it is possible to take a hanging stance on good, well-spaced, ice-screws.
3 21 metres. Climb up the groove, trending generally leftwards and

then straight up to finish.
M Lynden, J Sylvester, D Tunstall (VL) D Tunstall not present on day 3,
7-9 November 1987

About 100 metres west of South Face of Kent *is an obvious groove ending just above an overhang at 10 metres. This gives the start of* The Fog.

★★32 **Space Odyssey** 72 metres VI†

Some 30 metres right of *The Fog* is a steep wall capped by a row of roofs, which form the edge of a large terrace at mid-height with a superb corner marking its right-hand end. Start slightly left of a line directly below the corner. A wild excursion on excellent chalk.
1   27 metres.   Trend slightly right up the bulging wall, passing a shallow niche (rest) above a bulge at 15 metres, and step around the short arête just below the top. Continue, to gain the terrace immediately right of the roofs and directly below the corner. Move up the slab to a good stance.
2   15 metres.   Climb the slab and belay just left of the corner.
3   30 metres.   Climb the corner on hard chalk, moving onto the right wall at the bulge and continue to the top.
D Wills, D Hornby (VL), 8 December 1991 & 2 February 1992

★★33 **The Fog** 75 metres VI

A very fine route with a serious finish.
1   27 metres.   Climb the groove to the overhang; this is passed by moving onto the arête on the left. Move back right across the overhung ledge forming the top of the overhang and belay at the foot of a steep, smooth, right-trending ramp/slab.
2   24 metres.   Climb the ramp to overhangs and move right to belay on the arête, which is actually the left edge of an area of tufty ground stretching rightwards to a prominent corner with a crack at the back cleaving the upper part of the cliff – the top pitch of *Space Odyssey*.
3   24 metres.   Ascend the wall with projecting flints, trending left until it is possible to step left onto very loose ground, which leads in 6 metres to the final overhangs. Traverse horizontally left for 6 metres, the last 3 being overhanging (and overhanging the base of the cliff), until it is possible to pull over onto a slab leading to the top.
M Fowler, M Lynden (AL), 8 February 1987

About 400 metres west of The Fog *is a grassy slope protected by a 15-metre wall. Three climbs start from here:*

34 **White Man in Hammersmith Palais** 96 metres IV/V†

An alternative way of reaching the first belay of *Escape Hatch* climbing good quality chalk. Start in the centre of the wall right of

Escape Hatch.
1   21 metres. Go up 5 metres and then traverse a slab to the left for
3 metres. Now go up again for 3 to 5 metres to a ramp and follow
this slightly rightwards to a point underneath a small roof in a corner.
Pull round to the right (hard) onto a steep pebbly wall and traverse
across this rightwards to the first belay of *Escape Hatch.*
2   75 metres. As for *Escape Hatch* or *No Surrender.*
T Brady, A Trendall, 19 January 1992

*Escape Hatch has little merit and was first climbed as an escape from
an incoming tide. The start to it and No Surrender has changed since
the first ascent, making it more difficult than it used to be.*

35 Escape Hatch   98 metres IV
1   23 metres. Move up easily for a few metres until it is necessary to
traverse steeply right to a resting place. Climb back up left to gain the
left edge of the vegetated slope.
2   75 metres. Hack rightwards through the jungle, then continue up
the grassy slope to where a steepening on worrying, tufty vegetation
leads to a final easy exit chimney.
P Thornhill (solo), 13 December 1982

36 No Surrender   108 metres IV
1   23 metres. As for *Escape Hatch.*
2   18 metres. Climb a short wall and follow easier-angled vegetated
ground into a shallow depression.
3   27 metres. Traverse delicately rightwards to a steep rib. Climb
the rib and move left to belay at the foot of a corner.
4   40 metres. Climb the corner and follow a ramp to finish.
D Tunstall, S Brookes, 8 February 1987.

*About 200 metres further east is a grey shield-like formation rising to
half-way up the cliff. This is all that remains of Dover Patrol, the debris
at its foot having long been washed out to sea. Continuing on for some
450 metres towards Dover is one of the most unmistakable features on
the cliffs – a man-made 1.5-metre-wide, parallel-sided chimney which
cuts deep into the top of the cliff. This is taken by The Tube.*

★★★ 37 The Fortress   104 metres VI
Approximately 150 metres east of *The Tube* are two buttresses with a
shallow depression between them, which is more prominent in the
upper section of the cliff. Start from the beach directly beneath the
depression, just west of an old grass/chalk slide. A small letter 'F' is
carved in the rock. An extremely fine and varied climb.
1   43 metres. Climb straight up for 12 metres before trending left to
enter the obvious depression-line. Follow this steeply and continue

delicately on more unstable ground to a ledge on the left beneath obviously solid ground.
2 24 metres. Traverse 3 metres right and climb up for 18 metres (just left of poorer quality chalk) before traversing 3 metres right to belay.
3 37 metres. Move back left and climb up steeply on flaky chalk to gain a depression beneath a disjointed crackline. Step right and continue to the top. A hard pitch.
M Lynden, N Craine, 8 March 1987

38 The Cormorant 104 metres IV/V††
The first pitch has collapsed. Start 120 metres east of *The Tube* in a small cave at the foot of a rightward-trending ramp leading to the bottom right-hand corner of a large grassy depression.
1 43 metres. Climb the ramp to an obvious narrowing, which gives the crux. Above this, move left to a large ledge.
2 43 metres. Climb up left, then trend right into a vague gully-line leading to a niche beneath a steepening.
3 18 metres. Make a detour to the right to avoid 'dinner-plating' chalk and regain the gully above, which is followed to the top – or climb the 'dinner-plating' direct at a higher standard.
P Thornhill (roped solo), 6 March 1983

★★**39 The Tube** 95 metres IV
A good route up a prominent, interesting feature. Start at a short steep wall directly below the tube proper.
1 37 metres. Climb straight up, then move left just below the tube and then back right to belay at the foot of the chimney.
2 58 metres. Continue up the chimney using a wide variety of techniques and passing a number of man-made obstacles *en route*.
P Thornhill, M Fowler (AL), A Meyers, 8 January 1983

About 200 metres west of The Tube *is a striking and highly impressive prow, which is climbed by one of the most spectacular routes in the area,* The Great White Fright.

★★★**40 The Great White Fright** 88 metres VI
A magnificent route on very steep chalk. Start 5 metres left of the arête.
1 30 metres. Climb to a small ledge at 5 metres. Ascend diagonally rightwards and swing round the arête to gain a shallow depression. Follow this trending slightly right and surmount a gently overhanging bulge on the left to gain a good stance on the arête itself.
2 21 metres. Follow the leftward-trending ramp with increasing difficulty to a superb stance on a dubious pillar.
3 37 metres. Climb the white overhanging wall above, trending

slightly rightwards to beneath large, square-cut overhangs. Cross the
thin crack on the right and climb the grey shield of rock for 6 metres
until it is possible to move out left onto the wall above the overhangs.
Continue directly to the top. A phenomenal pitch.
P Thornhill, M Fowler, C Watts (VL), 23/24 April 1983 (Watts did
not climb Pitch 3)

★★ **41 The Ferryman** 73 metres VI
This excellent route climbs the shallow depression immediately left of
The Great White Fright. Start 15 metres left of that route.
1 34 metres. Climb to a ledge at 3 metres then continue to the
right-hand end of a grassy ledge above. From the left end of this
climb steeply left and then back right to follow a vague groove on
dubious rock to the foot of a shattered pillar.
2 18 metres. Traverse round the pillar and ascend its right-hand
side to a rubble-covered ledge.
3 21 metres. The vertical wall above is climbed trending slightly
leftwards to the top.
P Thornhill, C Jones (AL), 12/13 March 1983

Some 75 metres left of The Great White Fright *is a large pile of boulders
which used to give* Jive Chalkin' *and* The Furious Tax Collector.

42 Fisherman's Friend 61 metres V
An obvious feature in the cliff is a steel-plated door inset a metre
above the shingle (whose level can vary considerably) some 125
metres west of *The Great White Fright*. This route takes a right-to-left
slanting line above the door. Start 5 metres right of the door.
1 18 metres. Climb the deceptively steep left wall of a groove until
the angle eases slightly and, after a further 3 metres, traverse left for
3 metres to a belay ledge.
2 37 metres. Continue left on dubious chalk to cross a small loose
overhang and gain the toe of a prominent grass-tufted ramp, which
leads more easily to a belay below the final wall.
3 6 metres. The final wall – a convenient bush provides a belay
well back.
M Lynden, M Fowler (AL), 1 February 1987

The next route was Dry Throat, *which began 25 metres west of the steel
door and is now a pile of boulders at the foot of the cliff.*

*Approaching from the west, the foreshore walk passes the toe of a
buttress some 165 metres east of the zigzag path. The toe has a
through-tunnel which must be squeezed past to get through. This point
is impassable at mid to high tide. Some 100 metres east of this the cliff*

falls back in a shallow bay with long strands of cable hanging over the edge on the west side. To the right of these cables, the cliff consists of a short rock step at sea-level, a long intermediate grassy slope, and a grey headwall approximately 46 metres high. This headwall has two prominent rightwards-slanting grooves in its centre. Dover Soul takes the right-hand groove, having approached it from the lower wall and grass.

43 Dover Soul   121 metres   V

Start some 400 metres west of *Fisherman's Friend*.
1   46 metres.   Climb anywhere to reach the vegetated slope, which is ascended via a shallow leftward-leaning depression.
2   30 metres.   Traverse right and move up a vague groove to the foot of the upper wall.
3   15 metres.   Follow the ramp, passing a cave on the left, and take a hanging belay on warthogs.
4   30 metres.   Continue steeply up the ramp to the top.
P Thornhill, J Tinker, 22/23 January 1983

44 Some Like it Hot   125 metres   V†

This route takes the obvious groove-line running all the way up the cliff 30 metres left of *Dover Soul*. Fine varied climbing.
1   46 metres.   Climb an earth-bank to gain mixed ground and the start of the depression-cum-groove. Follow this on mixed ground to the belay.
2   43 metres.   Continue up mixed ground to the foot of a wall. Climb this into the upper groove and continue to a good cave belay.
3   18 metres.   Continue up the groove on the right to a belay.
4   18 metres.   Follow the groove to the top.
M Fowler, C Jones, 4 July 1993

45 Sentiera Luminosa   137 metres   IV/V†

The quality of the route is rather varied but protection (where it matters) and belays are excellent. Only ice-screws need be carried. Start below a system of clean, open grooves 33 metres west of the toe of the buttress with the through-tunnel.
1   30 metres.   Climb the slabby, slightly left-slanting groove until it is possible to break right to easier-angled, slightly vegetated slabs and a belay ledge below another short groove-system.
2   21 metres.   Gain the base of the groove and climb to where it steepens. Step left to a green slab, go over a bulge and then right to a ledge and belays.
3   35 metres.   Climb leftwards up steep, rotten 'rock' for 3 metres to a crumbly cornice. Pull left onto vegetated easier-angled slabs. Climb straight up these to a good belay below steep white walls.
4   40 metres.   Traverse some 9 metres left below the wall on vegetated ledges to gain a steeper slab. Climb the slab on chalk and

solid clumps of vegetation to belay below a final wall.
5 11 metres. Move slightly right to a fine finish on excellent chalk.
A Wielochowski, J Temple, 22 November 1992

46 The Verdant Tube   101 metres   III

The route follows a faint man-made, rightward-leaning channel
(reminiscent of *The Tube*) starting some 10 metres to the east of the
zigzag path and some 4 metres above the beach; it is most visible
from the cliff-top. Start by a leftward-leaning groove slightly to the left
of the bottom of the channel.
1 37 metres. Climb the groove to a delicate pull-round onto the
turf. Aim back right towards the channel, crossing it between two
small chalk outcrops and belaying just before a steepening of the
bush-filled channel.
2 40 metres. Continue straight up and then slightly left to regain the
channel, which is followed to a stance, preferably not in the line of
fire of the channel.
3 24 metres. Climb up the channel to the top.
D Barlow, P Drew, 27 November 1994

CLIFFS TO THE WEST OF DOVER

The following route is currently the only one west of Dover Harbour. The
chalk here is considerably harder than on the other Dover cliffs; the angle
of the climb is such that on the two ascents so far etriers or foot-slings
have been used attached to ice-axes. This makes the climbing feel more
like artificial work, hence the unusual grading for the area.

★ 47 Dukes of Hazard   80 metres   V/A3

The climb is on the first cliffs to the west of the harbour. At the point
where the cliff top footpath leaves the road, cross the railway by
means of a footbridge and walk west along the beach for 200 metres
to a very overhanging 37-metre high wall, which leads up to a mixed
rock and grass arête. Start directly beneath the wall.
1 37 metres. Trend diagonally rightwards to the bottom right-hand
side of the overhanging wall. Ascend this (foot slings on ice axes
used) to gain a shallow niche where the angle relents to vertical
(possible belay). Continue up the gently overhanging wall above to
its highest point. Good belays on the left.
2 43 metres. Climb the mixed arête above direct to the top.
S Ballantine, A Perkins (VL), 21/22 November 1987

Hastings

Although the serious (in all senses of the word) climbing lies on sea-cliffs or 'near sea-cliffs', the few small inland outcrops in this area are also described in this section.

On the seafront at the eastern end of Hastings old town lies an outcrop of sandstone sculptured by numerous caves and giving a more conventional style of climbing than the chalk cliffs.

The vein of sandstone continues eastwards to tempt the adventurous climber again. About ½ mile to the east of Hastings, and just east of Ecclesbourne Glen, the cliffs consist of bands of sandstone and clay interspersed with various indeterminate materials. The clay tends to fill any corners and pile up on ledges thereby making progress difficult and requiring ice gear. A slightly different approach is needed here. Whereas at Dover the chalk gives climbing akin to steep water-ice, at Hastings the climbing is analogous to 'mixed' climbing – less steep and spectacular but more delicate. The most useful form of protection here seems to be the warthog-type drive-in ice-screw, but great care should be taken not to test them as any protection on this cliff is highly suspect. All in all a serious place.

WEST HILL   OS Ref TQ 822 095
On the east side of the castle is a rocky area reminiscent of Wellington Rocks, providing easy scrambles. The crags below the castle are inaccessible, rising straight out of the gardens of houses and having loose material and vegetation at the top. Some climbing has been reported.

EAST HILL   OS Ref TQ 829 097
At the eastern end of the seafront at Hastings is a car-parking area. Fifty metres along a no-through road is a prominent rack-railway going about 50 metres up the hillside. This is the scene of a clandestine route:

1 Railway Crack   40 metres   Hard Very Severe 5a
In the west wall of the rack-railway is an obvious crack splitting a smooth wall. The route climbs the crack and proves more difficult than it looks. Fully open to public gaze, and climbing is actively discouraged by the authorities.
M Fowler, M Morrison, 1983

2 One in the Eye for Harold 24 metres Hard Very Severe 5a
On the hillside above the dry yacht enclosure is an obvious deep
chimney (bottleneck at one-third height) in the outcrop east of the
caves. Climb the chimney direct.
 P Thornhill, L Cole, 12 June 1983

*The yacht club car-park terminates at a concrete breakwater. Up the
grassy hillside behind this is a leftward-slanting crackline giving* The
Battle of Hastings, *whilst to the right is the striking corner-line of* Norman
Corner.

3 The Battle of Hastings 30 metres Very Severe 4a
Follow the leftward-slanting crackline to finish in a vague gully. Climb
this and the vegetated corner in the short upper tier to finish.
P Thornhill (roped solo), 30 May 1983

4 Norman Corner 24 metres E1 5a/b
Climb the prominent corner-line.
P Thornhill (second did not follow), 11 June 1983

ECCLESBOURNE GLEN OS Ref TQ 838 103
There are one or two miniature outcrops in the Glen itself.

ECCLESBOURNE GLEN TO FAIRLIGHT GLEN
OS Ref TQ 837 100 to 853 105
The next routes are on the sea-cliff beyond Ecclesbourne Glen, a lowering
of the cliff with a distinctive waterfall. To the east, stretching for
approximately 1 mile, the cliff has two bands of soft sandstone which
outcrop along its entire length. The lower band is about 24 metres high
and the upper band about 12 metres. Steep mud and clay intersperse
the outcrops and form the finish to most routes. The cliff can be
approached at lowish tide by walking along the beach from Hastings.
It can also be approached from Fairlight Glen, which gives non-tidal
access to *Reasons to be Fearful*.

The following routes require great caution: if the clay is wet it is like paste
and if it is dry it just falls apart. The †† distinction accorded to certain
of the following routes is marginal, since to a greater or lesser extent all
of these routes are in a continuous state of transition due to 'mud flows'
rather than rockfalls as such. This is particularly the case with *Reasons
to be Fearful*.

5 Monster Raving Loony   61 metres   IV/V††

This route takes a direct but not particularly obvious line up steep clay and very broken rock. Start about halfway between Ecclesbourne Glen and a large grassy mound at the base of the cliff, below three well defined corners in the upper band. Note – the right-hand corner provides the finish to *Reasons to be Fearful*. Climb up through the smooth band at the base of the cliff, striking out from a pile of rocks in a short shallow corner. Move left onto easier ground then find a way up the muddy shattered rocks above, with a short steepish clay slope giving access to easy grass slopes. From beneath the upper tier of cleaner sandstone trend left to a prominent corner capped by a final 'cornice'. Finish up a short clay slope.
P Thornhill (roped solo), 6 August 1983

6 The Green Ghastly   61 metres   IV/A1††

Start midway between Ecclesbourne Glen and *The Prow*, at what appears to be the easiest way up this area, a series of vegetated corners between terraces about 450 metres east of Ecclesbourne Glen. From the shore move easily up and right a little and then left, via a clay slope, to easy ground. On the left is an obvious vegetated corner with a rock step at the top; follow this to a ledge. Move left and go up a very short rock step to easy ground. Continue, with aid, up a rightward-slanting corner to a broad ledge beneath the upper tier. Traverse about 11 metres right to a grass-filled corner/groove and follow this, using some aid, towards the top.
P Thornhill (roped solo), 10 September 1983

On the western side of The Prow, *the distinct clay ridge that is clearly seen from Hastings, is an obvious gully,* Gully of the Godless. *Further west the cliff juts out slightly before becoming slightly recessed.* Screaming Lord Sutch *finds a devious way up this recessed area.*

7 Screaming Lord Sutch   64 metres   IV††

Start at the foot of a clay-cone-filled corner situated at the base of the cliff about 90 metres west of *Gully of the Godless*.
1   46 metres.   Go up the corner and follow a vague depression above to a steepening. Traverse right to another (deeper) clay-filled corner, which gives access to a broad ledge beneath the upper tier. Move right and belay beneath a corner.
2   18 metres.   Climb broken ground to the foot of the corner. Climb the corner for about a metre, then traverse right for a metre or two to gain a crack/groove leading to the top.
P Thornhill, A Saunders (AL), 30 August 1983

8 Duffyman's Dusk   61 metres   IV†

The route takes the easiest-looking line between *Screaming Lord Sutch*

and *Gully of the Godless*. Ascend the lower tier by a series of rightward-trending grassy corners to gain the *Reasons to be Fearful* traverse-line. Challenging tufting leads into a corner and the top.
P Thornhill (roped solo) July 1984

9 Gully of the Godless 76 metres III
Just to the west of *The Prow* is a large unpleasant-looking gully, which gives a route of fine character, avoiding any difficulties by making excursions to the left.
P Thornhill (roped solo) 20 August 1983

10 The Prow 76 metres IV
From the car-park this can be seen as the far skyline and proves to be a route of good quality. Climb the clay in two pitches to the base of the sandstone band, which provides the crux of the route.
P Thornhill (roped solo)

11 Reasons to be Fearful 1250 metres (33 pitches) IV††
An outstanding feat by the first ascensionists. A single continuous ascent of this route would be a major undertaking. Start to the east of *The Prow*, where the cliffs run into vegetation. Scramble up and left to gain the line where the first pitch (III) is soon encountered. Easier ground follows, then more III to gain *The Prow*, which is reversed a short way to just above the rock step. Traverse a wide clay band into *Gully of the Godless*. Climb this to regain the horizontal band and follow this for about 300 metres (pitches of II and III) to the first crux section. About 100 metres further on is a second crux area, which is followed by mainly easier ground to reach two blunt prows just before *Monster Raving Loony*. Here the band loses definition somewhat. Nevertheless, continue at roughly the same level until the second prow is reached; ascend this close to the arête to belay at the foot of the upper tier beneath a prominent crackline. Move left one metre and climb a gully/chimney round the corner to finish. The climb was originally described in 26 sections, varying in length between 15 and 167 metres.
A Saunders, P Thornhill (AL) between 26 October 1983 & 8 January 1984 in six parts.

FAIRLIGHT GLEN
There are two small outcrops, one an ex-quarry (OS Ref TQ 857 115) and the other in the upper car-park (OS Ref TQ 859 118). There is also a small outcrop (OS Ref TQ 856 109) hidden by trees just below the western edge of the plateau of Lover's Seat and just east of the path down to the sea.

CLIFF END   OS Ref TQ 885 125

The sandstone cliffs here are 20 metres high, but are mostly capped with clay and dense undergrowth, so that climbs would be difficult to finish. There is a lower tier with a few possible crack-climbs. The horizontal lines of weakness are equally prominent and in places look woefully rotten.

ORE ROCKS   OS Ref TQ 846 116

On the north side of the Ore-to-Fairlight road, half a mile from Ore and near to the prominent aerial. A small rock wall below the road might give a short climb or two. There is also a small quarry on the south side of the road.

TOOT ROCK   OS Ref TQ 887 129

An ancient sea cliff line, now inland, occurs at Pett Level. It reaches 7 metres in height, and some routes have been climbed here close to an old coastguard look-out.

RYE   OS Ref TQ 91/2 20

One or two short climbs have been reported on small rock walls in and around the town. All are strictly private.

Beachy Head to Brighton

BEACHY HEAD   OS Ref TV 584 952

Beachy Head is the highest and most spectacular precipice on the entire southern coast of England and presents a most impressive sight for anyone looking over its edge down the 120-metre drop below. Between Beachy Head itself and Birling Gap, 4 miles to the west, the cliffs form a continuously perpendicular wall easily viewed from the beach below. Particular care should be taken with the tides as there is no easy way whatsoever up this section of cliff. As at April 1995 there were steps down to the beach at Birling Gap.

To the east of the lighthouse the cliffs ease to high-angled grass and chalk leading to a steep headwall. Here lies the famous *Etheldreda's Pinnacle*, with *Crowley's Crack* prominent in the main wall behind. *Albino* follows the smooth groove 100 metres to the west of the pinnacle. *Monster Crack* takes the mind-blowing face-crack in the right-hand flank of Beachy Head itself, with *Passion Flake*, *The Ghost* and *Sunday Sport* taking lines up the walls on the west side of the Head and overlooking the lighthouse.

Access: due to its popularity for public/general recreation and the fact that Beachy Head is a Site of Special Scientific Interest, the access situation is sensitive. Please observe the following points carefully:

1. The base of the cliffs is best reached by descending grass slopes east of the main, and highest, car-park just east of Beachy Head.

2. It is very important that the coastguard at **MRCC Dover** (Telephone 01304 210008) is informed of any climbing activity as all routes are clearly visible from below and from the helicopters that fly past regularly.

3. Avoid damaging the cliff edge in the few instances when it may be necessary to place anchor stakes. Do not leave anchors or ropes in place longer than necessary.

4. There are important coastal sea-bird populations at Beachy Head: during the nesting season (1st February to 30th June) climbers should ring the Downland Ranger on 01323 41000 to find out if there are any access restrictions.

★★★ **1 Sunday Sport**   138 metres   Extremely Severe
A magnificent route taking the full challenge of the head. Most rewarding. Ice-screw protection *in situ*. The route takes a slab followed by a 75-metre corner-line finishing about 75 metres west of the lighthouse cables. The line can be seen form the clifftop from a point just east of the west end of the fenced-off area (the route finishes 75 metres east of the end of the fence). Start from the boulder beach (accessible at most states of the tide), about 150 metres west of the lighthouse and directly beneath the upper corners.
1   12 metres.   Scrambling leads to a good stance beneath overhangs guarding the slab.
2   46 metres 5c.   A short wall leads to the first overhang, which is crossed by a very long reach. The second band of overhangs is climbed via a crack with a large dubious block and leads to the bottom left-hand corner of the slab. Traverse the lower edge of the slab for 8 metres and tend up to its right arête. Follow this to a stance below overhanging walls. A superb pitch.
3   50 metres 6a.   Climb the overhanging groove to the left of the stance to where the finger-crack in the back runs out. Climb direct on flints for 9 metres to where the fault-line re-appears and continue up this to a ledge on the right. Another superb pitch.
4   30 metres 5b.   Move back left into the corner and climb up to a

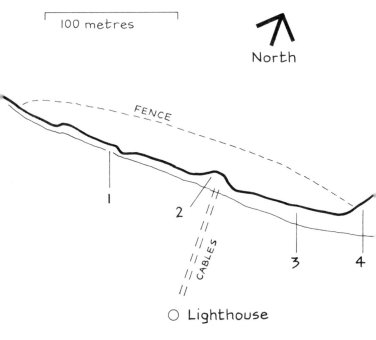

100 metres

North

FENCE

1

2

CABLES

3

4

○ Lighthouse

wider crack (overhanging in places), which is followed to below the earthy finish. Step right to gain the top.
M Fowler, F Ramsay, S Sustad (AL), 1 March 1990

2 The Ghost 60 metres   Mild Extremely Severe†
This climbs the left (east-facing) wall of the corner directly below the cables which link the cliff with the lighthouse. Reach the base of the corner via 150 metres of steep grass and easy-angled chalky rubble. The last 45 metres of the approach was climbed roped and involved a long right-to-left traverse below the headwall. Belay on a ledge just left of the corner.
1   30 metres.   Free climb the rotten cracks splitting the east face of the corner to big footholds below a steepening. *In-situ* stake and other belays.
2   30 metres.   Either climb the crack direct (steep and rotten) or climb up to the arête (thread runner) and traverse back right to the

BEACHY HEAD

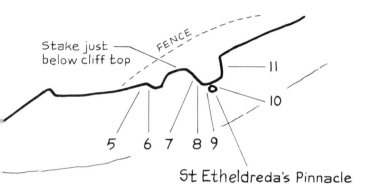

Stake just below cliff top

FENCE

11

10

5   6 7 8 9

St Etheldreda's Pinnacle

crack. Follow the crack till it ends at overhanging rubble. Traverse right across the steep headwall using huge buckets cut out of the rubble. Finish up the arête overlooking the wires and belay 15 metres back.

J Temple, A Wielochowski (AL), 4 November 1990

★ **3 Passion Flake** 66 metres   Extremely Severe
This route takes the elegant flake-line just east of the lighthouse cables. Approach by scrambling up steep grass and one mixed 5b pitch to reach the base of the vertical walls, or more easily by traversing from the grass slope on the left.
1 23 metres 5c. Climb up into a shallow groove and continue until it is possible to move leftwards beneath a small overhang to the base of the flake-crack, hanging stance.
2 12 metres 5b. The crack starts as a narrow hand-jam and develops into an off-width. Belay at a small ledge.
3 23 metres 5a. Continue up the wider crack passing an overhanging section to gain a ledge on top of the flake.
4 8 metres 4c. Step left and climb loose material to the top and belay on the fence.

F Ramsay, M Fowler (AL), 18 November 1990

***4 **Monster Crack**   101 metres   Extremely Severe
Piercing the centre of the eastern face of Beachy Head itself is an
extremely impressive crackline. Protection throughout is by ice-screws
and nuts. From the beach opposite the lighthouse ascend grass slopes
to the foot of the crack.
1   16 metres 5a   Follow a line of discontinuous grass tufts diagonally
leftwards to reach a small cave with excellent thread/hex belays (and
protection from the debris!).
2   38 metres 5b.   Climb the left-hand side of the grassy depression
to gain a grass ledge 3 metres to the left of the start of the crack
proper. Move up diagonally right to the foot of the crack. Climb the
crack for 5 metres, to reach good holds and a small cave. Continue
directly up the crack above to reach a stance and ice-screw belays
beneath a large roof.
3   23 metres 5a.   Cross a slab on the left and move up to gain a
niche in the crackline. Continue straight up, passing some dubious
flakes, to belay at the foot of a surprisingly large niche.
4   24 metres 5c.   Ascend rubble in the floor of the niche to gain a
narrow foot-ledge in the right wall. Traverse this to the arête
(ice-screw runner in place) and climb with difficulty on flints, passing
a second ice-screw, to reach a ledge at the foot of the upper crack.
Follow this crack, which leads steeply to the top.
M Fowler, M Morrison, C Watts. Pitches 1-3: 20 November 1982,
Pitch 4: 1 December 1982. Pitch 2 was originally climbed with 2
Friends for aid – climbed free by A Popp, F Ramsay in July 1989

*To the right of Monster Crack the steep section of cliff is lower. A
prominent feature at the highest point of the grass slopes leading up right
from that route is the deep vertical chimney of* Vaginoff *with the elegant
slim groove-line of* Albino *6 metres to the right.*

* 5 **Vaginoff**   46 metres   Extremely Severe
Scramble up rightwards to below the obvious chimney.
1   40 metres 5b.   Climb up past several loose chockstones until it is
possible to move deep inside and on up to the bottleneck at 24
metres. Bridge and jam up the outside (crux) to gain the easier upper
section, which is followed to a belay where the chimney becomes
mud-choked and overhanging.
2   6 metres 4c.   Start by back- and-footing and continue by wide
bridging on very loose rock.
M Fowler (second did not follow), 20 November 1982 (pitch 2
soloed with back-rope)

6 **Albino   46 metres   Extremely Severe
The attractive groove to the right of the chimney gives an excellent
main pitch protected with nuts and ice-screws, although not

recommended for asthma-sufferers. Start 6 metres right of *Vaginoff*.
1 40 metres 5b. Follow the deceptively steep groove, using mostly
hand-jams. Surmount an overhanging bulge at 21 metres (crux) and
enter the easier-angled upper groove above. This provides further
interest until a short slab is crossed to gain the upper chimney of
Vaginoff.
2 6 metres 4c. Finish as for that route.
M Fowler, L Cole, 6 March 1983

*Jutting well out from the main cliff the stubby thumb of Etheldreda's
Pinnacle can clearly be seen from above and below. Separating the wall
behind the pinnacle from Albino is the left-to-right-trending grassy ramp
which provides the exit from Chalk Farm Toad. On the right of the
pinnacle the wall sports an historic route, the steep and daunting line of
Crowley's Crack.*

7 Chalk Farm Toad 37 metres HVS 5a
Immediately west of the pinnacle is a gully-line below a left-to-right
ramp giving a route of dubious worth. Climb the gully to gain a ledge
at 21 metres with difficulty. Continue up to a large block belay on the
left at the head of the gully. Scrambling remains up the grassy ramp.
S Lewis, J Deakin (AL), P Thornhill, 20 November 1982

8 West Chimney 21 metres Very Severe 4b
The best method of access to the neck of the pinnacle. Climb the
prominent chimney facing the lighthouse on the western side of the
pinnacle.
M Fowler, M Morrison, 13 April 1980

9 Etheldreda's Pinnacle Route 1 8 metres Very Severe 4a
Crowley's original route on the pinnacle. From the neck climb straight
up for 2 metres, then trend right to the right arête of the pinnacle,
which is followed to the top.
A Crowley, 1894

10 Etheldreda's Pinnacle Route 2 9 metres Very Severe 4b
Start lower down the West Chimney than *Route 1*. Climb up and out
onto the block wedged across the chimney. From this gain the right
arête of the pinnacle and follow it to the top.
A Strapcans, G Forward, 1979

★ 11 Crowley's Crack 61 metres Mild Extremely Severe
Start below a groove on the east side of Etheldreda's Pinnacle,
beneath the impressive crack from which Crowley was rescued.
1 18 metres. Climb the groove on loose rock (The East Chimney)
until it is possible to move right and belay on ice-screws below the

crack.
2   43 metres 5a.   Follow the crack to the top.
Pitch 1: A Crowley, 1894. Pitch 2: M Fowler, M Morrison, B Wyvill,
13 April 1980

*To the right of the Etheldreda's Pinnacle area is an obvious gully running
the full height of the cliff. This, and the cliffs to the east, gave three routes,
which were destroyed by a landslide in 1989/90:* Aunt Ethel's Gully,
Croydon Club Route *and* Demolition Man, *and subsequently the
short-lived* Demolition Men.

SEVEN SISTERS   OS Ref TV 53 96
To the west of Birling Gap are the Seven Sisters. The only route here so
far is on the most westerly Sister.

1 Yorkie   90 metres   VI
Hard, serious and very fine climbing. Walking along the beach
eastwards from Cuckmere Haven (towards Beachy Head) the cliffs of
the first Sister increase gradually in height and a series of buttresses
project onto the beach. After approximately 300 metres, a buttress
projects further than the others. Directly above this are two
left-to-right-slanting ramps separated by a vertical wall and capped by
a short overhanging wall. Start at the toe of the buttress which forms
the right edge of the lower ramp.
1   24 metres.   Climb onto the buttress crest from the right and follow
it to belay where it steepens.
2   21 metres.   Pass the steepening above by climbing the slab on the
left and return to the crest, which leads to ledges below very loose,
shattered rock. Traverse 3 metres left into a vertical groove and
ascend this for about 9 metres until it is possible to move right to a
good ice-screw belay above the shattered rock.
3   21 metres.   Step back left and continue up the groove to gain the
foot of the upper ramp. Ascend diagonally up the ramp to belay on
the far side.
4   24 metres.   Climb the ramp to the capping overhangs. Traverse to
the right edge and climb a short wall to the top.
M Fowler, C Watts (AL), A Chaudry, 25 January 1987

SEAFORD HEAD   OS Ref TV 004 978
This cliff lies between the town of Seaford and Cuckmere Haven, and is
about 80 metres high. Access is best by parking the car on the Seaford
promenade due east of the Martello Tower. Either walk under the cliffs
5 hours either side of low tide, or walk over the Head, past the golf
course, to Hope Gap Steps just below a fence to the cliff edge and a
stile.

About 50 metres west of the point wherethe fence reaches the cliff edge is an obvious brownish slab above an overhanging cave leading to a grassy ramp:

1 Dead Choughed   65 metres   IV†
1   45 metres.   Either climb an arete of good chalk or bridge up the cave above a weak crackline. A rising traverse right leads just under a broken niche to the grass ramp meeting the headwall. Follow this line to a poor stance (the best belay is on the end of a pre-placed rope from the top).
2   20 metres.   Continue up the line of weakness on poor chalk to the top. Belay on a stake.
N Atkinson, F Berwick (AL), July 1995

QUARRIES NEAR LEWES
CABURN PIT   OS Ref TQ 447 088
A disused quarry, which has provide a girdle traverse.

BEDDINGHAM PIT   OS Ref TQ 440 062
This has in the past provided some climbing but is now being land-filled.

SALTDEAN   OS Ref TQ 385 018
In the vicinity of Brighton the chalk cliffs are featureless landscaped banks above a concrete promenade stretching from Brighton through Rottingdean to Saltdean. Where the under-cliff walk terminates at Saltdean, the cliff resumes its natural state and provides the climber with some interest. Easily identifiable by lime green colouring at its left end, the area provides several fine lines and *Saltdean Slab* is a good introduction to chalk climbing.

Access: for most of the western routes it is best to park at the Saltdean Lido and gain the undercliff walk by a subway beneath the A259. Follow this eastwards to its end, where a sloping ledge leads round a corner onto an artificial boulder-field. The climbs are accessible up to half tide by this approach. Concrete fence-posts offer excellent belays at the top of the cliff. Precision abseiling is a good alternative method of reaching climbs but beware – the cliff is about 55 metres at its highest point.

The Brighton Police Event Office should be notified of your intention to climb: ring 01273 606744 as well as MRCC Dover.

All the climbs are protected using ice-screws or ice-pitons only. The chalk is generally soft and reliable on the lower half of the cliff, variable towards the top and occasionally capped with a short rotten headwall.

It is wise to place an extended sling on a fence-post to provide protection for the final moves on some climbs; where this is important PS (for Protection Sling) has been added to the description.

Saltdean Slab starts some 40 metres east of the promenade, towards the right-hand end of the artificial boulder field. Thirty metres further east a tunnel entrance marks the start of *Jailhouse Rock*. Forty metres further east a very distinct slender ridge points out to sea; this is climbed by *Prunes*, the left-bounding corner gives the line of *Exlax*, and the right-bounding slab is *Relax*. Thirty metres east is the steep buttress climbed by *Greenhouse Effect*. After a further 40 metres the cliff gains its maximum height and, 120 metres east of *Prunes*, just beyond the out-jutting toe of *Turbo Buttress*, there is a slight bay. A steepening slab leads up to a very steep and unstable headwall. *Lime Wall* climbs the slab and then breaks right up steep greenish rock to avoid the headwall.

A further 60 metres beyond *Lime Wall* is a slight bay with a gentler-angled and rightwards-trending slab leading almost to the top. This is the line of *Brighton Rock*. Just left of this is the steeper, more direct and more vegetated slab of *Tiptoe Through the Tulips*, and to the right the steep corner of *Stormy Seas*. Both of the last-mentioned routes, and *St. Jerome*, are best reached from the east, where a footpath and steps lead down to the beach next to the Southern Water plant. Access from this direction is almost non-tidal. The first two routes are some 250 metres from the Water Works. *St. Jerome* goes up a slight, black buttress 100 metres west of the Southern Water plant.

1 Saltdean Corner 20 metres III
This climbs the vague corner above the centre of the boulders.

★**2 Saltdean Slab** 30 metres II
Gain the slab just right of the corner and follow it, trending right, to a steeper finish and the top. Although there is some loose rock this is an excellent introductory route.
P Thornhill (solo), 4 November 1983

3 Direct Route 30 metres IV
Start 5 metres right of *Saltdean Slab* and climb up a very steep wall on good chalk to gain the slab. Continue directly up to a loose, steep finish.

★**4 Jailhouse Rock** 40 metres IV PS††
Climb easily up to gain the entrance to the tunnel (possible belay point at high tide). Climb the corner to a steepening, move onto the left wall and then go diagonally up left to a ledge on the arête. Climb a shallow corner to the top. A rotten finish but still a fine steep route

on good chalk.
A Wielochowski, C Fox, 31 January 1994

★ **5 Exlax** 45 metres IV/V PS†
A good route.
1 25 metres. Climb, on good chalk, the prominent, steep corner
just left of the slender arête to gain a good stance astride the top of
the arête.
2 20 metres. Climb the narrowing slab above to a less stable finish.
D Clarke, J Hayward-Cripps, Spring 1992

★★ **6 Prunes** 45 metres IV/V PS†
An entertaining, good-quality route.
1 25 metres. Climb the seaward face of the arête to a ledge with a
block – possible belay. Continue up the steeper arête to where it
becomes vertical. Traverse right (on the east face) to the stance
astride the top of the arête.
2 20 metres. As for *Exlax*.
A Ekins, J Hayward-Cripps, January 1992

★ **7 Relax** 45 metres IV/V PS†
Start at the corner right of *Prunes*.
1 25 metres. Climb the corner to the arête stance of *Prunes*.
2 20 metres. Climb *Exlax* to where it takes the narrow slab to the
right. Break out leftwards to a very short but steep finish.
A Gordon-Seymour, A Wielochowski (AL), February 1995

8 The Bill 50 metres V††
Start about 15 metres right of *Prunes*, directly below the centre of the
hanging, pale brown slab.
1 35 metres. Climb a left-trending fault/ramp for 5 metres – now
partly partly buried by rockfall. Move up steeply left to gain a ledge
and hence a left-facing corner. Go up this and then more easily
leftwards to gain the slab. Climb the centre of this to a small stance
below the headwall.
2 15 metres. Climb the steeper, right-trending, narrow white slab
to the top.
A Wielochowski, A Brummeler, J Folkes, J Spancken, 2 December
1993

★★★ **9 The Greenhouse Effect** 50 metres VI PS†
Good chalk and technical climbing on the first pitch combined with a
steep sustained final pitch make this a fine climb. Excellent protection.
Start 10 metres left of the toe of the buttress 40 metres right of *Exlax*,
at the right-hand end of a pleasantly-angled slab of excellent chalk.
1 20 metres. Climb the right edge of the slab to where it steepens.

Step right to the base of a slim corner and climb the right-retaining narrow slab (awkward) to an overhang. Pull through this leftwards (*in-situ* ice-screw), to a good stance and belays.
2   15 metres.   Follow the easy, greenish slab above to belay below the headwall and at the top left-hand corner of the slab. This pitch could be combined with pitch 1.
3   15 metres.   Move to the right edge of the slab and climb the steep wall above (2 *in-situ* ice-screws) to the top.
A Gordon-Seymour, A Wielochowski (AL), March 1995

9A Turbo Buttress   60 metres   V+   PS†
Start left of the toe of the buttress 120 metres east of*Prunes*.
1   15 metres.   Climb left of the arête of the buttress to a good ledge.
2   45 metres.   Follow the arête trending leftwards to a steep blocky finish.
N Atkinson (second did not follow), 1994

★★ **10 Lime Wall**   60 metres   V   PS†
An excellent route. It is possible to start the climb on small ledges 2 metres above the beach if the sea threatens to wash over your feet.
1   30 metres.   Climb the centre of the steepening slab till a traverse right leads to a small stance below the headwall.
2   30 metres.   Traverse steeply right and up on excellent, green chalk to gain a slab. Climb this to the left end of green ledges. Go steeply left, then up rotten rock to a short, steep finish.
A Wielochowski, A Brummeler, February 1994

★★ **11 Tiptoe Through the Tulips**   55 metres   IV†
A pleasant route with a safe finish.
1   45 metres.   Climb the slab keeping a few metres to the right of the left-retaining corner to a patch of thicker vegetation (beautiful, fragrant flowers in the spring). Move right to avoid damaging the flowers and then step left to belay immediately above them.
2   10 metres.   Continue rightwards to the top.
A Gordon-Seymour, A Wielochowski, 24 May 1994

12 Brighton Rock   60 metres   IV
The easy-angled, grey, left-to-right sloping slab.
1   40 metres.   Follow the slab and move across to a niche on its left-hand side to belay.
2   20 metres.   Traverse out right and slightly up (*in-situ* protection spike) to find the easiest way through the short but steep 'barrier' at the top of the cliff, which gives the crux.
P Thornhill (solo), 14 November 1983

** **13 Stormy Seas** 50 metres V†
This takes the right-bounding corner of *Brighton Rock*.
1 35 metres. Climb the steep corner, first on the left and then on the right wall, to a stance below an overhang.
2 15 metres. Bridge up the corner until a breath-taking traverse leftwards leads onto the final slab of *Brighton Rock*.
A Wielochowski, C Mockett, January 1995

* **14 St. Jerome** 25 metres III†
A good-quality route on good chalk, which can be well-protected. Start to the left of the slabby grey, triangular buttress. Climb the slabby left side of the buttress up solid grey chalk trending rightwards to the shoulder at two-thirds height, possible belay. climb straight up to a clean finish.
A Gordon-Seymour, P Morgan, 11 April 1994

Special Considerations for Group Use

These guidelines are provided for people in charge of beginners' groups, and are additional to the general guidelines described elsewhere in the introduction.

PREPARATION BEFORE A CLIMBING TRIP
Beginners' groups can spend useful sessions indoors or at a climbing wall before a visit. Familiarisation with equipment, techniques and belaying can be extremely worthwhile, and allow a better appreciation and understanding of the outdoor experience. Particular reference should be made to suitable belay equipment and footware for sandstone. Keep groups small so that every member is involved in an activity. Consider ratios of assistant leaders to group members

CHOICE OF SITE
Please consider:

(a) the specific access arrangements and conditions

(b) the size of the site, and its popularity with individuals and other groups.

(c) the day of the week – please avoid popular crags at the weekend, and particularly Sundays

(d) the range and type of climbs in relation to ability of your group

(e) the parking arrangements: park considerately especially if you have a large vehicle and don't block roads or drives – if there is a problem with space find somewhere suitable even if it means walking a bit further.

THE CLIMBING ENVIRONMENT
Encourage group awareness and personal responsibility about the environment. No matter what the age or level of interest of your group it should be possible to cover some aspect of the following by showing examples on site:

(a) history of the site

(b) why the sites are special for conservation, climbing and general recreation

(c) erosion problems on Southern Sandstone

(d) how the sites are being looked after by local users

(e) good climbing practice.

GROUP MANAGEMENT DURING YOUR VISIT
Ensure group members are properly supervised before, during and after climbing. Keep the group involved in some form of activity, e.g. belaying, assisting, etc. Set specific boundaries and do not allow members to run off. Give consideration to:

(a) noise and language from your group

(b) noise from the instructor in managing the group

(c) other users/climbers needs

(d) storage of the group's equipment – keep equipment/bags out of the way so as not to take up large areas of ground space

(e) litter – leave the site in a better state than you found it – take a bin-bag and gloves for group collection

(f) the amount of time your group occupies routes or a section of crag

(g) toilet facilities – ensure group members have access to toilets before they visit the crag

(h) relations with the general public – the outcrops and their surroundings are popular recreation sites and give a very visible image of climbing.

GROUP SIZE
Keep groups small so that every member is involved in an activity. Consider ratios of assistant leaders to group members.

CHOICE OF CLIMBS
Choose climbs to suit the ability of the group. If group members are having trouble on a climb they will be causing increased wear with their feet. Move them onto something easier. Don't leave ropes set up if you have no one on the climbs.

TOP-ROPING/BELAYING
If, when setting up a belay and top-roping system, you feel the position of the karabiner will lead to an unsafe finish for your climbers, either make additional safety arrangements at the top or choose a more suitable route.

ABSEILING
This practice is discouraged on sandstone and banned at most outcrops.Consider the use of artificial structures or climbing walls (see list on page 265).

QUALIFICATIONS
Group leaders are encouraged to participate in the national Single Pitch Supervisor's Award (SPSA) or the Southern Sandstone Supervisor's Award (SSSA) schemes. The SPSA is nationally recognised, was set up by the BMC, and is administered by the Mountain Leader Training Board. Further details are available from the MTLB, 177-179 Burton Road, West Didsbury, Manchester, M20 2BB. Tel: 0161 445 4747. The SSSA is one which local authorities, schools and youth groups in Kent, East Sussex, West Sussex, and Surrey insist upon, and is specific to the local considerations of supervising climbing on Southern Sandstone. Details of the SSSA Training and Assessment courses are available from Kent, East Sussex, West Sussex, and Surrey County Councils.

EVALUATION
Review your group's visit – are there further ways you can reduce the impact of your group and improve their outdoor experience?

Climbing Walls

There are a number of climbing walls in the South-East, some of which are included here for those interested. The list is a guide and is not intended to be comprehensive. Those who need further information should contact the BMC Development Officer, Tel: 0161 2735835.

Basildon: Eversley Leisure Centre, Crest Avenue, Pitsea, Basildon, Essex, SS13 2EF. Tel: 01268 583076.

Bexhill-on-Sea: Bexhill Leisure Centre, Down Road, Bexhill-on-Sea, East Sussex, TN39 4HS. Tel: 01424 731171.

Canterbury: The Sports Centre, University of Kent, Canterbury, Kent. Tel: 01227 764000.

Canterbury: King's School Recreation Centre, 1 St Stephens Road, Canterbury, Kent, CT2 7HU. Tel: 01227 595602.

Chelmsford: Dovedale Sports Centre, Moulsham Street, Chelmsford, Essex. Tel: 01245 269020.

Folkestone: Folkestone and District Leisure Centre, Radnor Park Avenue, Folkestone, Kent, CT19 5HX. Tel: 01303 52686/58222.

Guildford: Campus Sports Centre, Surrey University, Egerton Road, Guildford, Surrey, GU2 5XH. Tel: 01483 509201.

Lewes: Lewes Leisure Centre, Mountfield Road, Lewes, BN7 2XG. Tel: 01273 486000.

London: Brixton Recreational Centre, 27 Brixton Station Road, London, SW9 8QQ. Tel: 0171 274 7774.

London: Brunel University Sports Hall, Brunel University, Kingston Lane, Uxbridge, Middlesex, UB8 3PH. Tel: 01895 252361.

London: The Castle, Green Lanes, London N4 2HA. Tel: 0181 211 7000. To open in October 1995.

London: Crystal Palace National Sports Centre, Ledrington Road, Crystal Palace, London, SE19 2BB. Tel: 0181 778 0131.

London: Hayes School Sports Centre, West Common Road, Bromley, Kent, BR2 7DB. Tel: 0181 462 2767.

London: Jubilee Sports Centre, 30 The Piazza, Central Market Square, Covent Garden, London, WC2E 8BE. Tel: 0171 836 4007.

London: Lee Valley Leisure Centre, Picketts Lock Lane, Edmonton, London, N9 0AS. Tel: 0181 803 9292.

London: Michael Sobell Sports Centre, Hornsey Road, Holloway, London, N7 7NY. Tel: 0171 609 2166.

London: Monks Hill Sports Centre, Farnborough Avenue, South Croydon, CR2 8HD. Tel: 0181 651 0984/5.

London: North London Rescue Commando, Bow Outdoor Pursuit Centre, Cordova Road, London, E3 5BE. Tel: 0181 980 0289. (Known as the Mile End Wall.)

London: Sadlers Sports Centre, Goswell Road, London, EC1U 7EJ. Tel: 0171 253 4399/9285.

London: Stubbers Outdoor Pursuits Centre, Ockendon Road, Upminster, RM14 2TY. Tel: 014022 24753.

London: Westway Sports Centre, 1 Crowthorn Road, London, W10 6PR. Tel: 0181 969 0992.

London: all the following walls are 'natural' brick walls and as such are generally limited to brick-edge type holds. Nonetheless, they offer an interesting (and cheap) alternative for those who seek them out. Repointing or redevelopment may of course render these walls useless or non-existent at any time. An A-Z mapbook is useful (essential) for locating these esoteric diversions. For further information see articles in High, April and July 1985.

(1) Cottage Grove Wall, Cottage Grove, London SW9 - close to Clapham North Tube Station. Apparently, offering good sustained traversing and some good boulder problems.

(2) Emmanuel Road Railway Arches, London SW12 - large railway arches, often wet.

(3) Regents Canal Area, Islington, London N1 - a number of venues all very close or adjacent to the Canal including:

(a) Magician Area – near the junction of Noel Road and Wharf Road - a big corner line and some other nearby problems.

(b) The Playground by Packington Street bridge – a number of thin finger cracks.

(c) George's Columns, Baring Street – a series of narrow pillars and a nearby bridge.

(d) De Beauvoir Walls, on Whitmore Road bridge and abutting retaining walls right next to the canal.

(4) Hornsey Wall, between Hornsey Rise, Crouch End Hill and Haslemere Roads, Islington – just over a mile from the Sobell Centre; a series of rising arches, some requiring a top-rope, in quite pleasant surroundings.

Maidstone: Maidstone Leisure Centre, Mote Park, Willow Way, Maidstone, Kent, ME15 7RN. Tel: 01622 761111.

Redhill: High Sport Unit, 6 Orchard Business Centre, Bonehurst Road, Salfords, Nr Redhill, Surrey, RH1 5EL. Tel: 01293 822884.

Rochester: Arethusa Ventura Centre, Lower Upnor, Rochester, Kent, ME2 4XB. Tel: 01634 296358.

Rochford: Clements Hall Leisure Centre, Clements Hall Way, Hawkswell, Rochford, Essex, SS5 4LN. Tel: 01702 207777.

South Ockendon: Ockendon School Sports Centre, Erriff Drive, South Ockendon, Essex, RM15 5AY. Tel: 01708 851309.

Sunbury: The Heights, Sunbury Leisure Centre, Nursery Road, Sunbury, Middlesex, TW16 6LG. Tel: 01932 772287.

Swanley: White Oak Leisure Centre, Hilda May Avenue, Swanley, Kent, BR8 7BT. Tel: 01322 662188.

Witham: Bramston Sports Centre, Bridge Street, Witham, Essex. Tel: 01376 517620.

Worthing: Worthing Leisure Centre, West Park, Shaftesbury Avenue, Worthing, West Sussex, BN12 4ET. Tel: 01903 502237.

Bibliography

SANDSTONE CLIMBING

(1) *Guide to the Climbs at Harrison's Rocks, near Groombridge, Sussex*, by M O Sheffield and H Courtney-Bryson, privately pub, 1934.

(2) *Oxford Mountaineering 1935*, pp.92-93 (note only).

(3) *Rock Climbs Round London*, by H Courtney-Bryson, privately pub, 1936.

(4) *Oxford Mountaineering 1937*, p.81 (note only).

(5) *Sussex County Magazine Vol.13* (January 1939). pp.29-33. Rock Climbing in Sussex, by R W Clark.

(6) *Sussex County Magazine Vol.18* (June 1944), pp.146-150. Recent Developments in Sussex Rock Climbing, by E C Pyatt.

(7) *Cambridge Mountaineering 1944*, pp.19-24. Harrison's Rocks, by A R H Worssam.

(8) *Sandstone Climbs in South-East England*, by E C Pyatt, privately pub, 1947.

(9) *Kent County Journal Vol.7* (April-June 1947). pp.124-126. Rock Climbing in Kent, by E C Pyatt.

(10) *Cambridge Mountaineering 1959*, pp.32-35. Sandstone, by D G Fagan.

(11) *Recent Developments in South-East England*, by J V Smoker and D G Fagan, privately pub, 1963.

(12) *A New Rock Climbing Guide to Harrison's Rocks*, by T S Panther, privately pub, 1967.

(13) *Mountain 1* (January 1969), pp.18-21. Who Digs Harrison's? by I McNaught Davis.

(14) *A New Rock Climbing Guide to Harrison's Rocks* (Second Edition), by T S Panther, privately pub, 1969.

(15) *Climbing and Walking in South-East England*, by E C Pyatt, David & Charles, 1970.

(16) *A New Rock Climbing Guide to Harrison's Rocks* (Third Edition), by T S Panther, privately pub, 1971.

(17) *Mountain 35* (May 1974), pp.13-19. Confessions of a Sandstone Addict, by M Boysen.

(18) *Crags No.20* (August/September 1979), pp.22-26. Sandstorm, by M Fowler.

(19) *The Climbers' Club Journal 1981*, pp.100-107. 'Top-Roping is now a Southern Disease...', by L R Holliwell.

(20) *Mountain 83* (January 1982), p.19. Southern Sandstone, by D Jones.

(21) *Rock Action One* (February 1983), pp.23-27. South-East Action, by D Jones.

(22) *Harrison's Rocks 1986*, by T Panther, privately pub, 1986.

(23) *High No 70* (September 1988), pp. 40-43, Forbidden Sandstone, by D Cook.

(24) *Mountain 144* (March/April 1992), pp.14-15. South-East England, by M T Vetterlein.

(25) *Climber & Hillwalker* (June 1991), pp. 24-25, South from the Smoke, by D Hobbs

(26) *On the Edge 30* (June 1992), pp.30-41. To See Heaven in a Grain of Sand, various authors.

(27) *Climber & Hillwalker* (September 1994), pp.18-21. The Forcing Ground: A Review of Sandstone, by C Mellor.

SEA-CLIFF AND CHALK CLIMBING

(1) *Climbing in the British Isles – England*, by W P Haskett Smith. Section on Chalk, by A F Mummery, 1894.

(2) *Scottish Mountaineering Journal, Vol.3* (May 1895) p.288. Chalk Climbing on Beachy Head, by E A Crowley.

(3) *Climbers' Club Journal* (Old Series), Vol.1 (February 1899), p.91. Chalk Climbing on Beachy Head, by H S Bullock.

(4) *Cambridge Mountaineering, 1925-26*, p.56. Cherryhinton, by I M Waller.

(5) *Cambridge Mountaineering, 1934*. Cherryhinton Chalkpit, by E J C Kendall.

(6) *Sussex County Magazine, Vol.9* (November 1935), p.688. Climbing on Beachy Head, by A Member of the Alpine Club.

(7) *Sussex County Magazine, Vol.26* (March 1952), p.131. Beachy Head in Mountaineering Literature, by E C Pyatt.

(8) *Climbers' Club Journal* (New Series), Vol.10 (1952), p.55. Chalk – a Miniature Anthology, by E C Pyatt.

(9) *Mountain 11* (September 1970), pp.12-14. The Brief Mountaineering Career of Aleister Crowley, the Great Beast 666.

(10) *Crags No. 26* (August/September 1980), p.23. Chalk & Cheese, by B Wyvill.

(11) *Mountain 91* (May/June 1983), p.17. Short feature with three photographs.

(12) *High No. 13* (November/December 1983), pp.26-27. Kings of the Wild Frontier, by C Jones.

(13) *Climber & Rambler* (September 1984), pp. 24-27. Over-use of Chalk, by P Thornhill.

(14) *Climber & Hillwalker* (November 1988), pp.20-22. After the Great White Fright, by A Perkins.

(15) *On the Edge 14* (Oct/Nov 1989), pp.36-40. A Battle at Hastings, by P Thornhill.

(16) *Climber & Hillwalker* (December 1993), pp.12-16. Loose Living, by C Mellor.

GEOLOGY

(1) *The Fossils of the South Downs*, by G A Mantell, 1822.

(2) *Geology of The Weald*, by W Topley, 1875.

(3) *Geology of London and South-East England*, by G M Davis, Murby, 1939.

(4) *The Wealden District*, 1st ed, by F H Edmunds, HMSO, 1934.

(5) *The Wealden District*, 2nd ed, by F H Edmunds, HMSO, 1948.

(5) *The Wealden District*, 3rd ed, by F H Edmunds, HMSO, 1954.

(6) *The Wealden District*, 4th ed, by R W Gallois, HMSO, 1965.

GENERAL

(1) *Highways and Byeways of Sussex*, by E V Lucas, 1904 (new edition 1950).

(2) *The Weald*, by S W Wooldridge and F Goldring, Collins (New Naturalist Series), 1953.

Graded List of Selected Climbs

In a change from previous practice the climbs are listed in descending order of 'total' difficulty. This takes into account the cumulative effect of all the difficulties encountered on a given climb, and not just the hardest single move. Hence a climb such as the strenuous and sustained *Monkey's Necklace* 5b, appears higher in the list than the technically harder, but otherwise less demanding, *Far Left* 5c. The list is composed of all the starred routes plus selected others. Almost all of the climbs in the top two technical grades have been included as those who climb at such a standard have a greater interest in such things – competitive as they tend to be. The following abbreviations have been used to help locate the climbs:

BF – Bassett's Farm Rocks
HRC – High Rocks Continuation Wall
Bo – Bowles Rocks
HRA – High Rocks Annexe
BH – Bulls Hollow Rocks
HV – Happy Valley Rocks
CW – Chiddinglye Wood Rocks

Pe – Penns Rocks
EG – Eridge Green Rocks
RF – Ramslye Farm Rocks
Ha – Harrison's Rocks
SF - Stone Farm Rocks
HR – High Rocks
UR – Under Rockes

Routes in italics are those yet to be soloed, while the dagger symbol (†) indicates unrepeated routes.

7a *Chimaera* (HR)†
6c *Bone Machine* (HR)†
6c *Cool Bananas* (HR)
6b *The Second Generation* (HR)
6c *Them Monkey Things* (Bo)†
6c *Unforgettable* (HR)
6c *Kinda Lingers* (HR)

6c *Lager Frenzy* (Ha)
6c *Carbide Finger* (Bo)
6c *Guy's Route* (SF)†
6c *Tempestivity* (Ha)
6b *Renascence* (HR)
6c *Nonpareil* (EG)
6c *Karate Liz* (BF)
6c *One Nighter* (Bo)
6c *Caped Avenger* (EG)†
6b *The Crunch* (EG)
6b *Nutella* (Bo)
6b *Missing Link* (HR)†
6c *I'll Be Back* (HR)
6b *Judy* (HR)
6c *A Killing Joke* (Ha)
6c *Woolly Bear* (Ha)
6c *Gentle Giant* (HRC)†

6c What Crisis? (Ha)
6b *Lager Shandy* (Ha)†
6b *Boonoonoonoos* (HR)
6b *Birdie Num-Nums* (SF)†
6b *Kinnard* (Bo)
6b *The First Crack* (HR)
6c *Moments of Pleasure* (EG)

6c *Quoi Faire* (SF)
6c *The Gob* (HR)†
6b *Powder Monkey* (Ha)
6c *The Wrecker* (Bo)
6c *Porg's Progress* (HR)†
6b *Nemesis* (HR)
6b *Recurring Nightmare* (Bo)
6b *Fungal Smear* (HR)†
6b *Time Waits for No One* (BH)
6b *Oliver James* (Ha)
6b *Knucklebones* (Bo)†
6b *Krait Arête* (HR)
6b *Flail Trail* (EG)
6b *The Thing* (Bo)
6b *One of Our Buzzards...*(Bo)
6b *Dr. Pepper* (Ha)
6b *Zugzwang* (EG)†

6b The Beguiled (EG)
6b *Educating Airlie* (HR)
6b *The Purvee* (HR)
6b Peapod (HR)
6b *Firefly* (HR)
6b Higher Purchase (EG)
6b Funnel Web (UR)
6b Lou (EG)
6b Stubble (Ha)
6b *Bowles Girdle* (Bo)†
6b Temptation (Bo)
6b Leglock (HR)
6b Double Top (HRA)
6b *Dyno-Sore* (HR)
6a Forgotten Crack (EG)
6b *Identity Crisis* (Pe)†
6b Diagonal (EG)

6b Meaty Thighs (EG)
6a Infidel (HR)
6b A Touch Too Much (HR)
6a Lionheart (UR)
6b *Telegram Sam* (HR)
6b Cheetah (HR)
6a Monkey's Bow (Ha)
6b Snail Trail (EG)
6b The Limpet (Ha)
6b *Salad Days* (HR)
6a Sandstorm (EG)
6b *So What?* (HR)
6b *Death Cap* (HR)
6b Roofus (HR)
6a More Cake for Me (EG)
6b Scirocco (EG)
6b *Lazy Chive* (EG)

6a Sossblitz (Ha)
6b *Moving Staircase* (HR)
6a *Dislocator* (BF)
6b Kathmandu (SF)
6b Shattered (HR)
6b *Harlequin* (CW)
6b *Too Hard for Dave* (HR)
6b Honeycomb (HR)
6a *Love* (Bo)
6b Blue Murder (Ha)
6b The Republic (Ha)
6a Coronation Crack (Ha)
6b Meridian (UR)
6b *Mervin Direct* (HR)
6b Kicks (Ha)
6a *Adder* (HR)
6b Top Cat (SF)

6b Cardboard Box (Bo)
6b *Kraken* (HR)
6a *Firebird* (HR)
6b Enigma (EG)
6b Waffer Thin (EG)
6b *Prowess* (EG)
6b Easy Life (EG)
6a *Lobster* (HR)
6a The Flakes (Ha)
6b Sandman (Bo)
6b Smile of the Beyond (EG)
6a *Dan's Wall* (BF)
6b *Skin Job* (Ha)
6b Illusion (SF)
6b *Rag Trade* (HR)
6a *Scorpion* (EG)
6a *The Shield* (BH)

6a Meat Cleaver (Ha)
6a *Bulls Hollow Girdle* (BH)†
6a *The Prang* (HR)
6a Yellow Soot (HR)
6a Craig-y-blanco (HR)
6a *Over the Hill* (UR)
6a Finale (Bo)
6a *Stone Ape* (Pe)†
6a *Mellow Toot* (EG)
6a *Attack of the Killer Pigs* (Pe)
6a Steamroller (EG)
6a Digitalis (Bo)
6a Robin's Route (HR)
6a Patella (Bo)
6a South-West Corner (Ha)
6a *Tilley Lamp Crack* (HR)
6a *Good Route...Poor Line* (EG)

6a Boysen's Crack (HR)
6a The Dragon (HR)
6a Serenade Arête (Bo)
6a Muscle Crack (Ha)
6a Hate (Bo)
6a *Touch Down* (EG)
6a The Entertainer (HRA)
6a Fly by Knight (EG)
6a Fandango Right Hand (Bo)
6a Flakes Direct (Ha)
6a *Nigel Mantel* (EG)
5b Amphitheatre Crack (EG)
6a Philippa (Ha)
6a Hangover III (Ha)
6a *Dogs of War* (UR)
5c Mulligan's Wall (HR)
6a Celestial's Reach (Ha)

6a *Going Turbo* (Pe)
6a *Baboon* (Ha)
6a *Too Tall for Tim* (HR)
6a *In One Hole…*(UR)
6a *Revelations* (EG)
6a *Poofy Finger's Revenge* (EG)
6a *The Scoop* (BH)
6a *Magic Pebble* (UR)
5c *Pseudonym* (BH)
5c *Streetlife* (Pe)
6a *A.W.O.L* (Pe)†
6a *Right Unclimbed* (Ha)
6a *Stirling Moss* (EG)
5c *Wailing Wall* (Ha)
5c *Fork* (HR)
6a *The Knam* (Ha)
6a *Belle Vue Terrace* (SF)

6a *Hottie* (EG)
6a *Graveyard Groove* (HR)
6a *Camelot* (HRC)
6a *Juanita* (Bo)
6a *Nightmare* (Bo)
6a *Afterburner* (EG)
6a *Steelmill* (EG)
5c *Fireball* (UR)
5c *Orangutang* (Ha)
6a *Dr. Kemp's Cure* (EG)
6a *Bassett's Farm Girdle* (BF)
6a *Desperate Dan* (Ha)
6a *Obelisk* (EG)
6a *Stem Son* (EG)
6a *Cat Wall* (SF)
6a *Grant's Wall* (Ha)
5c *The Pillar* (EG)

6a *Banana* (Bo)
6a *Crack and Wall Front* (HR)
6a *Boysen's Arête* (Ha)
6a *Earthrise* (EG)
6a *Iron Man Tyson* (EG)
5c *Knife* (HR)
6a *Sputnik* (HR)
6a *The Mank* (Ha)
5c *Bludgeon* (HR)
6a *The Sphinx* (HR)
6a *Genesis* (EG)
5c *Target* (Bo)
6a *Engagement Wall* (HR)
6a *Edwards's Effort* (Ha)
6a *Grant's Groove* (Ha)
6a *Unclimbed Wall Variations* (Ha)
6a *Toevice* (Ha)

5c *Dysentery* (HR)
5c *Slanting Crack* (Ha)
5c *The Wall* (BH)
5c *Toxophilite* (Ha)
5c *Counterfeit* (Ha)
5c *Pie an' Ear-ring* (Pe)
5c *Coronation Crack* (HR)
5c *Umbilicus* (Bo)
5c *Fandango* (Bo)
5c *Bonanza* (Ha)
5c *Crusaders* (Pe)
5c *Amethyst* (CW)
5c *Demon Wall* (EG)
5c *Inspiration* (Bo)
5c *Dinner Plate* (HR)
5c *Cowgirl in the Sand* (Pe)
5c *Control* (SF)

5c *Asterix* (EG)
5c *Lady of the Light-bulb* (HR)
5c *Fandango* (EG)
5c *Huntsmans' Wall* (Pe)
5c *Drunkard's Dilemma* (HRC)
5c *Piecemeal Wall* (Ha)
5c *Diversion* (Ha)
5c *High Traverse* (Ha)
5c *Knott* (BH)
5c *The Touch* (UR)
5c *Girdle Traverse* (Bo)
5c *Excavator* (BF)
5c *Cut Steps Crack* (HR)
5c *Odin's Wall* (HR)
5c *Branchdown* (EG)
5c *Salamander Slab* (Bo)
5b *Monkey's Necklace* (Ha)

5c *Coathanger* (Bo)
5c *Playtex Girdle* (Pe)
5c *Simian Mistake* (HR)
5b *Monkey Nut* (HR)
5c *Perspiration* (Bo)
5c *Leech* (EG)
5c *North-West Corner* (Ha)
5c *Pig's Ear* (Bo)
5c *Poltergeist* (BH)
5c *Last Chance* (Ha)
5c *Clenched Buttocks* (Pe)
5c *Brenva* (HR)
5c *Dark Crack* (UR)
5c *Pinchgrip* (HR)
5c *Green Fingers* (Ha)
5c *Girdle Traverse* (SF)
5c *Central Crack* (UR)

5c Navy Way (HR)
5b Step's Crack (HR)
5c Dynamo (Ha)
5c Quiver (Ha)
5c Crowborough Corner (Ha)
5c Little Sagittarius (Ha)
5b Birchden Wall (Ha)
5c Locust (EG)
5c Shodan (Ha)
5c Vulture Crack (Ha)
5b *Lord Chumley Pootings* (CW)
5c Antoninus (EG)
5c Jaws (HR)
5b R-Maker (CW)
5c Rift (Ha)
5c Chalet Slab Direct (Bo)
5c *Headhunter* (RF)
5c Portcullis (EG)

5c Lucita (HR)
5c Marquita (HR)
5b Girdle Traverse (UR)
5c Good Route...Good Line (EG)
5c Slim Finger Crack (Ha)
5c Lee Enfield (Bo)
5b Lady of the Lake (HRC)
5c Stone's Route (CW)
5c Uganda Wall (UR)
5c Celebration (HR)
5b The Niblick (Ha)
5b Forester's Wall (Ha)
5c Orr Traverse (Bo)
5c West Wall (Ha)
5c Bulging Wall (Ha)
5b Swastika (Bo)
5c Elementary (Ha)

5c Co-Co (HRC)
5c The Scoop (Ha)
5c *Doing the Dirty* (RF)
5c Mohrenkop (Bo)
5c *Orca* (HR)
5b Mammoth Wall (EG)
5c Thin (SF)
5c Bludnok Wall (HR)
5b Effie (HR)
5c *Brian's Corner* (EG)
5c Birchden Corner (Ha)
5b Advertisement Wall (HR)
5b Henry the Ninth (HR)
5b Krankenkopf Crack (HR)
5c Far Left (Ha)
5c Pine Buttress (SF)

5c Blue Peter (Ha)
5b Jockey's Wall (Pe)
5b Drosophila (Bo)
5b Simian Face (HR)
5b Cave Wall (Ha)
5b Set Square Arête (Ha)
5b Spider Wall (Ha)
5b Unclimbed Wall (Ha)
5b Front Face (SF)
5b Slab Crack (Ha)
5b Hennessy Heights (Bo)
5b Swing Face (HR)
5a Abracadabra (Bo)
5b Concorde (EG)
5b Seltzer (Bo)
5b Siesta Wall (EG)
5a Herbal Abuse (CW)
5b Burlap (Bo)

5b Jackie (Bo)
5b Broken Nose (BH)
5b Battleship Nose (HRC)
5b Impossibility (BH)
5b Trapeze Crack (Pe)
5a Pig's Nose (Bo)
5b Evening Arête (UR)
5b Scooped Slab (EG)
5b Pussyfoot (HR)
5b Woodpecker Crack (Pe)
5b Pinnacle Buttress Arête (SF)
5b Dying for a Tomtit (Pe)
5b Thin Wall (RF)
5b Left Edge (HRC)
5a Simian Progress (HR)
5b Hipposuction (EG)
5b Thin Layback (EG)

5b *Gilt Edge* (CW)
5b Belts and Braces (Ha)
5a Larchant (Bo)
5b Usurper (Ha)
5b Karen (CW)
5b Birthday Arête (HR)
5b Middle Stump (HRA)
5b Stupid Effort (Ha)
5b Pull Through (Bo)
5b Cough Drop (HR)
5b Sliding Corner (Ha)
5b Twin Slabs (EG)
5b Devaluation (Bo)
5a Upwards Scoop (Pe)
5b Trouble with Rubble (UR)
5b Half-Crown Corner (Ha)

5b Hadrian's Wall (EG)
5a The Helix (HR)
5b Diagonal Route (SF)
5b Equilibrium Wall (EG)
5b Innominate Crack (EG)
5b Pinnacle Buttress (SF)
5a Battlements Crack (EG)
5b Pelmet (Ha)
5b E.S. Cadet Nose (Bo)
5b Z'mutt (HR)
5b Signalbox Arête (Ha)
5b Nose One (HRA)
5b Dival's Diversion (Bo)
5b Elastic Headbands (EG)
5b Augustus (HRA)
5a Sagittarius (Ha)
5a Long Layback (Ha)
5a North Wall (HR)

5a Hanging Crack (EG)
5a Roof Route (HR)
5a Panty Girdle (Pe)
5a Windy Wall (HRC)
5a Spook (CW)
5a Waistline (BH)
5a Leg Stump (HRA)
5a Leaning Crack (SF)
5a Bell Rock T.P. Route 1 (HR)
5a S.W. Corner Scoop (SF)
5a Garden Slab Right (Ha)
5a Four-by-Two (Bo)
4c Orion Crack (HR)
5a Cave Crack (Bo)
5a Bell Rock T.P. Route 2 (HR)
5a Middle and Off (HRA)
5a Girdle Traverse, Isolated Buttress (Ha)

5a Two-Toed Sloth (Ha)
5a Todd's Traverse (Ha)
5a Key Wall (SF)
5a Zig-Zag Wall (Ha)
5a Pegasus (Bo)
5a Run Out (HRA)
4c Isolated Buttress Climb (Ha)
5a Bald Finish (HR)
5a Grant's Crack (Ha)
5a Degenerate (HR)
5a Giant's Ear (Ha)
5a Senarra (Ha)
4c Backyard (EG)
5a Garden Slab Left (Ha)
5a Purgatory (HRA)
5a Peter's Perseverance (Bo)

5a Hear No Evil (UR)
5a Murph's Mount (Bo)
5a Hell Wall (Ha)
5a Fragile Arête (Bo)
5a Wander at Leisure (Ha)
4c Going Straight (Pe)†
4a Anaconda Chimney (HR)
4c Remote (SF)
4c Deadwood Crack (Ha)
4c Cowardly Custard (Pe)
4c Nealon's (Bo)
4c Dusk Crack (EG)
4c Slab Direct (Ha)
4c Six Foot (Bo)
4c October (Bo)
4c Sunshine Crack (Ha)
4c The Sewer (Ha)
4c Centurion's Groove (BH)

4c Bramble Corner (BH)
4c Valhalla Wall (HRA)
4c Remus (EG)
4c Sapper (Bo)
4b Long Crack (Ha)
4c Slab Variant (BH)
4c Alka (Bo)
4c Starlight (Ha)
4b Turret Face (HRC)
4c High Traverse (Bo)
4c Off Stump (HRA)
4b Gytrack (CW)
4c Crack Route (HR)
4c The Vice (Ha)
4b Barbican Buttress (EG)
4b Port Crack (HRC)
4c Moonlight Arête (Ha)

4b Babylon (Bo)
4c Hidden Gem (HV)
4b Split's Groove (Pe)
4b Conway's Crack (BH)
4b St Gotthard (Ha)
4b Primitive Groove (SF)
4b Pot-hole Crack (HRC)
4b Ricochet (Bo)
4b Kemp's Delight (Bo)
4b Cottonsocks Traverse (Ha)
4b S.E. Corner Crack (SF)
4b Eyelet (Ha)
4b The Sandpipe (Ha)
4b Sabre Crack (Ha)
4b Stone Farm Crack (SF)
4b Ashdown Wall (SF)

4a Lawson Traverse (Bo)
4b Tiger Slab (EG)
4b Possibility Wall (BH)
4b The Bearded Clam (Pe)
4b Long Man's Neighbour (EG)
4a Limpet Crack (HRC)
4b The Juggler (Pe)
4b Sylvie's Slab (Bo)
4a Hound's Wall (CW)
4b Recess Chimney (Pe)
4a Kennard's Climb (Bo)
4b Scirocco Slab (Bo)
4a Gap Traverse (SF)
4a Crack and Cave (Ha)
4a Sashcord Crack (Ha)
4a Rota (EG)
4a Right-Hand Crack (Ha)
4a Right Circle (Ha)

4a Dib (Bo)
4a Yoyo (Bo)
4a Netwall (Bo)
4a Ejector (Ha)
4a Fragile Wall (Bo)
4a Stone Farm Chimney (SF)
4a Bow Window (Ha)
4a Undercut Wall (SF)
4a Chelsea Traverse (Bo)
4a Funnel (Bo)
4a The Buzzard Years (HV)
4a Ordinary Route (HR)
4a Simplon Route (Ha)
4a Curling Crack (SF)
4a Corbett Slab (Bo)
4a Root Route 1 (Ha)
4a Slab Direct (SF)

3b Warning Rock Buttress (HR)
3b Cut Holds (RF)
3b Wellington's Nose (Ha)
3b Birch Tree Crack (Ha)
3b Stalactite Wall (HRC)
3b Snout Crack (Ha)
3b Bulging Corner (SF)
3b Pine Crack (SF)
3b First Visit (CW)
3b Chalet Slab Left (Bo)
3b Nose Three (HRA)
3b Conway's Variation (BH)
3b Horizon Wall (HRA)

3b Outside Edge Route (HR)
3b Reclamation Slab Left (Bo)
3b Conway's Buttress (BH)
3a Hut T.P. Rufrock Route (HR)
3a Sing Sing (Bo)
3a Gangway Wall (BH)
3a Horizontal Birch (Ha)
3a Charon's Chimnney (Ha)
3a Charlie's Chimney (Bo)
3a Skiffle (Bo)
3a Wells's Reach (Bo)
3a Easy Cleft Right (Ha)
3a Garden Wall Crack (SF)
2b Flotsam (Ha)
2b Shelter Chimney (HR)
2b The Chimney (Ha)
2b Boulder Bridge Route (Ha)
2b Grotto Chimney (Bo)

2b Jackson Hole (Pe)
2b Reclamation Slab Right (Bo)
2b Brushwood Chimney (HR)
2b Big Cave Route 1 (Ha)
2b Tame Variant (Ha)
2b Holly Route (HR)
2b One of Our Chimneys...(HR)
2b Open Chimney (Ha)
2b Left Edge (Ha)
2a Dark Chimney (Ha)
2a Windowside Spout (Ha)
2a Short Chimney (HR)
2a Big Cave Route 2 (Ha)
2a Easy Crack (HR)
2a Harden Gully (Bo)
2a Giant's Staircase (Ha)
2a Smith's Traverse (Ha)

2a Easy Crack (SF)
2a Introductory Climb (SF)
2a Slab Arête (SF)
1b Medway Slab (SF)
1b Dinosaurs Don't Dyno (SF)
1b Birch Crack (Bo)
1b November (Bo)
1b Junend Arête (Ha)
1a Yew Break (BH)
1a Scout Chimney Right (Ha)
1a Reclamation Gully (Bo)
1a Isometric Chimney (Ha)
1a Scotland Slab (HRC)

Index

5.11 Crack	68	Back Passage	116	Birch Tree Crack	118

5.11 Crack 68
6.0 a.m. Route 64
A Killing Joke 98
A Lady in Mink 49
A Touch Too Much 142
A.W.O.L. 196
Abracadabra 43
Achilles' Last Stand 74
Acrobat, The 195
Adder 128
Advertisement Wall 138
Afterburner 71
Agent Orange 110
Aladdin and the Ramp 196
Albino 254
Alka 48
All Quiet on the Western Front 192
Amethyst 182
Amnesian 64
Amphitheatre Chimney 67
Amphitheatre Crack 66
Anaconda Chimney 127
Anchor Chain 158
Annexe Slab 159
Another Wet Bank Holiday 77
Antoninus 73
Apex, The 202
Apis 54
Apis Variation 54
Araldite Wall 116
Archer's Wall 95
Archer's Wall Direct 95
Arnold Anyways 195
Arnold Thesanigger 160
Arrow Crack 94
Arustu 109
Ashdown Wall 174
Assault 201
Asterix 73
Attack of the Killer Pigs 195
Augustus 161
Auxiliary Arête 195
Avalanche Arête 57
Avalanche Route 57
Awkward 155
Awkward Corner 145
Baboon 102
Baby Boulder 48
Babylon 37
Back of Beyond 184

Back Passage 116
Backyard 72
Bad Finger 113
Badger's Head 33
Balcony Direct 134
Bald Finish 142
Baldrick's Boulderdash 114
Balham Boot Boys 175
Ballerina 48
Banana 37
Barbed Wire Fence 146
Barbed Wire Kiss 146
Barbican Buttress 77
Bare Essentials 171
Bare Necessities 171
Barefoot Crack 156
Barham Boulder 49
Baskerville 119
Battery Wall 201
Battle of Hastings, The 247
Battle of the Bulge 114
Battlements Crack 77
Battleship Nose 158
Beacon Wall 186
Beanstalk 137
Bearded Clam, The 195
Beech Corner 90
Beef Curtains 195
Beer Gut Shuffle 147
Beguiled, The 68
Bell Rock Passage 131
Bell Rock Transverse Passage Route 1 131
Bell Rock Transverse Passage Route 2 131
Bell Rock Transverse Passage Route 3 131
Belle Vue Terrace 172
Belts and Braces 106
Bertie 178
Bertie Bothways 194
Beyond Our Ken 179
Biceps Buttress 117
Big Cave Route 1 114
Big Cave Route 2 114
Big Fat Tart 62
Big Toe Wall 96
Bill, The 259
Billy the Bong 161
Birch Crack 45
Birch Nose 107
Birch Tree Buttress 57

Birch Tree Crack 118
Birch Tree Variations 118
Birch Tree Wall (BH) 57
Birch Tree Wall (Ha) 118
Birchden Corner 112
Birchden Wall 112
Birdie Num-Nums 176
Birthday Arête 143
Birthday Buttress (HRC) 152
Birthday Buttress (UR) 201
Bishop and the Actress, The 97
Bitch and the Meal Ticket, The 57
Bivouac Chimney 64
Black Crack 71
Blackeye Wall 88
Blasphemy 55
Bloody Fingers 113
Bloody Sunday 99
Bludgeon 141
Bludnok Wall 144
Blue Helmet 194
Blue Moon 34
Blue Murder 90
Blue Peter 90
Bluebell 159
Boa by the Back 127
Boa-Constrictor Chimney 127
Bolder Route 113
Bolt Route 127
Bolts, The 100
Bonanza 104
Bone Machine 128
Boonoonoonoos 141
Bootless Buzzard 106
Bostic 102
Bottle Chimney 154
Boulder Bridge Route 112
Boulder Chimney 62
Boulder Wall 175
Boundary Gully 164
Bovril 49
Bower Boot 116
Bow Crack 145
Bow Locks 204
Bow Window 94
Boysen's Arête 112
Boysen's Crack 134
Brain Dead 232
Brain's Missing 160

Bramble Corner 55
Branchdown 67
Breakknife Buttress 85
Breakfast 148
Brenva 150
Brian's Corner 69
Bridge Crack 52
Bright Eyes 136
Brighton Rock (EG) 77
Brighton Rock 260
   (Saltdean)
Brittle Arête 196
Broken Crack 51
Broken Nose 56
Brouillard 188
Brushwood Chimney 142
Brushwood Chimney – 140
   Outside Route
Bugbear Buttress 75
Bulging Corner (EG) 65
Bulging Corner (SF) 174
Bulging Wall 174
Bulging Wall/Zig Nose 120
Bull's Nose 33
Burlap 40
Bush Arête 144
Buzzard and the Purple 55
   Fish, The
Buzzard Years, The 187
Buzzard's Breakdown 157
Buzzard's New Saw 65
   Gets Christened
Cabbage Patch Blues 116
Caesar 56
Camelot 156
Cannibals 101
Caped Avenger 67
Capstan Wall 75
Capstone Chimney 157
Carbide Finger 43
Cardboard Box 43
Careless Chalk Costs 237
   Lives
Caroline 105
Carpet Slab 179
Carrera 87
Carry on Up the Tower 192
Casement Wall 93
Cat Wall 168
Caught between Two 52
   Stools
Cave Chimney 64
Cave Climb 79
Cave Corner 79
Cave Crack 44
Cave Wall 115
Cave Wall Traverse 114
Celebration 141

Celebration Hangover 140
Celestial's Reach 91
Cellar Wall 54
Cenotaph Corner II 36
Central Crack 202
Central Groove 85
Central Jordan 172
Central Route 84
Centurion's Groove 56
Ceylon 78
Chalet Slab Direct 33
Chalet Slab Left 33
Chalet Slab Right 33
Chalk Farm Toad 255
Chalker Spur, The 237
Chalybeate 188
Channel Holes 239
Channelsea Crack 203
Charlie's Chimney 45
Charon's Chimney 118
Charon's Staircase 164
Chasm, The 52
Cheetah 137
Chelsea Chimney 36
Chelsea Traverse 46
Chez Moi 199
Chiddinglye Chimney 184
Chimaera 128
Chimney One 160
Chimney Two 160
Chimney Wall 160
Chimney, The (HV) 188
Chimney, The (Ha) 109
Chipperydoodah 170
Chockstone Chimney 129
Chossy Arête 178
Chris 45
Chute and Chimney 161
Chute, The 131
Circus Act 194
Claire 48
Clamp, The 107
Cleanliness 184
Clear Conscience 78
Cleft 187
Clenched Buttocks 190
Close to You 61
Clown, The 195
Co-Co 153
Coal Cellar 54
Coast to Coast 36
Coathanger 37
Cobra Chimney 128
Coffin Corner 100
Colorado Crack 136
Columnar Buttress 61
Communist 72
Concentration Cut 173

Conchita 134
Concorde 75
Condom Corner 64
Conjuror 43
Contortionist, The 194
Control 170
Conway's Buttress 55
Conway's Crack 55
Conway's Variation 55
Cool Bananas 136
Corbett Slab 46
Cormorant, The 242
Corner 117
Corner Crack (HRA) 161
Corner Crack (HV) 187
Corner Layback 35
Corner Shop, The 231
Coronation Crack (Ha) 92
Coronation Crack (HR) 137
Corridor of Uncertainty 89
Corridor Route 107
Cottonsocks Traverse 88
Cough Drop 144
Counterfeit 88
Courts Climb 34
Cowardly Custard 196
Cowgirl in the Sand 192
Crack and Cave 115
Crack and Wall Front 140
Crack Route 143
Crackpot 77
Craig-y-blanco 146
Cretin 192
Crossing the Rubicon 130
Crossply 57
Crowborough Corner 112
Crowley's Crack 255
Crucifix 117
Crunch, The 66
Crusaders 191
Crypt Crack 138
Cunning Stunts 116
Curling Crack 170
Cut and Blow Job 194
Cut Holds 197
Cut Steps Crack 130
D.J. Face the Music 84
Dagger Crack 146
Dan's Wall 180
Dark Chimney 92
Dark Chimney Buttress 93
Dark Crack 204
Dave 86
Dead Choughed 257
Deadly Lampshade, The 188
Deadwood Chimney 130
Deadwood Crack 106
Death Cap 140

Degenerate	145	
Déjà Vu	192	
Demon Digit	158	
Demon Wall	65	
Departure Slab	205	
Descent Chimney	65	
Descent Gully	194	
Designer Label	129	
Desperate Dan (Ha)	119	
Desperate Dan (Dover)	238	
Devaluation	44	
Devastator	148	
Diagonal	61	
Diagonal Route	175	
Dib	46	
Didshi	161	
Digitalis	39	
Dilemma	71	
Dinner Plate	148	
Dinosaurs Don't Dyno	174	
Dinosaurus	89	
Direct Route	258	
Dirty Dick	138	
Disillusion	171	
Dislocator	179	
Dival's Diversion	46	
Diver, The	147	
Diversion	112	
Docker's Armpit	180	
Dogs of War	202	
Doina da J'al	183	
Doing the Dirty	198	
Don	86	
Double Top	160	
Doug's Come-uppance	186	
Doug's Dilemma	194	
Dougnacious	78	
Dover Soul	244	
Down the Huntsman	157	
Downfall	96	
Dr. Kemp's Cure	64	
Dr. Pepper	109	
Dragon, The	132	
Drosophila	37	
Drunkard's Dilemma	154	
Dry Ice	236	
Dubonnet	49	
Ducking Fesperate	175	
Duffyman's Dusk	248	
Dukes of Hazard	245	
Dumpy	162	
Dusk Crack	67	
Dutch Cap Arête	65	
Dying for a Tomtit	189	
Dynamo	85	
Dynamo Deltoid	195	
Dyno-Sore	138	
Dysentery	133	
E Chimney	129	
E.S. Cadet Nose	44	
Ear-ring	114	
Earthrise	69	
East Jordan Route	173	
Easy Cleft Left	118	
Easy Cleft Right	118	
Easy Crack (HR)	142	
Easy Crack (SF)	171	
Easy Life	65	
Eckpfeiler	188	
Educating Airlie	140	
Edwards's Effort	111	
Effie	136	
Ejector	87	
El Loco	103	
Elastic	86	
Elastic Headbands	77	
Electric Rainbow	194	
Elementary	119	
Elephant's Head	61	
Elephant's Tail	61	
Elephant's Umbrella	155	
Embarkation Crack	68	
Emerald	68	
Empty Vee	69	
Encore	48	
Engagement Wall	138	
Enigma	65	
Entertainer, The	161	
Equilibrium Wall	62	
Equinox	199	
Eric (EG)	76	
Eric (Ha)	109	
Eridge Tower Route	78	
Escalator	47	
Escape Hatch	241	
Etheldreda's Pinnacle Route 1	255	
Etheldreda's Pinnacle Route 2	255	
Eureka	164	
Even Better than the Real Thing	230	
Evening Arête	203	
Excavator	180	
Exlax	259	
Eyelet	86	
Eyewash	56	
Face, The	169	
Fahrenheit	160	
Fallen Block Eliminate	97	
Fallen Block Mantelshelf	97	
Fallen Block Wall	97	
Fandango (EG)	76	
Fandango (Bo)	37	
Fandango Right Hand	37	
Fang	89	
Far Left	119	
Far South Wall	121	
Fat and Middle-Aged	107	
Fernkop Crack	76	
Ferryman, The	243	
Fig Roll	161	
Final Solution?	180	
Finale	48	
Finance	67	
Finger Fiend	158	
Finger Popper	117	
Finger Stain	94	
Finger Wall	153	
Fingernail Crack	89	
Fire-Eater, The	195	
Fireball	202	
Firebird	141	
Firefly	141	
First Crack, The	126	
First Visit	183	
Fisherman's Friend	243	
Flail Trail	66	
Flake Crack	63	
Flakes Direct	92	
Flakes, The	92	
Flatus Groove	162	
Flotsam	106	
Flower Power Jules	105	
Flutings	76	
Fly by Knight	73	
Flying Doctor, The	238	
Foam Dome	180	
Fog, The	240	
Fontainebleau	76	
Footie	167	
Forester's Wall	104	
Forester's Wall Direct	104	
Forget-Me-Not	114	
Forgotten Climb	198	
Forgotten Crack	67	
Fork	148	
Fortress, The	241	
Fortuitous	57	
Four-by-Two	44	
Fragile Arête	47	
Fragile Wall	47	
Free Willy	50	
French Tickler	228	
Frêney	188	
From Behind	188	
Front Face	171	
Fruits	75	
Full Monty, The	148	
Full Moon	56	
Fungal Smear	127	
Funnel	46	
Funnel Web	204	
Gall Stone	113	

Gamekeeper, The 194
Gangway Wall 57
Gap Traverse 174
Garden Slab Left 116
Garden Slab Right 117
Garden Wall Crack 170
Garden Wall Traverse 170
Gardeners Question 94
Time
Garlic Chives 196
Gascape 183
Genesis 72
Genevieve 138
Gentle Giant 152
Geoff's Route 34
Geronimo 64
Get Orf Moi Land 179
Getafix 67
Ghost, The 252
Giant's Ear 96
Giant's Staircase 94
Giant's Stride 131
Gibbet, The 136
Gibbons Progress 153
Gilbert's Gamble 87
Gilt Edge 184
Girdle Traverse (BF) 180
Girdle Traverse (BH) 58
Girdle Traverse (Ha) 113
Girdle Traverse (SF) 168
Girdle Traverse (UR) 203
Girdle Traverse (Bo) 50
Glendale Crack 98
Gob, The 146
Going Straight 196
Going to the Pub 156
Going Turbo 192
Going Turbot 186
Golden Crack 121
Golden Nose 194
Good Friday 99
Good Route...Good 74
Line
Good Route...Poor Line 74
Googly, The 163
Gorilla Wall 161
Grandad Goes Bird 198
Watching
Grant's Crack 115
Grant's Groove 115
Grant's Wall 115
Graveyard Groove 148
Greasy Crack (Ha) 96
Greasy Crack (HR) 146
Greasy Slab 68
Great Bald Turkey 73
Meets a Dwarf with
a Problem, The

Great Escape, The 228
Great Exploit 238
Great White Fright, The 242
Green Bollard Chimney 73
Green Crack 79
Green Fingers 113
Green Ghastly, The 248
Green Gilbert 157
Green Groove 164
Green Slab 154
Green Wall 176
Greenhouse Effect, The 259
Grist 94
Grotto Chimney 39
Grotty Groove 34
Gully of the Godless 249
Gully Rib 79
Gully Wall 45
Guy's Problem 90
Guy's Route 175
Gytrack 183
Hadrian's Wall 73
Half-Crown Corner 117
Handfuls of Dirt 196
Handle with Care 56
Handvice 107
Hanging Crack (BH) 55
Hanging Crack (UR) 199
Hanging Crack (EG) 63
Hangman's Wall 157
Hangover II 91
Hangover III 91
Harden Gully 47
Harlequin 183
Hartleys 76
Hate 45
Headhunter 199
Hear No Evil 203
Hector's House 117
Heffalump 61
Helix, The 149
Hell Wall 118
Helter Skelter 33
Hennessy Heights 47
Henry the Ninth 133
Herbal Abuse 184
Hibiscus 33
Hidden Arête 132
Hidden Gem 186
High Traverse (Bo) 36
High Traverse (Ha) 113
Higher Purchase 67
Hipposuction 74
Holly Leaf Crack 170
Holly Route 150
Holly Tree Chimney 120
Holly Tree Wall 179
Honest Toil 78

Honeycomb 146
Horizon Wall – Routes 162
1 and 2
Horizontal Birch 96
Hottie 62
Houdini 230
Hound's Wall 183
Hour Glass 68
Humphrey 184
Huntsmans' Wall 190
Hut Transverse Arête 140
Hut Transverse Passage 141
– Central Route
Hut Transverse Passage 140
– Ordinary Route
Hut Transverse Passage 141
– Rufrock Route
'Hyphenated' Jones 76
Hypothesis 180
I'll Be Back 140
I'm a Dutchman 156
Ian's Answer 180
Icarus 38
Ice Cream Garden, The 189
Icicle Passage 157
Identity Crisis 189
Ides of March 146
Illusion 171
Impacted Stool 69
Impossibility 54
IN 164
In Limbo 98
In One Hole... 202
Incisor 89
Increment Excrement 157
Independence 154
Index 50
Indian Face, The 179
Infidel 133
Inimitability 90
Innominate Crack 62
Inside or Out? 171
Insinuation Crack 132
Inspiration 39
Into the Groove 231
Introductory Climb 174
Iron Man Tyson 72
Isolated Buttress Climb 111
Issingdown 136
It Came From Beneath 105
the Slime
It May Be Green but 105
It's Not a Teenage
Mutant Ninja Turtle
J.P.S. 150
Jackie 41
Jackson Hole 196
Jagger 114

Jailhouse Rock	258	Lamplight	205	Magic Pebble	202
Jamber	198	Larchant	47	Malcolm McPherson's	188
Jaws	134	Last Chance	115	a Very Strange	
Jennifer	184	Last of the Pie an' Ears,	191	Person	
Jetsam	106	The		Mamba Crack	136
Jockey Shorts	190	Last of the Summer	62	Mammoth Wall	61
Jockey's Wall	190	Wine		Mania	171
Juanita	40	Lawson Extension,The	48	Manita	41
Judy	129	Lawson Traverse	48	Mank, The	108
Jug Arête	154	Layaway	74	Manteloid	205
Jug of Flowers	142	Lazy Chive	73	Mantelpiece	90
Juggler, The	192	Leaning Crack	175	Marathon Man	147
Jughandle	75	Ledge Climb	191	Margate Chimney	226
Jumping Jack Flash	96	Lee Enfield	44	Marquita	134
Junend Arête	96	Leech	67	Mastercard	204
Jungle Book, The	196	Left Circle	99	Max	120
Karate Liz	180	Left Edge (Ha)	96	Meager's Right Hand	41
Karen	183	Left Edge (HRC)	154	Meander	160
Karen's Kondom	109	Leg Break	163	Meat Cleaver	120
Kathmandu	168	Leg Stump	164	Meaty Thighs	67
Kemp's Delight	38	Leglock	130	Medway Slab	167
Ken Clean Air System	72	Leisure Line	173	Mein Herr	70
Ken's Wall	179	Libra	63	Mellow Toot	71
Kenian Crack	179	Lichenous Language	197	Mental Balance	36
Kennard's Climb	46	Life Begins at 30	233	Mercator's Projection	49
Kestral	204	Life in the Old Dog Yet	76	Meridian	204
Key Wall	172	Lime Wall	260	Merlin	204
Keystone Crack	76	Limpet Crack	153	Mervin Direct	140
Keystone Face	76	Limpet Wall	155	Mick's Wall	38
Keystone Wall	76	Limpet, The	92	Mick's Wall Arête	38
Kicks	106	Lion Tamer, The	194	Mick's Wall Variation	38
Kinda Lingers	140	Lionheart	201	Middle and Off	164
Kinetix	69	Little Cave	97	Middle Stump	164
Kinnard	39	Little Cousin	116	Middleclass Ponce	69
Kippers	186	Little Sagittarius	95	Midway Chimney	156
Kiss, The	238	Liz's Layback	78	Midway Traverse	157
Knam, The	108	Lobster	133	Midweek Chimney	191
Kneeling Boulder	167	Locust	67	Mike's Left Knee	142
Knife	148	London Corner	75	Milestone Arête	173
Knight's Gambit	108	London Wall	75	Milestone Stride	173
Knight's Move	108	Long Crack	95	Minotaur	52
Knott	55	Long Layback	92	Miss Embassy	150
Knucklebones	36	Long Man's Neighbour	66	Missing Link	126
Koffler	45	Long Man's Slab	66	Mist	187
Krait Arête	137	Long Reach	100	Mocasyn	134
Kraken	132	Long Stretch (Ha)	100	Mohrenkop	33
Krankenkopf Crack	132	Long Stretch (HR)	144	Moments of Pleasure	65
Krypton Factor	113	Longbow Chimney	94	Monkey Nut	148
Kukri Wall	85	Look Sharp	138	Monkey's Bow	102
Kukri Wall Direct	86	Loose Living	232	Monkey's Necklace	101
L.H.T.	116	Lord Chumley Pootings	184	Monkey's Sphincter	149
La Cicciolina	232	Lou	72	Monolith Crack	163
Labyrinth	131	Love	45	Monolith Girdle	163
Lady Jane	105	Low-Level Girdle	176	Monolith Left Buttress	162
Lady of the Lake	156	Lucita	134	Monolith Right Buttress	163
Lady of the Light-bulb	124	Lunar Music Suite	195	Monster Crack	254
Lager Frenzy	91	Luncheon Shelf	91	Monster Raving Loony	248
Lager Shandy	91	Lunge'n'Shelf	146	Moonlight Arête	102

Moonlight Variation (Brookslight) 102
Moray 186
More Cake for Me 66
More Funkey than Monkey 69
More Neck than Simon Ballantine 231
Moroccan Roll 78
Mosquito 65
Moss 54
Moss Wall 167
Motza 154
Moving Staircase 128
Mr Angry 236
Mulligan's Wall 141
Murph's Mount 41
Muscle Crack 117
Mysteries of the Orgasm 147
N.E. Corner 175
Nail, The 71
Nativity Relativity 157
Natterjack 140
Navy Way 145
Nealon's 49
Nelson's Column 46
Nemesis 142
Neptune Arête 54
Nero 42
Netwall 35
Neutral 120
New Hat 85
Niblick, The 104
Nigel Mantel 70
Nightmare 43
No Ghosts 205
No Surrender 241
Nob Nose 163
Noisome Cleft No.1 103
Noisome Cleft No.2 103
Noisome Wall 103
Noisome Wall Direct 103
Nonpareil 63
Norman Corner 247
North Wall 149
North-West Corner 110
Nose and Groove 120
Nose Direct 172
Nose One 160
Nose Three 161
Nose Two 160
Nosh 154
November 48
NS (Not Skinnered) 188
Nut Tree 93
Nutella 39
Nuthin' Fancy 62

Nuts, The 100
Obelisk 70
Obscene Gesture 167
Obverse Route 156
Ockendon Slab 136
October 47
Odin's Wall 145
Off Stump 164
Oily Bird 228
Old Red Eyes 237
Oligarchy, The 137
Oliver and His Amazing Underpants 76
Oliver James 102
Oliver's Twist 49
One Bit 155
One Flew over the Buzzard's Nest 195
One Hold Route 167
One in the Eye for Harold 247
One Move 164
One Nighter 40
One of Our Buzzards Is Missing 47
One of Our Chimneys Is Missing 131
One Out, All Out 194
One Up All Up, Except Mat 204
One Up the Rectum Don't Affect'em 191
One-Two Traverse 103
Ones Traverse 160
Open Chimney 174
Open Chimney 87
Open Groove 144
Optical Racer 77
Orangutang 101
Orca 134
Ordinary Route (HRC) 156
Ordinary Route (HR) 147
Original Route 96
Orion Arête 126
Orion Crack 126
Orr Traverse 38
Orrer Crack 145
Out 164
Outfall Crack 203
Outside Edge Route 149
Oven Ready Freddy 147
Over the Hill 201
Over the Rainbow 194
Overboard 158
Overhanging Crack 57
Overlap Centre 197
P.E. Traverse 147
Paisley 76

Panther's Wall 90
Panty Girdle 191
Parba Nangbat 195
Parisian Affair 64
Parrot's Parasol 155
Parrot's Wing 155
Pascale 100
Passage Chimney 103
Passion Flake 253
Pastry 38
Pat's Progress 49
Patella 39
Patrick's Wall 162
Paul Skinback 158
Peace on Earth 124
Peapod 137
Pedestal Wall 77
Pegasus (HR) 129
Pegasus (Bo) 42
Pelmet 94
Penis Door Slam 156
Penknife 85
Percy Pustule Went to Town 184
Peregrine 204
Perspiration 42
Pete's Reach 105
Peter's Perseverance 42
Philippa 117
Phoenix 199
Photinia 85
Pie an' Ear-ring 190
Piecemeal Wall 109
Pig's Ear 45
Pig's Nose 45
Pigs on the Wing 194
Pillar, The 69
Pillow Biter 78
Pincenib 104
Pinchgrip 143
Pine Buttress 169
Pine Crack 169
Pink Pengster, The 72
Pinnacle Buttress 171
Pinnacle Buttress Arête 171
Pinnacle Chimney 172
Pipe Cleaner 101
Plagiarism 103
Plank, The 236
Plantagenet 147
Playtex Girdle 191
Plumb Line 113
Poacher Corner 154
Poetic Justice 78
Polly Ticks 72
Poltergeist 52
Ponytail Pearson (and His Shorts of Doom) 142

Poofy Finger's Revenge 73
Pop's Chimney 47
Porg's Progress 138
Port Crack 158
Portcullis 77
Possibility Wall 52
Pot-belly 187
Pot-hole Crack 152
Powder Finger 113
Powder Monkey 101
Prang, The 133
Prickle Corner 157
Primitive Groove 175
Primrose 61
Profiterole 145
Prow, The (HRA) 162
Prow, The (Hastings) 249
Prowess 63
Prunes 259
Pseudonym 56
Pull Through 44
Pullover (Pe) 192
Pullover (Ha) 118
Punch 129
Pure Arête 124
Purgatory 161
Purple Nasty 116
Purvee, The 124
Pussyfoot 143
Puzzle Corner 146
Pyramid Route 167
Python Crack 137
Quasimodo 107
Quentin's Crisps 195
Quickset 162
Quirkus 138
Quiver 95
Quoi Faire 172
R-Maker 183
Rad's Cliff 49
Rag Trade 129
Railway Crack 246
Rake Buttress 155
Rake's Progress 153
Ramp, The (SF) 169
Ramp, The (Ha) 84
Rampant Erosion 228
Rapunzel 204
Rattlesnake 136
Rattlesnake II 127
Reach for the Sky 108
Real White Cliffs 230
  Experience, The
Reasons to be Fearful 249
Recess Chimney 192
Recess Wall 129
Reclamation Slab Left 36
Reclamation Slab Right 36

Recurring Nightmare 43
Red Peg 48
Red Snapper 186
Relax 259
Remote 170
Remus 74
Renascence 128
Renison Gully 48
Republic, The 104
Revelations 73
Reverse Traverse 109
Rhapsody Inside a 107
  Satsuma
Rhino's Eyebrow 144
Rhododendron Route 144
Rhody-O 188
Rib 46
Rich Bitch 233
Ricochet 44
Rift 120
Right Circle 99
Right Unclimbed 119
Right-Hand Crack 88
Ring Master, The 195
Ringlet 86
Robin's Route 132
Rocket Man 192
Rockney 143
Rodomontade 189
Roger's Wall 205
Roman Nose (Bo) 34
Roman Nose (EG) 74
Romulus 74
Roobarb 140
Roof Route 143
Roofus 144
Root Chimney 169
Root Route 1 88
Root Route 1.5 88
Root Route 2 88
Root Route 3 88
Rota 65
Rotpunkt 187
Rotten Stump Wall 89
Rough Boy 114
Rough-legged Buzzard, 184
  The
Route Minor 188
Rowan Tree Wall 100
Rubber Panty 157
Rum and Coke 116
Rum and Ribena 116
Rum, Bum and Biscuits 145
Run Out 164
Running Jump 35
Rupert and His Chums 160
S.E. Corner Crack 175
S.W. Corner Scoop 175

Sabre Crack 105
Sacrifice 183
Sadness Is: 35 and 65
  Living at Home
Safe Sex 64
Sagittarius 95
Saint's Wall 98
Salad Days 130
Salamander Slab 42
Saltdean Corner 258
Saltdean Slab 258
Sand Piper 87
Sandbag 108
Sandcastle 52
Sandman 45
Sandpipe, The 101
Sandstone Bogey 184
Sandstone Hell 68
Sandstone Safari 188
Sandstorm 66
Sandy Wall 57
Santa's Claws 36
Sapper 40
Sashcord Crack 94
Scimitar 126
Scirocco 66
Scirocco Slab 35
Scoop, The (Ha) 118
Scoop, The (BH) 52
Scooped Slab 70
Scorpion 73
Scotland Slab 156
Scout Chimney Left 116
Scout Chimney Right 116
Scouter, The 46
Scratch 64
Screaming Lord Sutch 248
Seaman's Wall 144
Seat Climb 164
Second Chance 115
Second Generation, The 128
Seltzer 48
Senarra 118
Senile Walk 131
Sentiera Luminosa 244
Sentry Box 54
Sentry Box Arête 54
Sequins of Cosmic 143
  Turbulence
Serenade Arête 39
Serendipity 88
Set Square Arête 108
Seventh Heaven 157
Sewer Wall 101
Sewer, The 101
Sewer-Rowan 101
  Connection
Sex Buzzards 196

Shalot	157	Smoke	141	Steeple Direct	156
Shanty Wall	75	Smooth Chimney	133	Stem Son	72
Sharp Dressed Man	103	Snail Trail	68	Stepped Buttress	156
Shattered	142	Snake's Crawl	97	Steps Crack	128
Shelter Arête	137	Snap, Crackle...	71	Sticky Wicket	89
Shelter Chimney	137	POP!... Splat		Sting, The	96
Shelter Passage	137	Snout	90	Stinging Nettle	197
Shelter Slabs	138	Snout Crack	90	Stirling Moss	70
Shidid	159	So What?	132	Stone Ape	192
Shield, The	55	Sod, The	103	Stone Farm Chimney	168
Shirt Rip	78	Soft Cock	106	Stone Farm Crack	169
Shodan	117	Soft Rock	88	Stone's Route	183
Short Chimney	138	Soft Rock'er	109	Stonefish	186
Short Chimney II	136	Solo (BH)	55	Stormy Seas	261
Short Sharp Cock, The	187	Solo (HR)	145	Stranger than Friction	89
Short Wall	198	Solstice	120	Strangler	130
Short Work	77	Solution	180	Streetlife	191
Shorter than the A3	196	Sombrero Wall	153	Stubble	120
Shytte	87	Some Like it Hot	244	Stupid Effort	95
Siesta Wall	61	Something Crack	145	Sullivan's Stake	87
Signalbox Arête	97	Sonny Dribble Chops	77	Sun Ray	120
Silly Arête	179	Sorrow	128	Sunday Sport	251
Simian Face	148	Sossblitz	104	Sunshine Crack	108
Simian Mistake	149	Sound Effects	236	Swastika	43
Simian Progress	148	South Boulder	121	Swing Face	143
Simpering Savage	176	South Face Of Kent	239	Swingtime	196
Simplon Route	100	South-West Corner	111	Sylvie's Slab	47
Sing Sing	41	Space Odyssey	240	T.N.T.	37
Singlet	86	Speak No Evil	203	T.T.	45
Sinner's Progress	97	Spermatozoa	196	Tallywackle's Climb	65
Sinner's Wall	97	Sphinx, The	149	Tame Variant	106
Six Foot	47	Spider Wall	115	Target	44
Skiffle	38	Spider's Chimney	131	Tartan Custard	190
Skin Job	108	Spleen Slab	160	Taurus (BH)	52
Slab	90	Split's Groove	192	Taurus (HRC)	157
Slab Arête	170	Spook	183	Teddy Bear's Picnic	85
Slab Buttress	169	Spook's Groove	192	Telegram Sam	129
Slab Chimney (HR)	132	Spot the Dog and the	69	Tempestivity	102
Slab Chimney (BH)	56	Breath of Death		Temptation	39
Slab Crack	91	Spout Buttress	93	Ten Foot Pole	103
Slab Direct (SF)	170	Spout Crossing	93	Tequila Mockingbird	197
Slab Direct (Ha)	90	Sputnik	149	Them Monkey Things	43
Slab Variant	56	Squank	103	Thin	170
Slant Eyes	136	Square Cut	57	Thin Layback	64
Slanting Crack (EG)	70	Squirter	198	Thin Wall	197
Slanting Crack (Ha)	88	St. Gotthard	100	Thing, The	40
Slapper	198	St. Jerome	261	Thingamywobs	115
Sliding Corner	89	Stag	107	Thingy	116
Slim Finger Crack	95	Stalactite Wall	153	Thinner	161
Slowhand	134	Stalactite Wall Direct	154	Thirteenth Light, The	201
Slug	66	Starboard Chimney	158	Thorny Crack	205
Slyme Cryme	37	Stardust	91	Thoroughly Kentish	188
Small Chimney	99	Starlight	102	Three Cheers for Pooh	185
Small Wall	99	Station Master Leroy	195	Three Hands Route	78
Smear Campaign	89	Winston		Thrutch	69
Smile of the Beyond	67	Steamroller	77	Thug	161
Smiliodon	90	Steelmill	73	Tiger Moth	65
Smith's Traverse	114	Steeple Back	156	Tiger Slab	78

Tight Chimney	86	Tumble	197	Wellington's Nose	105
Tight Chimney Slab	87	Tunnel Chimney	157	Wells's Reach	46
Tilley Lamp Crack	142	Turbo Buttress	260	West Chimney	255
Tim Nice but Dim	178	Turfed Off	195	West Wall	111
Esquire		Turret Face	154	What Crisis?	95
Time Waits for No One	56	Turret Wall	155	What the Buck	204
Time Warp, The	231	Tusk	61	Whatsaname	115
Tiny White Tremble	227	Tweedle Dee	72	Whiff Whaff	145
Tiptoe Through the	115	Tweedle Dum	72	Whiplash	157
Lichen		Twiglet	86	White Man in	240
Tiptoe Through the	260	Twin Slabs	78	Hammersmith Palais	
Tulips		Twinkle Toe Slab	155	White Sail	232
Tiptoe Thru the Tulips	117	Twitch	160	White Verdict/The Ly'in	41
Titch Arête	160	Two Bit	155	Why Fronts?	190
Toad	86	Two Mantelshelves and	156	Wide Crack	201
Toad Arête	57	Cave		Wildcat Wall	106
Toad Wall	57	Two Step (Bo)	33	William's Layback	49
Toadstool Crack	72	Two Step (HV)	188	Winch Me Up Scottie	189
Todd's Traverse	120	Two-Toed Sloth	109	Wind and Wuthering	205
(Boundary Wall		U.N.	46	Windowside Spout	93
Traverse)		Uganda Wall	202	Windy Wall	155
Toevice	107	Umbilicus	34	Wisdom	89
Tomcat/Simon's Wall	90	Uncertainty	52	Wishful Thinking	146
Too Hard for Dave	130	Unclimbed Wall	119	Witches Broomstick	120
Too Short	63	Unclimbed Wall	119	Wobble	77
Too Short to Mention	64	Variations:		Wobbler Wall	154
Too Tall for Tim	130	Undercut	198	Woodlice Crack	194
Tool Wall	148	Undercut Rib	189	Woodpecker Crack	190
Top Cat	168	Undercut Wall	171	Woodside Blossom	106
Torpedo Route	67	Unforgettable	141	Woodstock	65
Tortoise on a Spin Out	69	Up the Junction	157	Woofus Wejects	146
Touch Down	73	Upwards Scoop	192	Woolly Bear	110
Touch, The	202	Usurer	85	Wrecker, The	46
Tower Girdle	78	Usurper	85	Wye Chimney	132
Toxophilite	95	Vaginoff	254	Y Crack	61
Trainer Drainer	63	Valhalla Wall	161	Yellow Soot	71
Trapeze Crack	194	Valkyrie Wall	161	Yellowstone Crack	52
Travellin' Man	152	Venom	128	Yellowstone Wall	52
Traverse and Crack	174	Verdant Tube, The	245	Yer Greet Northern	152
Tree Climb (BH)	52	Vice, The	107	Basstud	
Tree Climb (EG)	64	Victoria	107	Yew Arête	170
Tree Route	178	Vingt-et-un	145	Yew Break	54
Triangle Arête	56	Viper Crack	142	Yew Crack	69
Triangle Climb	56	Vulgar Armadillo	237	Yew Tree Crack	159
Triceratops	69	Vulture Crack	96	Yew Tree Wall	159
Trident Arête	54	Waffer Thin	70	Yew Wall	52
Trident Chimney	54	Wailing Wall	112	Yom Kippa	154
Trident Left	54	Waistline	51	Yorkie	256
Trip of the Psychedelic	87	Wall, The	55	Yosemite Big Wall	94
Tortoise		Wallow, The	114	Climb	
Trivial Trappist, The	194	Wally	49	Yoyo	41
Trouble with Rubble	204	Waltzing Buzzard, The	204	Z'Mutt	150
Truncate	64	Wander at Leisure	118	Zig-Zag Wall	120
Trunk Route	61	Warning Rock Buttress	133	Zoom	36
Tubby Hayes Is a Fats	126	Warning Rock Chimney	131	Zugabe	48
Waller		Warrior	183	Zugzwang	68
Tube, The	242	Weeping Slab	89		
Tubesnake Boogie	103	Wellington Boot	106		

Rescue

SANDSTONE AREA
In the event of an accident where an ambulance is required **telephone 999.** The nearest telephones to the major outcrops are as follows:

Bowles Rocks: in the administrative office near the entrance, and in the house by the road.

Bulls Hollow Rocks: in the house about 100 metres to the east of the outcrop and numerous others a short distance away in Denny Bottom.

Harrison's Rocks: from Forge Farm (in the valley beneath the *Isolated Buttress Climb* (235) to *Unclimbed Wall* (316) area). It is advisable for one member of the party to wait at the level crossing by Forge Farm so as to direct the ambulancemen/women to the site of the accident.

Once the ambulance has been called, please could you also report the accident to Terry Tullis on 01892 864238 (mobile 0374 243888); or Chris Tullis on 01892 863659 (mobile 0860 462527).

High Rocks/Continuation Wall/Annexe: in the Hotel.

Stone Farm Rocks: in the house on the opposite side of the road to the start of the footpath to the rocks (Stonehill House).

SEA CLIFFS
In the event of an accident where further assistance is required, **dial 999** and ask for **The Coastguard.**